HOTEL HEAVEN

Confessions of a Luxury Hotel Addict

MATTHEW BRACE

Published in Great Britain in 2008 by
Old Street Publishing Ltd,
28–32 Bowling Green Lane, London EC1R 0BJ
www.oldstreetpublishing.co.uk

First published in Australia by Random House in 2007

A CIP catalogue record for this book is available from the British Library.

ISBN13: 978-1-905847-40-2

Printed and bound in Great Britain by J. H. Haynes & Co. Ltd., Sparkford
10 9 8 7 6 5 4 3 2 1

Front cover design by Darian Causby/www.highway51.com.au
Front cover image used by kind permission of Icons Hotel. Located in the
picturesque village of Imerovigli on the island of Thera (Santorini), Icons Hotel
enjoys spectacular views of Santorini's remarkable lagoon and caldera, the rem-
nants of a volcanic eruption about 3500 years ago. More information on Icons
Hotel can be found at www.santorinicons.gr
Back cover photo: Igor Terekhov

Contents

Foreword

DEFINING WHAT MAKES a truly luxurious hotel is like plucking a goose. It feels all soft and fluffy and like it might be a bit of fun, but the more you get stuck in to it the more complicated and messy it becomes. Before you know where you are, there are feathers everywhere.

The good news is that you can consider your goose well and truly plucked. *Hotel Heaven* has done the hard work for you, dashing feverishly all over the globe during the past decade in pursuit of the real definition of luxury in a hotel.

There are thousands of hotels in the world which claim to be luxurious. They are awarded lots of stars and ticks for practical things like having fax machines, spa baths and 597 different cable channels in their rooms, yet their service, design and overall ambience are little better than that of a beach shack on the Gulag Archipelago. In short, the wow factor is simply not there.

When I began reviewing luxury hotels in 1997, having upgraded from being a travel writer for the cheap, backpacker end of the market, I set out on a mission to discover the essence of a true luxury hotel. To my horror, I found myself more often than not being distinctly un-wowed by vastly expensive hotels that claimed to be the pinnacle of luxury but fell far short. The terrifying realisation that money does not necessarily buy hotel happiness made me even more determined to seek out the genuinely luxurious hotels of the world, the ones that leave their guests open-mouthed and thinking, 'Well, it might have cost £700 a night – but my word, it was worth it.'

I knew these hotels were out there. I just had to fight my way through the sickly soup of PR hype and the brochures that told me a hotel would 'change my life' and 'make me see paradise on Earth' and 'explode the inner heart of my mind'.

The result is *Hotel Heaven*, a frank, honest and highly personal account of what I consider to be the great luxury hotels of the world. It is by no means an exhaustive guide, and any fellow luxury hotel junkies out there might well disagree with my selection.

The 80-odd hotels in the book are here because they satisfy my criteria; they are memorable, character-filled, efficient, chic and fun. They exhibit the finest style, display immaculate attention to detail, exude finesse and confidence, and they run with the smooth precision of a Breitling wristwatch.

Hotel Heaven also lets you glimpse the secret, nomadic, frequently decadent but occasionally lonely and stressful world of the luxury travel writer. Jetting into far-flung airstrips on tiny planes, trying desperately to look fabulous on arrival after 36 hours in the air, speed-learning hundreds of years of history and culture in an afternoon, immersing oneself in the nightlife, breezing into diamond-encrusted soirées, mastering the finer points of beach fashion and etiquette in Cannes, Miami, Bali and Bora Bora, and being able to smile and say 'How do you do?' in seven different languages: all these are part of the daily grind of the five-star hotel reviewer.

People stop me at parties and demand to know my

favourite hotel, the best pool, the most romantic balcony, the suite with the best view, the most extravagant airport transfer I have had, or the most expensive place I have stayed. To give me a little more time at parties to enjoy myself, wolf down some devils-on-horseback and ask other people what they do for a crust, I have included all you need to know here in this book.

So grab your Porsche luggage, sling on your Prada in-flight satchel and come on a round-the-world glamour jaunt with an incurable luxury hotel addict.

Come with me to Hotel Heaven.

Matthew Brace
Suite 508, Londra Palace, Venice

Chapter 1

Getting Addicted

SEX, COCAINE, FOOTBALL, shopping ... we all have our addictions. Mine is luxury hotels.

This is no petty, passing obsession that can be cured with shock therapy, such as work experience as a Kontiki rep or an enforced stay in a backpacker hostel in Koh Samui. It is terminal. I must have my quota of luxury hotel fixes each year or there are serious side-effects, which range from mild hissy-fits and childish foot-stamping in the street to full-blown panic attacks and demonic moods.

Recently I failed to secure a stay at the Waldorf=Astoria in New York because every one of its 1,425 rooms was taken. My face was so full of rage on the subway that people moved away from me, suspecting a crime was about to take place. It took every ounce of my mental energy to stop from ranting about my predicament to the bag lady sitting opposite me. That day I worked out why there are so many crazy people in New York – because all the luxury hotels are full.

I know it is not politically correct to covet such extravagances as airport transfers in helicopters and Rolls-Royces, or free mini-bars, chocolate banquets and private butlers who iron a copy of *The Wall Street Journal* for you each morning. And I know it is probably sinful to turn my nose up at cheaper forms of accommodation that, if I weren't a travel writer and didn't get my hotel rooms for free, I might have to frequent. But I don't care ... because I am an addict, a bona fide, happily helpless luxury hotel addict.

I have fashioned my career to satisfy this addiction, turning down far more lucrative jobs in mainstream news journalism on the world's finest newspapers, and roles in PR agencies that would have seen me earning at least £80,000 a year by now, in order to be a poorly paid but definitely jetset luxury travel writer. When I am reviewing for a commission, hotels put me up for free, in the same way as film or restaurant critics get free tickets and tables, but I make it a point to inform every hotel manager that my pen can be as cutting as it can be kind so the hotel had better be as good as it says in the brochure.

I am not only an addict but also a long-term one. My first fix was in the early 1980s, when, aged 13, I stayed with my parents in a luxury hotel near Sevenoaks in Kent. We were heading home early from a seaside holiday that had been pretty much ruined by incessant rain, and my parents decided we could do with a slice of rare luxury. It almost cost them more for two nights there than the entire week we had just spent in no-frills B&Bs at the coast getting drenched, staring at the sea mists and playing hours of Monopoly every day.

The early signs of luxury hotel addiction were apparent the moment I walked in to the oak-panelled lobby. Oil paintings hung on the walls, portraits of hunting parties and society ladies taking tea at Ascot. A waiter glided softly by with china cups, saucers, a solid silver milk jug and a tea pot wrapped up in a striped woollen cosy. He was making his way to the conservatory, from which emanated the low, warm murmur of contented guests. Somewhere in there a string quartet was playing too. The waiter left behind him the lingering scent of Earl Grey tea and shortbread biscuits.

The man behind the desk called my father 'Sir' and – more importantly – referred to me as 'the Young Master', which I thought was entirely fitting and have been trying to persuade people to do ever since. He directed us to a wide, graceful staircase which led temptingly up to the rooms and passed, en route, a 10-foot stained-glass window, through which the afternoon light was shafting in a beatific fashion – coloured rays were lighting the stairs, as if nirvana lay just a few steps away. God, this was going to be good!

The stairs creaked under their crimson carpet as we climbed them, and the banister rail was smooth, polished by the hands of a century of guests.

Up in our room I stared at a view of the gardens and the fields beyond, flicked all the light switches on and off, tried to make the huge television come on, and jumped on my bed – which was the most comfortable I had ever felt and made me realise I had been sleeping on something little better than a sack of potatoes at home for the past decade. The pillows and sheets smelled of lavender and looked as if they had been purchased that afternoon from a bespoke linen emporium in London's Bond Street. Everything was dusted and polished and neat. The beds had wooden extensions on either side with radios built into them, offering exotic stations I had never heard of, like Radio Luxembourg.

I soon displayed the classic traits of the novice luxury hotel guest. I pocketed the posh soaps and little shampoo bottles from the bathroom along with the shower-cap-in-a-bag and other accessories. I convinced myself that the nail files in plastic wrappers might come in handy for some impressive craft project at school – and, as the wrappers carried the hotel insignia, they would double as proof to my classmates that I had stayed at a luxury hotel and they had not.

I tried in vain to steal the shiny silver bath plug, which was not attached by a chain, but it was too heavy. I begged my mother to stuff a fluffy white bathrobe in her suitcase. She refused and said I should be ashamed for even thinking of such a thing. It took me years to forgive her, and longer still to get over the underlying guilt of stealing hotel bathrobes. (For anyone else labouring under the same affliction, the good news is that this guilt does not last forever, and after a while you will become so adept at the practice that you'll be able to open a stall at your local market selling fluffy white robes from hotels on every continent.)

My two nights in Kent also introduced me to the wonders of maid service. The idea of someone picking up your smalls where you dropped them, then folding them and placing them in drawers, was every teenage boy's fantasy – well, one of their fantasies, at least; that and dancing with Olivia Newton-John in the video of 'Physical'. I merged these fantasies and kept expecting Olivia to knock on the door in a maid's outfit and whisk me off to the gym, but instead I got a large Cockney brunette who sang Broadway show tunes as she scrubbed the bath, and smuggled me chocolates from her cleaning trolley. It wasn't much of a trade-off but the chocolates were good.

I watched her clean and chatted to her while my parents walked in the garden, and in half an hour saw her transform the room from a slept-in squat back to an immaculate haven. Those musty sleep smells had vanished, there were more lavender pillows, fresh tea bags next to the kettle and not a scrap of dust to be seen. She even re-tuned the radio from Radio Three to Radio One, just for me.

There was no turning back. I was addicted. My parents

had to drag me kicking and screaming to the car when we left, and I vaguely remember the phrases, 'Now look what you've done ... Got him hooked on luxury hotels ... How do you suppose we can we afford that?!' being uttered between them before some rather cool, silent moments on the drive home.

Sadly but inevitably, this epiphany was followed by years of mediocre hotel experiences until a moment of clarity in the south of France in 1997. I was by then a professional travel writer for several national newspapers and magazines in England and unfortunately had established a reputation as a 'cheap stay' writer. If there was an editorial idea to feature 'Paris for Paupers', 'Bargain Brussels' or 'Venice on £5 per day' then I was the mug they sent. I flew economy, hauled my bags onto public buses, lost several days of my life waiting for delayed trains, was invariably allocated rooms with views of brick walls, fire escapes and pigeons, and lived a life enjoyed only by impoverished backpackers and incurable tight-arses.

I had to use my own money to pay for everything but the accommodation. I spent an average of four days on each assignment and was paid the princely sum of about £100 per article. I barely broke even, relying on my day job as a contracted freelance Fleet Street news journalist to pay rent and buy food.

In 1997 I was sent to Cannes to research an article. 'How to visit the Cote d'Azur without breaking the bank' should have been titled 'How to have a memorably crap time in France, surviving on one croissant per day and wondering why you bothered leaving home'. The film festival was on,

Hollywood was in town, the sun was shining and everyone apart from me was wearing Gucci sunglasses and enjoying themselves.

There was a bright side – a great family friend, the renowned *Evening Standard* film critic and Hollywood biographer Alexander Walker, invited me for lunch at the rooftop restaurant at the sumptuous Hôtel Méditerranée, from where we could gaze out over the port of Cannes and its fleet of super-yachts, glistening in the sunlight like neatly moored piles of gold and pearls. Beyond them stretched the impossibly glamorous sea-front known as the Croisette (or the Croissant if you want to upset the locals).

At the time, this was the hotel of choice for the more discreet and elegant Cannes clientele. Alex was one such client, an old hand at Cannes. He was also my surrogate uncle, a colleague and bosom buddy of my father, and an unfailingly debonair self-made man whose charm and panache had won him some A-list pals in Tinseltown, among them Elizabeth Taylor and Richard Burton.

The Méditerranée's menu told me, in elegant curly writing, that most dishes cost about the same as one night in the grotty pension-cum-brothel where I was holed up on the wrong side of town. Yes, Cannes has a wrong side – trust Fleet Street's faithful 'Cheap Day Return' reporter to have found it. But Alex was paying, or maybe the Evening Standard was paying. Either way, I was not; everything tasted far more delicious than it would have done had my wallet been required.

The yachts clinked at their moorings, a huge wooden steamer cruised in and sounded its horn, and Cannes glistened through a typically rich and star-studded May afternoon. After dessert and over exquisite petits fours and bite-size chocolate brioches I regaled Alex with stories from my misery tours to the bargain basements of Europe and Asia. He remained smiling but I knew that inside he was wincing at the hotel hell I had been through. However, he seemed genuinely amused by one desperate incident in a 50p-a-night hostel in Bombay, which I was sharing with about 200 wheezing Somalian labourers who had been brought in to work on the railways. We slept in one vast warehouse room with cardboard partitions for walls. During a power cut one night I made a necessary dash for the shared squat toilets and inadvertently introduced my left foot to the black and dreadful hole between the slippery foot-stands.

I told Alex I was sick of slumming it around the world. It's hard to maintain a belief that there is a glamorous side to travel writing when you are up to your ankles in someone else's shit.

'I want *this*,' I said, gesticulating at the Méditerranée's glamorous rooftop restaurant, its dramatic sun canopy, its spectacular views and its immaculately dressed waiters, who were looking back at me and wondering if they should throw me out because my crumpled trousers and cheap polyester shoulder bag were committing a Cannes fashion crime.

'I want the glamour. Where's the glamour?'

Alex uncrossed and re-crossed the legs of his silver-grey Savile Row suit and smiled knowingly.

'Well, Matthew, that's an easy one,' he said in his velvety County Down brogue. 'Upgrade yourself. Go five-star … luxury all the way. Don't look back. But not crass luxury – go for style and class, for finesse. That's where the real glamour is. And you can do it too – you're a travel writer, so just write about the good stuff, not the cheap stuff, and do it for *Tatler*, *Vogue*, *Harpers & Queen* and *The New York Times*. There are just as many five-star travel publications as there are bargain-basement ones. Now, I've got to dash – I'm interviewing Woody Allen in half an hour. I'll see you for your birthday. Cheerio.'

The answer had been staring at me from the shelves of every newsagency for years, but it had taken someone with Alex's stature, wisdom and experience to point it out. Only someone who dined out every night of the year, collected modern art and used his fridge solely to chill vintage champagne would have been able to advise me so knowledgeably.

Upgrade yourself. Five-star. Don't look back. Style, class, finesse. I let the words float about in my head as Alex signed the bill, made a joke in perfect French that had the waiters helpless with laughter, and was flourished away by the restaurant manager for his Hollywood appointment.

I felt like staying on and celebrating my revelation with a Méditerranée rooftop martini, but I calculated it would have cost me the entire fee I was being paid for my article. Instead, I deftly flicked the remaining brioches and two bright pink petit fours into a tissue, which I dropped into my shoulder bag with the practised skill of a cat burglar. I tried to scoop in a couple of beautiful silver teaspoons too, as mementos of this life-changing occasion and maybe to pawn at Portobello Market but I mistimed the move in my excitement and they dropped to the floor, tinkling on the terracotta tiles and bringing two waiters scurrying to assist – one to rescue each spoon.

I apologised and left. Unlike Alex's departure there was no flourish, and I failed to raise so much as a smile from the waiters let alone a laugh, but I felt refreshed and I walked confidently down the Croissant, grinning at the poodles. It wasn't going to be easy, I thought, resigning as Fleet Street's unofficial travel peasant. My editors were going to be furious that they now had to find some other idiot to do the job. But I knew it was the right thing to do. Far more glamorous things lay ahead.

I paused near a policeman who tutted at my sand-shoes and looked as though he wanted to fine me 100 francs for lowering the tone of the place. I gazed longingly at the palace hotels: the Carlton, the Martinez, the Majestic. The warm May afternoon light was dancing on their façades and I wondered: just how good could it get? I had seen cheap, so now it was time to visit the other end of the scale: how luxurious could a hotel be?

It was then that I made it my mission to get to the heart of the concept of the luxury hotel – to track down the world's very best, the most luxurious, the ultimate in decadence.

I set my own criteria, based largely on Alex's example. Above all, establishments had to be memorable for all the right reasons – for their class, character, finesse, imagination and uniqueness. Also, they would need to be able to prove a certain luxurious pedigree, possibly through an infamous reputation, a celebrity clientele or time as a cinematic backdrop. I wanted eccentricity, audacity and even pretentiousness, but I refused to admit into my little club any hotel that was bland, dull, classless or crass, regardless of its price tag. In short, I went looking for the essence that the novelist Arnold Bennett described in his 1902 novel *The Grand Babylon Hotel* – 'that mysterious quality known as "style".'

There have been some establishments in my decade of research which I would personally love to burn to the ground because they were so outrageously over the top and showy, but nevertheless they are clearly adored by other luxury hotel junkies so, in the spirit of objectivity, they passed the test.

I went searching for the best service, the finest interior design, the most poetic room views and the best privacy. I examined hotels made famous by film-makers and novelists, or by the eccentricities of their owners, and others that became infamous for the headline-grabbing orgies of sex, drugs and murder which took place there.

It's been an arduous ten-year mission, as I am sure you can appreciate, globetrotting from five-star suite to five-star suite, all in the name of research.

I am met at airports by men in peaked caps who chauffeur me in Rolls-Royces. Hotels offer me penthouse apartments and honeymoon suites with bathtubs big enough to fit all the members of a reasonably sized swingers club. Butlers 'butle' for me. Managers leave chilled bottles of Moët et Chandon in silver buckets in my room next to boxes of chocolates with red silk ribbons on the top, welcome cards and bowls of lychees and rambutans. Hotels give me gifts of bathrobes and towels, books, CDs and polo shirts, which I often have to decline because I cannot fit them in my luggage. Restaurants offer me not just a wine sommelier but one for olive oil as well.

Bath 'masters' come and fill my tub with rose petals and Middle Eastern spices, and leave a Romeo y Julieta cigar and a glass of Courvoisier XO Imperial cognac warming by the taps. Masseuses rub frangipani and ylang-ylang oil into my weary writing arms and shoulders. Yogis wake me before dawn for yoga and take me to rice paddies where they tie me in knots. Personal trainers take me for exhausting runs around the streets and parks of unknown cities.

After ten years of hard hotel slog, I now know how good it can get. I have experienced the ultimate luxury hotel highs, which have continued to fuel my addiction. I have stayed in hotels so beautiful and sublime that checking out has brought on bouts of depression. I have slept in penthouse eyries and underground caves, met movie stars in corridors, shared lifts with ex-presidents, fallen in love with panoramic views, and spent hours lazing by blissful pools trying in vain to write articles that do them justice.

Several managers have become good friends. Drivers, butlers and chefs have taught me the ways and beliefs of more than a dozen different cultures. And, most meaningfully to me, I found the love of my life standing at the entrance of one of the most luxurious hotels in the South Pacific.

Things have changed a lot in ten years. I remember checking in to The Ritz in London in the late 1990s and finding a nice, shiny fax machine in my suite and thinking, 'that's posh, I must be a VIP'. Now if a hotel hasn't got wireless broadband, or at the very least a high-speed data port, guests feel a blind panic spinning towards them like a summer squall at sea, and they have to sit down and breathe deeply until the concierge assures them there is internet in the hotel's 24-hour business centre at no extra charge.

Faxes look more like antiques in The Ritz today where high speed (100mb) broadband access is standard in all rooms with wireless connectivity in private meeting rooms.

En route through the hotel stratosphere, I have discovered that I am not alone in my addiction. I share it with a rapidly growing band of wealthy luxury hotel junkies, including hordes fleeing the miserable winters of their newly post-Communist countries. I have had caviar and Campari sodas with oil barons from Kazakhstan and property developers from Shanghai who are making speedy fortunes as their nations begin trading with the West and their economies boom. Some of them have been legitimate while others are no doubt exploiting the burgeoning black market in drugs, guns and protection. After these nouveau-millionaires have purchased a Lamborghini Countach and several dodgy timeshare apartments in Sevastopol, they spend their crisp (and very possibly laundered) hundred-dollar bills on luxury travel.

I have met confident thirty-something Australian designers and property developers who have made millions as their country has skyrocketed to the economic strato-sphere on the back of a resources boom. And demure British retirees who spent their working lives frugally and made a wise investment 30 years ago and now, on the advice of their jetsetting children, are embarking on a luxury travel lifestyle, flying business class between the world's finest hotels.

And everywhere there are Russian accents. They now rival Americans in their omnipresence in luxury hotels. They have fallen in love with London, New York and the Middle East. During their long, cold northern winter, they virtually take over balmy Dubai and the south of France. They are young and rich, and they spend their roubles like kids in a sweet shop, booking entire floors of hotels for weeks on end and ordering cases of champagne and lash-ings of caviar.

According to International Luxury Travel Market, the world's premier annual luxe shindig, there is some hard data behind the profusion of luxury hotel junkies. ILTM's marketing manager, Tim Latimer, said luxury travel had experienced robust growth over the last decade.

'Estimates show the market to be growing at over 10 per cent per annum, more than double that of the mainstream travel sector,' he said, as he prepared for a conference in Cannes. 'As economies prosper and the work–life balance becomes even harder to achieve, indulgent travel is increasingly becoming an antidote to hectic professional lives. Twenty years ago booking a five-star hotel was the preserve of the few. Nowadays a culture of 'treating' has evolved, meaning that even those without a high disposable income will save up to indulge themselves. As for the very affluent – the sky is the limit – they are looking for more and more personalised exclusive experiences.'

This accelerating demand means there are now more luxury hotels than ever before, and they are getting more and more luxurious. Five-star is not enough these days. Now we demand six-star and seven-star, even though the official star rating only goes to five, and we are willing to pay for it too. The luxury hotel is entering a second Golden Age.

Some of my fellow guests have been a constant source of entertainment and amazement, each checking in with their particular luxury hotel criteria. Some do not care if their view is of a soap factory as long as their beds have 500-thread-count cotton sheets as a bare minimum, and they have at least 40 television channels to keep them amused. Others put up with seriously substandard food and service just for the chance to stay on their own private beach. Some insist on private plunge pools, floral wallpaper and French Renaissance chintz in every corner, while others demand absolute minimalism and get chest pains if there is so much as a single flower in a vase to break up the emptiness of white walls and black functional furniture.

There are cultural differences too. Australians, Britons and Europeans are, in general, more private and keener not to integrate with their fellow guests, whereas Americans love nothing better than meeting complete strangers and recounting their life histories, along with photo albums of their offspring, their New York loft apartment and their condo in Miami, and graphic details of how they survived major heart surgery after a lifetime of devouring fast food.

Australians think it bizarre and unnatural for a luxury hotel not to have a swimming pool because it is such an integral part of their home culture. Germans really do like sneaking around shortly before dawn and spreading their towels on loungers by the pool to ensure they get a seat in the sun. English people like removing them.

And some guests crave a hotel policy of utter decadence and seek out hotels where excess is encouraged. The errant aristocrat Jamie Blandford told me years ago in a newspaper interview that his definition of luxury was the Hotel Byblos in St Tropez 'because you can do what you want – anything goes'.

To keep these wealthy jetsetters happy, the concept of the true luxury hotel has evolved into a number of subspecies – all of them stylish and classy, but all of them very different in look and feel.

There are hotels so devoid of furniture and pomp that it is hard to find the entrance. Others stand on their foundations decked in such lurid regalia that they scream at you to notice them, like a child suffering attention-deficit disorder.

Even though I have tried to experience them all, I have fallen short. Just as one is reviewed another seems to pop up from nowhere offering better in-room amenities, more Michelin stars at its restaurant, and posher sports cars for hire. The phenomenon changes daily, which is terrific news for any luxury hotel junkies because it gives us the perfect excuse to keep on using.

Chapter 2

Luxury Legacy

❧

SOME OF THE earliest luxury hotel junkies were the Romans, who brought a new meaning to the idea of excess. We know they were avid travellers, eagerly barging into far-flung, windswept kingdoms, bashing native brigands on the head, locking up druids, deposing fur-clad rulers and then claiming the territories for Rome. We also know that they built beautiful villas and palaces throughout their vast empire, which became private hotels for Caesars, senior politicians and commanders of legions. Here they held lavish week-long feasts, fuelled by a never-ending supply of wine, wild boar, grapes, courtesans and catamites, proving that you could be outrageously decadent and take over the world at the same time.

Roman authors left us in no doubt of the lengths to which their fellow Romans went to satisfy themselves. Their books tell of how the super-wealthy erected brick buildings in which they created atria, peristyles (colonnaded gardens and courtyards), and engineered running water, sewage disposal and hypocausts (ducted central heating under the floor tiles).

The Roman biographer Suetonius described Nero's palace as having vaulted supper rooms with walls inlaid with ivory and gold, and rooms that were designed to revolve like the heavens, all in order to make the emperor and his guests feel god-like. He recounts that Nero's entourage (of roughly 1,000 vehicles) took along 500 she-asses, so his wife Poppæa Sabina could bathe in their milk every day.

More than 600 Roman villas have been excavated in Britain alone, and many reveal clues to the lavish lifestyles led by the invaders. Three of the most extravagant – Chedworth in Gloucestershire, Lullingstone in Kent and Fishbourne Palace in West Sussex – boast intricate mosaics and complete bath complexes. Fishbourne, which was built in 75 AD, had no fewer than 20 mosaic floors.

I've got a lot to thank the Romans for. I would be out of a job were it not for their determination to create temples to aesthetic beauty and indulgence in as many countries and climates as possible. Without their international pioneering in the fields of gluttony, lust and several other deadly sins, the concept of enjoying grand luxuries away from home might never have been put into practice on a global scale and the luxury hotel might never have been born.

Unfortunately, Suetonius and his scholarly pals did not get together and write a Best Villa Guide, so we had to wait a couple of millennia before the luxury hotel came of age.

While it didn't emerge until the 1800s, its far more basic no-star predecessors have been around for thousands of years. Used out of necessity rather than for leisure purposes, they were anything but luxurious. Journeys taken by horse or on foot were laborious and required frequent overnight stops en route between towns. In England in the Middle Ages, these coaching inns were shabby, dangerous places frequented by highwaymen and other unsavoury ne'er-do-wells. They were dreaded by the well-born ladies who had to sojourn there while the horses were rested and the coachmen got drunk on warm ale and tore into fat haunches of beef in the bar.

Travellers often had to share sleeping quarters, and it was pot luck who you got as a bedfellow. Some quarters would have been directly over the tap room, so even if you could get to sleep (with one eye on your thieving, pox-ridden neighbour), you'd be woken several times during the night by the carousing of the drunkards downstairs in the never-closing bar. The concept of an innkeeper providing even a hint of privacy or cleanliness, let alone luxury, was not really grasped until the late eighteenth century when, also in England, the rise of manufacturing and trade (courtesy of the Industrial Revolution) meant more and more people were travelling on ever-improving roads and modernising modes of transport.

Inns suddenly got wise and started catering more to the increase in passing trade, but even after they improved tenfold and gained international reputations, the idea of such a thing as a luxury hotel – at least as we know it today, with butlers, jacuzzis, rose petals in bathtubs, mini-bars, and the like – was utterly alien.

But then some bright sparks had the idea of creating temporary luxury accommodation in London that would come close to the standard the aristocracy was accustomed to in their big country houses. They would be pieds-à-terre for wealthy country squires who came to the capital to do business and visit their money in the bank.

There was no immediate and widespread demand for accommodation of this nature, partly perhaps because England is small and because by the 1900s the rapidly developing railway system was shrinking it still further by allowing travelling dukes, earls and marchionesses to catch an evening steam train home to their shire. Subsequently the collected style, effort and money went into developing a small clutch of exquisite and truly luxurious, character-filled London hotels: the Ritz, the Savoy, the Langham, Claridge's, Brown's and the Goring.

There is a never-ending cat-fight over which was the first luxury hotel in London – mainly because nailing down exactly what defines a luxury hotel is more a loud debate than a scientific equation – but my money is on Brown's on Albermarle Street in Mayfair. It's the only hotel I have stayed at where I believe I actually smelled the sweet and evocative odour of natural wealth, when I briefly met a member of the English gentry in the English Tea Room. I also noticed that he managed masterfully to wangle his way out of paying for a cup of coffee, saying he'd settle up on his next stay, a trick I have been trying to perfect in hotels ever since in the hope it will allow me to amass a fortune similar to his. The problem is that Brown's knows very well that the gentleman in question will stay again and has enough money to buy a coffee plantation if he desires let alone a cup of the stuff, whereas I might not look like such a safe bet.

Brown's is not so much quintessentially English as quintessentially London. London properties that have been around for a few hundred years or so have a distinct character that is hard to define. It's not just the visual effect of the large blocks of limestone which make up so many buildings of this period. The character also comes from the many lives led within those protective, motherly walls. The collective history of world-changing events: wars, diseases, births, deaths, fortunes won and lost. The amassed joy and pain of numerous generations seeps into the walls of buildings like Brown's. Many of these lives were led before the building was opened as a hotel in 1837 and, as this is London's richest neighbourhood, a lot of them would have been pretty lavish.

This age and experience, this weight of years, adds a certain solidity to a hotel. Brown's actually feels like London – old, wise and rich; graceful and formal when it needs to be, but still with a youthful funky twist to it. The hotel's general manager, Stuart Johnson, told me that one distinguished guest, when asked at which hotel he stayed in London, replied with a wry smile: 'I don't stay in a hotel; I stay at Brown's.'

The hotel was opened by James and Sarah Brown, gentleman's valet and personal maid to Lord and Lady Byron respectively. In 1859, it was purchased and expanded by the innovative James John Ford, who installed fixed baths, electric lighting and one of the first lifts in England. To maintain the feel of a city retreat for country squires, he created a gentlemen's smoking room where lords, politicians, statesmen and captains of industry would puff away while contemplating what to do about the Austro-Sardinian War, how to celebrate the formation of the British Crown Colony of Queensland, or whether to invest in one of those newfangled American oil well thingies.

Ford also began a food revolution by opening a dining room at Brown's, the first public dining room in London. Before this, hotel guests would hire individual suites and dine on their own.

The hotel quickly became part of London's aristocratic scene. Kings, queens and presidents all clamoured to stay here. Theodore Roosevelt stayed at Brown's in 1886, just before his second marriage. Queen Elizabeth of the Belgians took refuge here during World War I. Ethiopia's Emperor

Haile Selassie also camped out within these walls, and King George II of the Hellenes stayed at Brown's for nine years after he was thrown out of Greece in 1924. That must have been some hotel bill.

Rudyard Kipling wrote a good chunk of *The Jungle Book* here, and Agatha Christie based her thriller *At Bertram's Hotel* on Brown's. Possibly the most famous event was in 1876 when the Scottish scientist and inventor Alexander Graham Bell checked in with his new contraption – the telephone – and made the first phone call in Britain.

This was just one of a catalogue of inventions that were being introduced to London hotels. The Langham, opened by the Prince of Wales on 10 June 1865 and, with seven floors and 600 rooms, one of the largest buildings in the city, was the first hotel to have hot and cold running water and hydraulic lifts. Over the years these luxurious amenities were enjoyed by Napoleon III, who spent much of his enforced exile from France there in a first-floor suite, Oscar Wilde, Mark Twain, Sir Arthur Conan Doyle, Noel Coward and Mrs Wallis Simpson, who stayed at the hotel during her controversial courtship of Edward VIII.

The Savoy, which was opened on 6 August 1889 by the opera impresario Richard D'Oyly Carte, boasted full electric lighting, 67 baths (for its 200 rooms) and possibly the most famous hotel manager and chef at the time: César Ritz and Auguste Escoffier. It was here in 1893 that Escoffier invented the Pêche Melba dessert in honour of the opera soprano Helen Porter Mitchell, whom you might know better as Dame Nellie Melba. The girl from Melbourne (hence the pseudonym) was by then the prima donna just around the corner at the Royal Opera House in Covent Garden.

Melba was, by some accounts, as much of a prima donna offstage as she was on it but she was undeniably a society figure, so Escoffier's gesture was both flattering and strategic, both for him and the hotel.

The Savoy was in many ways the pioneer of luxury hotels, mainly because it broke the tradition of charging separately for extras such as candles and baths, which was the practice in continental Europe and elsewhere around the world. When guests were given a rate for an apartment at the Savoy, everything was included except food and drink.

More recently the Savoy has installed rapidly filling bathtubs, which have been extremely popular with most guests – with one notable exception. Elton John left his running while he scurried back into the bedroom to answer the phone. As he merrily chatted on, the bath overflowed and caused some major damage to the rooms below Sir Elton's suite.

A few streets away in Mayfair is Claridge's, which was hosting well-heeled guests in apartments in 1812 but did not become a fully-fledged luxury hotel until the 1850s. Even then it was only temporary. It opened permanently in November 1898, after being completely rebuilt by D'Oyly Carte – fresh from his success at the Savoy.

Claridge's faced fierce competition from the Savoy and others, so it made sure it also had electricity, lifts and ensuite bathrooms. It came into its own in the Great Depression after World War I, when many British aristocrats were forced to sell their London homes. Renting a suite at Claridge's was far cheaper than shelling out mortgage repayments on a pile of bricks and mortar you only inhabited for six months of the year.

King Peter of Yugoslavia shacked up at Claridge's during his exile in 1941, and his son Crown Prince Alexander was born in Suite 212.

A lively after-dinner stroll from Claridge's is the Ritz,

which was opened on 24 May 1906 in Piccadilly, on the site of the former Walsingham House Hotel.

César Ritz contemplated how to outdo his own success at the Savoy and hit upon some even more luxurious innovations. To the jaw-dropping astonishment of his fellow hotel designers, Frenchman Charles Mewes and Englishman Arthur Davis, and no doubt of their collective accountants, Ritz decided that each guest room should have its own bathroom.

Double-glazing was introduced to block out the dreadful coal-fired smog of London and the clatter of traffic up and down Piccadilly. Early forms of air-conditioning and heating were pioneered, supplying cooler or warmer air to rooms depending on the weather and season. Every suite was furnished with a telephone that could be switched to a guest's next-door neighbour or to the furthest limit of the public exchange. Ritz also replaced the hotel's wooden beds with big brass ones, added Louis XVI-era furnishings and created the first walk-in wardrobes in guest rooms.

The hotel's excellent history book, written by the architecture correspondent of *The Times*, Marcus Binney, reports that:

> ... every bedroom was provided with a working fireplace, and the architects' sections through the building show the elaborate arrangement of flues which rise in the chimney breasts to the fifth floor and then ascend diagonally to become the central rooftop clusters of chimneys.

Every possible new or useful appliance was put at the disposal of guests. *The Sunday Chronicle* newspaper reported that 'in the vaults of the Ritz two pairs of silver-plated tongs for stretching the fingers of gloves have recently emerged – a very important accessory when gloves are wet'.

Keeping up the hype, that bastion of early twentieth-century journalism, *The Caterer and Hotel-keeper's Gazette*, reported in July 1906 that each floor of the Ritz 'is furnished with pneumatic tubes for the dispatch of notes, letters and keys'. Not to be outdone, *The Illustrated Carpenter* added: 'A visitor wishes to communicate with a resident in the hotel, and his card is pneumatically conveyed to the attendant on duty.'

After six years of design and building, the chateau-style Ritz opened with a grand flourish, a perfect example of the turn-of-the-century bonhomie between the old rivals England and France – the Entente Cordiale. Representatives from all the British newspapers were there, hopeful of a chicken leg or a cup of Earl Grey from the hotel's best chinaware, as well as those from *The New York Times*, the *Bombay Gazette* and the *Sydney Morning Herald*, guaranteeing the hotel had a worldwide reputation from day one. César whispered to the press that it was 'a small house to which I am proud to see my name attached'.

On the other side of Hyde Park, a corgi-walk from Buckingham Palace, the Goring opened on 2 March 1910, the last of the grand hotels of the Edwardian era. It offered the utmost in luxury – a radiator in every room. This, so the hotel's website claims, was a world-first. The devices were connected to a vast trembling boiler in the basement, which gurgled and spat and rumbled day and night to provide the Goring's cosseted guests with heat. This was not enough for the ambitious and imaginative owner, Otto Richard Goring, who also put in copper piping outlets on each of the four floors, into which his chambermaids could plug their vacuum hoses. All the muck and fluff they picked up was shooshed down tubes and out into the sewers.

Mr Goring was not going to let Brown's get away with hogging all the telephonic glory, so he insisted on adding a full, working telephone exchange in the lobby. Lines were fitted to each room through the walls and floors, allowing guests to call down and have a direct chat with the manager – probably to ask: 'How the devil do you use these new-fangled radiator whatnots?' Also, if a call came in for a guest from outside it could be connected to the appropriate room. Later, the hotel added a direct line to Buckingham Palace so the many royal guests who favoured the Goring while on official business at the palace could call through to check on the correct arrival times for garden parties and state suppers.

By the early twentieth century this small club of luxury London hotels was world-famous, and each was in fierce competition with the others. To maintain their A-list clienteles they had got into the habit of trying to out-luxe each other with outrageous parties, famous guests and celebrity events, especially lavish New Year's Eve parties.

The Savoy held a Gondola Dinner, hosted by champagne millionaire and Wall Street financier George Kessler, in July 1905. The staff worked hard to recreate Venice in the forecourt. At least 400 Venetian lamps were scattered about, and a full-size silk-lined gondola was decorated with 12,000 fresh carnations. A cake, specially baked for the occasion, stood five feet tall, and the famous tenor Enrico Caruso was hired to sing for the wallet-busting fee of £500.

The BBC managed to persuade the Savoy to host a radio show, *Dance Music from the Savoy Hotel in London*. The show became regular and was beamed out to millions of listeners all over the world, doing untold wonders for the hotel's PR. In 1925 George Gershwin took the seat at the piano in the hotel's ballroom to give London its first performance of 'Rhapsody in Blue'.

Over at the Ritz, Noel Coward was writing songs, Charlie Chaplin was being protected from his adoring fans by scores of bobbies, and – in the 1950s – Hollywood siren Tallulah Bankhead sipped champagne from her slipper during a press conference.

King Alfonso of Spain and Queen Amelie of Portugal met at The Ritz. Pavlova the Russian Prima Ballerina danced there, Paul Getty had a suite, and Churchill, de Gaulle and Eisenhower conducted summit meetings in the Marie Antoinette Suite during the Second World War.

Another frequent guest, King Boris of Bulgaria, had a passion for steam locomotives. Early one morning he returned to the Ritz from Euston, his face black with soot after riding on the footplate of the night express. He was told in no uncertain terms by the hall porter, George Criticos, to push off and make his coal delivery at the back of the building, away from the high society guests. Finally, he was recognised and was rushed through the lobby and up to his suite for a much-needed bath before the soot got on the furniture.

The Queen Mother was a frequent visitor to the hotel's restaurant, as was Prime Minister Harold Macmillan, who preferred Table 39. Jackie Onassis always asked for Table 9 by the window, while the Aga Khan III liked to dine at Table 1.

In 1936 *The Bystander* magazine reported that the Ritz was 'terrifically sophisticated and smart, especially at lunch time. If you're a woman, don't go there unless you've got the greatest confidence in your clothes'.

The Goring hosted a glittering list of European royals

for the coronation of George VI in May 1937, including the Crown Prince of Norway, who exclaimed that he much preferred staying there to the big house over the road because 'I never have a bathroom to myself in Buckingham Palace'. This turned out to be an inspired choice, for during World War II the Goring survived unscathed whereas poor old Buck House took at least six direct hits, which meant even fewer bathrooms for guests.

Despite London's small club of luxury hotels gaining a fabulous reputation around the world, England as a whole was lagging behind Europe and the USA in the great luxury hotel race. Apart from these magnificent half-dozen stylish and stand-out hotels, London is, unfortunately, now awash with mediocre, overpriced and badly serviced properties whose success baffles me.

The late nineteenth century in Europe was an era of great social decadence and big changes in fashion, architecture, technology and travel: La Belle Époque, as it was known. During this time, the first of the great luxury hotels were opening their doors, almost exclusively to aristocratic families who spent their summers doing the Grand Tour of Europe's antiquities and their winters bathing in the curative hot springs of Baden-Baden. These hôtels de luxe were very clearly temporary homes for the fabulously wealthy and off-limits to everyone else.

The Beau Rivage on the Riva degli Schiavoni, just a few steps from Piazza San Marco in Venice, opened to much Italian excitement in 1860, when the first guests clip-clopped across the white Istrian marble to check in. The Russian composer Pyotr Ilyich Tchaikovsky stayed at the hotel in 1877, and was so inspired by the view over the water to the island of San Giorgio Maggiore that he wrote the first three movements of his Fourth Symphony in its honour, from his desk in Room 106.

The unstoppable César Ritz was continuing his programme of world domination by hotels with the opening of Le Grand Hotel in Rome on a snowy 11 January 1894. It speedily became a hotspot for kings and queens, heads of state, movie stars and writers. In the Swiss Alps, in the small mountain town of Gstaad, which was becoming a hang-out for the well-heeled, the Palace Hotel opened in 1913. Inside the faux-Gothic architecture, complete with fairytale turrets and conical roofs, the hotel was ultra-modern and offered almost all the amenities of London's best hotels, including private bathrooms, electric lights and telephones. In Monte Carlo, no self-respecting European royal or aristocrat would be seen checking in anywhere but the Hôtel de Paris, which was built in 1864 right opposite the casino.

A leisurely hour's drive west along the Corniche in a Rolls-Royce Silver Ghost, the Cote D'Azur – and Cannes in particular – was accumulating an almost unbeatable collection of à la mode properties. The first was the Hotel Bellevue, built in 1861 to house the growing flocks of English holidaymakers migrating south each winter to escape the miseries of the weather back home. Then came the Grand Hotel in 1864, whose 230-foot arcade faced the glittering sea.

The Hôtel Carlton (1913) was the rather self-indulgent creation of local architect Charles Dalmas. During the project, Dalmas was so enamoured with Europe's most sought-after courtesan, the Spanish dancer Caroline Otero, that he sculpted the hotel's two corner tower domes after her breasts. This might have drawn La Belle Otero's many high-profile lovers – including Edward VII and the Duke of Westminster – to the Carlton, but I cannot help feeling that the lady herself would have been less than flattered. The domes are cone-shaped rather than nicely rounded spheres and more closely resemble the ends of two up-turned zeppelins.

The magnificent Martinez opened in 1929, just in time for the inaugural Summer Season in Cannes, when the hotels went head-to-head to charm guests. The openly polite but secretly deadly rivalry along the Croisette has been fierce ever since.

And so to Paris, where through the first half of the twentieth century two hotels dominated the luxury landscape. The Ritz (César's first triumph) had held court on Place Vendôme since 1898, entertaining nobles and A-list celebrities and generally being fabulous day after day. Cole Porter composed 'Begin the Beguine' at the bar, Fred Astaire sang 'Putting on the Ritz', there was dancing every afternoon and the bar poured no fewer than 100,000 glasses of champagne each year. Coco Chanel was so overwhelmed by the place that she moved in permanently in 1934 and lived there for more than 30 years, forever linking the hotel with haute couture and the pinnacle of Parisian chic.

The hotel's reputation for elegance and glamour only fell to Earth once, when, during the liberation of Paris in August 1944 and in a typically loutish outburst of bravado, Ernest Hemingway romped into the bar with some soldiers and canteen bottles full of gin and dry vermouth, and ordered the barmen to rustle up 73 martinis for his men. He would go on – modestly, of course – to tell his friends and anyone else who would listen that he 'liberated' the Ritz that day. The hotel named the bar after him.

Up the road, just off the Champs-Élysées, is the Ritz's

great rival, the George V (now a flagship Four Seasons property). It opened in 1928 in honour of George V of England, the current Queen's grandfather. It boasted magnificent art deco detail, marble mosaic floors and original seventeenth- and eighteenth-century tapestries, which remained from when the building was a Parisian palace. The beautiful stone building survived all Paris's wartime bombardments and served as US General Dwight Eisenhower's headquarters during World War II.

It was designed by French architects Lefranc and Wybo under the direction of its American owner, Joel Hillman. It was described in early press coverage as 'conceived in the spirit of modern and elegant luxury, and endowed with the latest technological innovations', which included the installation in each guest room of a telephone with both outside and hotel service lines. Some suites had two bathrooms, so modest couples could bathe at the same time and be ready to go down to supper together. Fitted closets were another boon, as were fire alarms, extra-wide corridors (to eliminate luggage gridlock), and an elaborate dumb-waiter system which shot hot room-service food several storeys up from the kitchens in the basement.

In 1930 Chase Bank opened a counter in the building, facilitating on-site transactions for guests. In the same year, the George V introduced an air taxi service between London, Berlin and Madrid on a three-seater Farman. Shorter flights to Deauville, Le Touquet and select golf courses were offered on a Nieuport.

Across the Atlantic, the USA was enjoying its first Golden Age of luxury hotels (the second is beginning as you read this book). And, with quintessentially American brashness, they were big, bold statements on the landscape – a world away from the more subtle, genteel establishments in London, Cannes or Gstaad. Industrialists, bankers and professional egotists chucked millions of dollars at projects to build limestone and sandstone hulks: monuments by which they would be remembered forever.

The Tremont House in Boston, which opened in 1829, was the first hotel in the world to have running water and indoor plumbing, indoor toilets and free soap. It is also credited with being the first hotel to offer a reception area, locks on the guest room doors and bellboys to fetch and carry luggage. It announced the arrival of the Massachusetts architect Isaiah Rogers, who went on to be one of the most in-demand hotel builders in the nation.

Almost 80 years later in New York, in 1902, the Algonquin Hotel opened its doors, and so began one of the USA's true success stories. The hotel was close to famous restaurants, theatres and nightclubs, and soon a battery of the city's most exciting and free-spirited writers and artists began frequenting the hotel.

Gertrude Stein, Simone de Beauvoir and Eudora Welty all stayed; William Faulkner drafted his Nobel Prize acceptance speech there in 1950; and the Broadway star and Hollywood actress Helen Hayes (remember the little batty old lady in Airport and the Herbie films?) was the hotel's longest permanent resident.

For one glorious decade from 1919 the hotel played host to the literary elite. A group of writers and humorists, including Dorothy Parker, George S. Kaufman and Robert Benchley, met daily for lunch at a round table in the hotel's restaurant. The Algonquin Round Table set the standard for literary style and wit in its era, and the table is still there today. (I had breakfast at it one morning and kept lifting the placemats to read the initials scrawled in the oak.) It was from this band of bright minds that the idea for The New Yorker sprouted. The magazine and its famous cartoons are now mainstays of New York literary society and specially commissioned cartoon wallpaper decks the walls of the hotel.

The Algonquin is the oldest continuously operating hotel in New York City, and despite its fervent passion for the arts, it has not stinted on modernity. It was the first in New York to introduce electronic keycards, smoke detectors and air-conditioning in all rooms.

Today, one of the most appreciated additions is nothing mechanical at all. It is a cat called Matilda. When the hotel was being built a cat wandered in, and the benevolent owner, rather than shooting the poor thing, decided this was her own Midtown Manhattan territory and that she had a right to stay.

The current Matilda is a Blue Point Burmese and, while not a direct descendant of the 1902 moggie, she is just as important to the hotel. She even has her own miniature chaise longue in the lobby, just opposite the reception desk, where she can be found luxuriating of an afternoon. Feel free to stroke her under her chin. If she is not there, you can find her snoozing among the warm fax machines on the reception desk itself.

Matilda is so famous now that she has her own fans. She also has an email address and business cards, and former guests regularly send her messages of love and support. The hotel even has management meetings about Matilda, to work out the best food for her, and how they can continue to accommodate her in the lobby and still run the hotel for the guests. At least one general manager has spent most of a day looking for her, especially just prior to an appointment with the vet.

I imagine poor Matilda has been feeling a little out of sorts as the Algonquin has undergone a major refurbishment, including the lobby, Round Table restaurant and guest rooms. Maybe Matilda has her own suite at last, complete with feline butler.

Impressive as the Tremont House and the Algonquin were, they were eclipsed two years later when the scaffolding was finally removed from a new building on Park Avenue in Manhattan. On 1 October 1931, just two years after the Wall Street Crash and in the depths of the Great Depression, the Big Apple presented the world's biggest hotel. The Waldorf=Astoria was born and the bar of excellence for luxury hotels was raised several notches in an instant.

No fewer than 50 red carpets were laid in front of the main entrance for the grand opening – a sight a modern-day Hollywood blockbuster premiere would have trouble matching. The hotel was vast, even for Manhattan. It covered an entire city block, filling the void between Park and Lexington avenues, and from Forty-ninth to Fiftieth streets. Then it went up 43 floors above Midtown, making it New York's first skyscraper hotel.

President Herbert Hoover broadcast a message of congratulations on the hotel's opening, which he delivered on radio direct from the Cabinet Room of the White House. He considered it a stunning endorsement of the USA's economic future, and said:

> Our hotels have become community institutions. They are the centre points of civic hospitality. They are the meeting place of a thousand community and national activities. They have come to be conducted in far larger vision than

mere profit earning. If we considered them solely from an economic point of view we should find them among the leaders of American industry. The opening of the new Waldorf=Astoria is an event in the advancement of hotels, even in New York City. It carries on a great tradition in national hospitality. The erection of this great structure at this time has been a contribution to the maintenance of employment and is an exhibition of courage and confidence to the whole nation.

Hoover's kind words ensured him impeccable service later on when, after leaving office, he packed his bags and became a permanent resident of the Waldorf Towers, the luxurious hotel-within-a-hotel that occupies floors 28 to 42 of the Waldorf=Astoria building.

But this was not the first Waldorf=Astoria Hotel. A previous incarnation had existed on Fifth Avenue near Thirty-fourth Street when the 13-storey Waldorf Hotel was linked by a corridor to the adjacent Astoria Hotel. The corridor was dubbed Peacock Alley, as it was chosen by the city's fashionable elite to parade and preen before fawning onlookers. The hotel's millionaire owner, William Waldorf Astor, also invited the couturiers of the day to use the space to show off their latest fashions. If you are wondering why the 'Waldorf' and the 'Astoria' are joined by a double hyphen rather than a single one, it is to signify the unity of the two former hotels. The '=' is the corridor.

The combined establishments won accolades from American society and a worldwide reputation for unbridled luxury. The buildings were later pulled down to make way for the Empire State Building, but not before Astor had opened the eyes of the world to just how opulent a hotel could be.

The new Waldorf=Astoria went even further, making the

famous hotelier Conrad Hilton (Paris's great-grandfather) determined to add it to his growing property portfolio. Hilton was so smitten with the Waldorf=Astoria that for years he kept a framed picture of it on his desk, with the words 'The Greatest of Them All' scrawled across it in his handwriting. He realised his dream in 1949 when he acquired control of the hotel by purchasing 68 per cent of its stock for $3 million. If it wasn't for great-granddad Conrad, little old Paris would not have been able to grow up in her suite at the Waldorf=Astoria. Goodness knows where the delicate flower might have had to slum down. At about the same time, across the country in a bean field in what is now Beverly Hills, another legendary hotel was having its dusty beginnings. On New Year's Eve 1927, the Beverly Wilshire opened its doors. This E-shaped hulk of a building was the tallest in Los Angeles and stretched a full 250 feet along Wilshire Boulevard. It was a $4 million French/Italian Renaissance extravaganza where smartly suited staff helped guests from their motorcars and then parked them in a huge underground car park. Doormen swept the guests into the palatial lobby through heavy bronze doors and past thick marble columns.

The hotel's developer, Walter McCarty, knew that luxury hotels in New York, Paris and elsewhere were getting more sumptuous, more outrageous, and that there was no place in this game for anybody who did not think very big. So he sent his scouts to Italy to find not only the finest Carrara marble but also a special stone from Tuscany that Roman architects were said to have used for imperial palaces. McCarty added sturdy marble columns, skylights made from mosaic glass, and gardens that rambled for 150 feet across the rooftop, where guests could sit on summer evenings and look down on the poor people. (That was a time when Beverly

Hills had poor people – of course, they have all gone now, apart from a tramp I saw just off Rodeo Drive looking only vaguely scruffier than me.)

The excesses at the Beverly Wilshire did not stop there. Models were shipped in each week from New York for fashion shows. Later, gaslights were imported from Edinburgh's Royal Mile to light the approach road. Headboards were sourced from remote Spanish villages, and bas-relief boxes and trays from somewhere in deepest, darkest Mexico. A Champagne Floor was created, with suites named after the big houses: Pol Roger, Bollinger, Veuve Clicquot, Krug, Moët et Chandon, and so on.

No expense was spared when wooing dignitaries. When Prince Charles arrived in 1974 US sailors lined the edge of the carpet, a Mexican mariachi band played deafening trumpet voluntaries from under their substantial sombreros, and Josie Wayne (John Wayne's granddaughter) presented him with an equally vast-brimmed hat. Having just spent time in Texas, where the local chilli-powered cuisine had not agreed with the royal digestion, Charles urgently called the general manager to his suite, thanked him for the Mexican welcome but begged him not to serve him any more hot food. Asked if he liked his hat, the prince put it on and it slid down over the royal ears, which is some feat. 'My head must have shrunk in Hollywood,' he said.

A similar spectacle was laid on for Queen Margrethe of Denmark. Some studious hotel employee had discovered that her highness's name means Daisy, so as she arrived chambermaids hurled handfuls of fresh daisies from the upper-floor suites. The daisy blizzard was a television sensation in Europe, giving you an idea of how gripping other television shows must have been in Europe that night.

The same crafty researchers found out that King Olav of

Norway was a sailing nut, so rather than merely opening the hotel's doors for him they borrowed a gangplank from a Los Angeles pier, hoisted an admiral's flag, and had a US naval commander and 30 cadets pipe him aboard the hotel. But the Beverly Wilshire must have had the B-team working on the night the grotesquely overweight King of Tonga came to stay, because all they could think of was to decorate his suite with 30 Big Macs.

No hotel has quite gone to these lengths for me yet, but I am expecting some pretty fabulous entrances in the future. If any concierges are reading and taking notes, I really like champagne, Calvados, oeufs cocotte, Annick Goutal fragrance pour homme and Cadbury's Dairy Milk bars. Also, please don't expect any posh toiletries to be left in the room after my stay for I must confess to an incurable case of hotel kleptomania. My home is stocked with more bars of soaps and bottles of shampoo than your average Crabtree & Evelyn outlet. I have a special cupboard for them and when writer's block hits I like to procrastinate by rearranging them.

Each one has a memory. Ah yes, the Hermes collection we snaffled over a two-night stay at the Mandarin Oriental in Hong Kong; no matter how often we vacuumed them up from the bathroom they were replaced. And, my word, didn't we do well with Bulgari from the Chedi in Muscat – we still have lots even after giving some away as Christmas presents.

I don't stop at soap. I have an impressive collection of shoe mitts, sewing kits, emery boards and shower caps, all in decorated boxes. Most of them I shall never use although I have been employing the shoe mitts lately to great effect. The most treasured possession is the luxury hotel slipper. I now have enough fresh and unused pairs to leave a pair by the bed in the spare room for each guest to use and abuse.

The last time I bought a pen was in the early 1990s. Since then I have been writing my articles and books courtesy of instruments swiped from palais de luxe around the world and embossed with their names. The one I took from my first visit to the Four Seasons Jimbaran Bay in Bali is still going – and that's getting on for six years ago.

While the US's luxury hotel Golden Age was glinting in the California sunlight, things were also shining brightly on the Florida shore, which was fast becoming a holiday haven for wealthy northerners fleeing the cold winds and piles of snow that froze New York, Chicago and Pittsburgh in winter. While Miami and Miami Beach were already gaining reputations as sexy, slightly risqué destinations, Palm Beach – 100 miles north up the coast – was always more genteel and refined. So when the oil magnate and railroad pioneer Henry Flagler was poking around for a site to build a stately and elegant hotel on the south-east coast, he chose Palm Beach.

His test run was the Royal Poinciana Hotel, which opened in 1894 and almost instantly attracted the USA's elite like very expensive filings to a magnet. Two years later, when Flagler had them hooked on his brand of seashore hotel, he built a second one, the Palm Beach Inn, right on the beach. Guests began to request – or more likely demand, given their status and bank accounts – rooms 'over the breakers'. Flagler did what all good hoteliers should do: he listened to his guests. Invariably, that is where the best ideas come from. When he doubled the hotel's size, not only did he maximise the number of beachside rooms, but he also renamed the place 'Breakers'.

Few hoteliers in the USA could match Flagler's clientele. The Rockefellers checked in to suites, the Vanderbilts too.

The Astors took breaks from making their millions in New York and spent some of their fortunes in Palm Beach. Andrew Carnegie popped in.

J. P. Morgan got sand between his toes. It became a retreat for vacationing US presidents and European kings and queens.

When the Breakers burnt to the ground in 1925, Flagler made a dash to Italy and rounded up 75 of the most highly regarded artisans, flew them back to Florida and set them to work modelling the new-look Breakers on the Villa Medici in Rome. The bewildered Italians made like Michelangelo and painted the ceilings of the 200ft lobby, and watched their cheques being written. Their families probably still talk about it.

Such one-upmanship among the USA's fabulously wealthy hoteliers could only mean one thing – more and more jaw-droppingly amazing hotels for lucky guests. The latest extravagant accommodation became a regular topic of chatter in society, wealthy and otherwise. Just how good could it get, they wondered.

Things were not quite as decadent in Australia but hotels there were pushing the luxury envelope all the same. Among the first luxury hotels Down Under was the Victoria in Melbourne, which opened for business on 1 November 1880 and was the first in the city to have electric lights. But its real coup was to be a dry hotel. That was different. That was its unique selling point. Melbourne, which was still finding its feet having only been founded as a city in 1835, was glutted with rough and lecherous pub accommodation – which was fine if you were rough and lecherous but not much fun if you wanted to go to bed at 9 PM with a good book and a cup of beef tea.

The Victoria was founded by a temperance league as a sanctuary away from stumbling gropers, hairy miners and the all too familiar presence of vomit in the grog-fuelled pubs. It does not rank as a luxury hotel today, and to be fair it does not advertise itself as such, preferring to state that it is three-and-a-half-star, but back in the 1920s and 1930s spending a night or two here must have been blissful. The porters did not just greet guests on arrival at the front door; they went down to the docks or Spencer Street Station to find their clients and shepherd them back to the hotel.

Singapore was determined to reflect London's fledgling luxury hotels in a tropical setting. Its major contribution to world hotels, Raffles, began quite humbly on 1 December 1887 as a 10-room bungalow hotel on the corner of Beach and Bras Basah roads. After twelve years of expansion the hotel came into its own when the main building was completed in November 1899. There were ceiling fans and electric lights and a French chef.

A bartender called Ngiam Tong Boon created the Singapore Sling cocktail, which is still served today. Somerset Maugham stayed here, making mental notes of the scandal and gossip he heard at cocktail parties and supper engagements, and then spending his mornings sitting under a frangipani tree in the Palm Court scribbling down all the juicy detail, which he used for his spicy stories of tropical intrigue and society goings-on.

When the Japanese swept down the Malay Peninsula in 1942, British families gathered up their gramophones and tea chests, fled south to Singapore and headed straight for Raffles. And as Singapore surrendered shortly afterwards they stood shoulder to shoulder in the hotel's lobby and defiantly sang 'There'll Always Be an England'.

World War II also played a major role in the South Pacific's first truly luxurious hotel, Aggie Grey's in Western Samoa. Aggie founded the hotel in 1933 as the British Club, and by the 1940s, as war raged in the South Pacific, it was virtually taken over by visiting US troops who were stationed there. Aggie made hamburgers and served cold beer, and the soldiers loved every minute of it. For many it was the only brightness and relief in an otherwise dark and dreadful war.

The returning US soldiers did most of Aggie's PR work for her, and before long Hollywood film stars were jetting in on old Catalina boat planes and staying for weeks. Gary Cooper was here to film the screen version of James Michener's Tales of the South Pacific. Michener had become a personal friend of Aggie, and it is widely accepted that she was the inspiration for the character Bloody Mary.

Marlon Brando has stayed at Aggie Grey's too, as have Denholm Elliot, William Holden, Cheryl Ladd and Robert Morley. British royals have breezed in, US presidents too, and prime ministers from many nations.

In its heyday it was one of the most romantic spots in the world, and it still is today – I have concrete proof of that. Aggie Grey's is where I met my wife, on the front steps one sun-kissed April morning. I was an exhausted, unshaven foreign correspondent at the end of a tiring and frustrating assignment for *Geographical Magazine*. She was fresh, beautiful, captivating and … Australian. The world stopped, I lost the power of speech, the hotel and the frangipani trees spun around my head, and life was instantly more exciting. It was the birth of love and the death of my career as a foreign correspondent, and I hold Aggie Grey's responsible for both.

Aggie Grey's was proof that by the 1940s the luxury hotel was a global phenomenon. For the first time, people talked about holidaying 'at Aggie Grey's' rather than 'in Samoa'; 'at the Breakers' rather than 'in Palm Beach'; 'at the Algonquin' rather than merely 'in Midtown Manhattan'. The hotel was becoming the destination.

But travelling between these decadent boltholes was still difficult and time-consuming. Passenger flights did not begin until the 1950s and were heart-stoppingly expensive. Ships were still the main means of international travel, and so the ocean liner companies realised that if you can have unbridled luxe on land, then you can also have it at sea.

The first-class cabins of ocean liners like the *Mauretania*, the *Ile de France* and the *Normandie* epitomised luxury on the waves during the first half of the twentieth century. One shipping line even kept a cow on board to provide guests with fresh milk, although the poor thing must have been dry as a desert at the end of every voyage.

The French were particularly suave in their liner designs, and when champagne was broken on the bow of the *Ile de France* in 1927 people fainted with delight. The ship later inspired that great globetrotter and bon viveur of the day, Noel Coward, to pen the song 'These Foolish Things'.

But then came the *Normandie*, the Waldorf=Astoria of the high seas. To everybody's amazement it had a swimming pool on board – 'Surely the water would slop out!' cried the doubters – a gym, a library, a merry-go-round, a kids' playroom and a Winter Garden stuffed full of exotic plants and birds. There was a nightclub for dancing, a cinema that showed films before they were on general release, and a shooting gallery for bored army generals to get in some target practice instead of aiming at seagulls off the starboard bow.

Guests could spend hours browsing in the shops. You might bump into Fred Astaire at the florist, Gloria Swanson at the beautician, or David Niven having his moustache trimmed at the barber.

The French had taken a leaf from César Ritz's book – on how to make your guests cry with joy – by designing every state room individually. The most sumptuous had four bedrooms, a dining room and pantry, servants' quarters and five baths (a different one for every day of an Atlantic crossing). Doors to suites and cabins were made from hand-wrought iron, while sculptures and tapestries further accentuated the shamelessly elaborate décor. And, lest the poor guests got bored during their voyage, grand pianos were heaved aboard and wheeled into the more luxurious suites, so guests could entertain themselves and their friends with show tunes in the middle of the Atlantic.

The *Normandie* was a floating monument to art deco. There were great gilded glass panels, lacquered plaster reliefs, and bronze and cloisonné vases.

The irony of this outrageously lavish liner was that the *Normandie* was named after a northern French peasant. They even advertised the fact by putting up an 8-foot statue to 'La Normandie' in the main hall. Maybe this piece of snobbery tempted fate. When the liner was languishing in New York during World War II, unable to return to Nazi-saturated France, an accidental fire gutted her. This graceful floating palace de luxe which had cost $60 million to build was sold in New York harbour for scrap, fetching a mere $161,000.

But the liner, along with the early luxury hotels of the modern world, had shown what could be done. They had revealed the lengths to which hoteliers were prepared to go to create temples to decadence, and they showed that guests were insatiable in their desire for more lavish temporary surroundings.

Imagine this lust for decadence and this vibrant rivalry between hotels massively amplified and diversified, and elevated to a world scale, and you will get some idea of the size and importance of the luxury hotel industry today.

Add a restless, rich and savvy globetrotting clientele to the mix and you have the makings of a worldwide phenomenon – exactly what we are now experiencing.

Chapter 3

Infamous

PSYCHOTHERAPISTS COULD EARN plenty of overtime ana-
lysing our global lust for staying in hotels where terrible
murders, drug-fuelled suicides and sexual escapades have
taken place. For thousands of us, the very proximity to a
scandal, even if it happened ten or fifty years ago, is enough
to count as luxury, and on the surface that sounds neither a
normal nor healthy condition for the human mind.

To be there – in the very room where Michael Hutchence's body was found, where Sid Vicious murdered Nancy
Spungen, where John Belushi overdosed with the call girl,
where Fatty Arbuckle indulged in the orgy that cost him
his career, or where some of Led Zeppelin took part in one
which enhanced theirs – is to be almost part of that famous event. It is the chance to feel history and notoriety all
around you. It's not just the ghosts of people but the ghosts
of the event itself, the echoing note of infamy which can
take decades to fade. Such is the indelible mark that some
events leave on their location.

Ask anyone over 40 and with even a vague interest in
1970s music why the Chelsea Hotel in New York is famous
and they will doubtless tell you: 'That's where Sid Vicious
stabbed his girlfriend to death.'

How about the Chateau Marmont on Sunset Boulevard in Hollywood? 'John Belushi and the hooker – he had a heroin and cocaine overdose.' Or the Sunset Tower just down the road, of which guest Truman Capote wrote: 'I am living in a very posh establishment, the Sunset Tower, which, or so the local gentry tell me, is where every scandal that ever happened happened.'

There are more. The Ramada Inn on Union Square in San Francisco got instant fame on 22 January 1949 when the cops burst in to Room 203 and found jazz giant Billie Holiday nestling a stash of opium. The Landmark Hotel on the Twenty-nine Palms Highway in Hollywood earned similar status when Janis Joplin was found dead in Room 105 on 4 October 1970.

Room 501 at the Sheraton Plaza La Reina (now the Sheraton Gateway) near Los Angeles's international airport was splashed on newspapers worldwide after the car designer John DeLorean was set up and videotaped there by the FBI in a cocaine sting in 1979. The feds had gutted a television and filled the space with a hidden video camera. DeLorean won in court using entrapment as a defence. A television is back in there now with all 1596 channels of glorious cable television. Maybe they should have left it empty.

Luxury hotels are wide open to scandals such as these because of their transient and often famous clientele. If you are a Hollywood movie star or international rock deity, it is far more convenient to shag your bit on the side or take your drugs in a hotel room rather than at home, where you might have, for instance, a family, who wouldn't consider it entirely appropriate behaviour.

Such notoriety can make or break a hotel's reputation and its future, and in the above examples – and in many more – scandal has brought the hotel incomparable publicity, future bookings and economic success.

The lonely and lovely Joshua Tree Inn in the desert of Southern California was little more than a highway pit stop before rock musician Gram Parsons (from the Byrds and the Flying Burrito Brothers) settled down alone in Room 8 to a leisurely evening of booze and drugs. He overdosed and died, aged 26.

I remember Parsons's death because it happened the day after my sixth birthday, and although he meant nothing to me at the time, I became instantly obsessed with the beauty of the motel's design and the wide open spaces beyond it that I saw on crackly black-and-white television reports.

Architecturally low-set in classic desert 1950s style, the hotel was built in a horseshoe shape but with sharper angles and a big roof easing down either side from an adobe-style central chimney stack. It was bathed in sunlight and had vines draped over the porch and awnings. It was different and striking and I wanted to go there and check in. It took me another 20 years but I finally went and slept in Room 8, which has been renamed the Gram Parsons Room. I drank as much of a bottle of tequila as I could without throwing up, smoked a joint and, rather pathetically, fell asleep in a chair. Not exactly a hard-core rock 'n' roll evening, but I felt the Parsons spirit wafting through the room before my eyelids fell.

Some desperate-to-be-hip establishments actually go looking for this sort of trouble. Getting on the front pages for the wrong reasons can sometimes be a deliberate attempt by the hotel to foster an edgy reputation. The owners and managers calculate that it is worth the risk. Anything for a bit of publicity.

For the most part, however, infamous hotels have had notoriety thrust upon them. They were merely going about their daily business of welcoming guests, serving tea, checking in and checking out, when trouble came knocking at their revolving lobby door, mainly in the guise of errant movie stars and long-haired rockers with plenty of Jack Daniel's, girls and pharmaceutical hors d'oeuvres.

While some of these hotels are lavish and exotic, others are – or at least were, on the day their fame-makers came to stay – quite unprepossessing places. Targeted by fate, you could say, and destined for greatness by means of orgies, overdoses and other over-the-top behaviour. Some were picked at random, and many at the last minute, by demented tour managers, often because every self-respecting establishment in town had said, 'No way are these guys staying with us.'

Despite suffering the headaches, the press clamouring at the door, and the vice-squad detectives in cheap suits camped out in the lobby, almost every one of these hotels became an overnight success. Their names were on everybody's lips and their pictures and logos were everywhere. A scandal was the perfect advertisement and usually cost only the price of a new set of furniture, a television or two, some fresh carpet and a fumigator.

The managers and staff at the Ritz-Carlton on Cross Street in the plush suburb of Double Bay in Sydney, Australia, had more than your average cleaning job on their hands in Room 524 on Saturday 22 November 1997. They had a body to remove, and a very famous one at that.

The room had been booked under the name of Mr Murray River, an alias for the rock god Michael Hutchence. The front man for INXS, Australia's most successful band, was dead.

Hutchence had been preparing for INXS's twentieth anniversary tour. He had also been battling a clinically diagnosed depression, which was being exacerbated by a child custody row in London over his daughter Tiger Lily. Hutchence wanted her and her two sisters, Peaches Honeyblossom and Fifi Trixibelle (whose father is Sir Bob Geldof), and their mother and Hutchence's partner, the British television personality Paula Yates, all with him in Australia for Christmas.

According to the inquest report, Hutchence had returned to his hotel at 10.30 PM the previous night after an evening out with his father. He continued a low-key party with two friends in his room. They stayed as emotional supports for Hutchence, who was expecting a phone call from London.

They hit the mini-bar and Hutchence also took some cocaine (it was found in his system during the post mortem), but this was not a boozing session – more a casual couple of drinks.

Oddly, rather than the large suite that you might think a multi-millionaire rock star would stay in, Room 524 was just a room. It was certainly luxurious, as one would expect at a Ritz-Carlton, and had the best aspect, offering a view of the harbour (at least it had the night I stayed and I don't believe the hotel has been sneaky and changed the numbering). But it was not excessive or extravagant, and neither was the trio's behaviour. They talked about Hutchence's plans for a career as a Hollywood actor, and listened to his fears over the court case.

After his friends left in the early hours of Saturday morning, Hutchence was alone in this room with depressive thoughts massing around him.

Phone calls to and from London proved the custody battle

was not going well for Hutchence and his situation was becoming more and more desperate.

Almost six hours later, at 11.50 AM, an unsuspecting chambermaid pushed her cleaning trolley down the hushed, carpeted corridor of the fifth floor and arrived outside 524 to make up the room. Her knocks on the door went unanswered. When she tried to open the door she found it jammed, and she needed to push with all her might to move it. Hutchence was lying naked on the floor, dead. Clothes were scattered around the room and his bed was half-made.

The coroner's report said he had been kneeling against the door with a leather belt nearby. In the room was a Ventolin inhaler, along with Nurofen painkillers, Zovirax 200 tablets, Prozac capsules and other pills.

Police said a leather belt was found inside the room but there were 'no suspicious circumstances', which is police-speak for suicide. Hutchence, stressed and depressed by the news from London and further affected by alcohol and drugs (both prescription and the other variety), had been pushed over the edge.

The managers of the Ritz-Carlton went into damage control, fielding calls from journalists around the world. The hotel had to get this right in the media to maintain its image as edgy – it had a strong reputation as Sydney's rock'n'roll celebrity hotel, having played host to Kylie Minogue, Kiss, Alice Cooper, Dionne Warwick, Engelbert Humperdinck and scores more. It had also served as a temporary Sydney address for Winston Churchill, Bill Clinton and Princess Diana.

The news sped around the globe. Hutchence's face, full of vigour but hiding trauma, was on the front pages of newspapers and magazines for days, as was that of the grieving

Yates. Adding to the tragedy was the news that the two were to be married in Bora Bora the following January.

The fear was that, after Hutchence's demise, the hotel would turn into a gawking shop for tourists (and travel writers) hell-bent on visiting the room where he died, disturbing the other paying guests. Despite the fears of the owners and managers, Hutchence's death did nothing but good for sales. The hotel continued to woo rock bands, some of whom might have chosen to stay there partly as a result of Hutchence's death.

I visit Shakespeare's grave in my home town in England more than once a year for inspiration, so I can fully understand rock bands wanting to get a Hutchence vibe from Room 524 in this hotel.

The property changed hands in 2000 when the Singaporean-based Stamford chain took over, renaming it the Stamford Plaza. But the stars kept coming. During the filming of *Mission: Impossible II* at Sydney's Fox Studios, the hotel was a temporary home for Tom Cruise. Add Madonna and Keanu Reeves to the mix (in separate rooms, thank you) and it is easy to see how the hotel's celebrity reputation has survived.

Today the hotel proudly shows off its clientele with signed photographs and letters hanging in frames on the walls of Winston's Lounge. Tucked away in the cigar room, next to the humidor and its racks of Cubans, is a gold frame containing a photograph of Hutchence on stage wearing a sleeveless denim jacket. Underneath the picture is a small plaque.

That it is there, subtly placed away from the main public areas, is proof that the hotel does not want to revisit that incident from its past – possibly for fear of being (wrongly) accused of milking the death for publicity, possibly just out of respect. I asked two staff members if this was the former Ritz-Carlton where Michael Hutchence died. They politely smiled and confirmed it used to be a Ritz-Carlton, but on the other matter: 'I wouldn't know about that, Sir.'

Hutchence was not a rock god to me, although I was a fan of INXS and remember vividly when he bounced down to the front of the stage at Manchester's G-MEX centre in 1990 and briefly gripped my outstretched hand. He was the first Aussie I ever met. Back then, I used to like my music a little harder. A decade later, although a one-night stay at the Stamford Plaza in Sydney was a bit of fun and a chance to squeeze into my black leather trousers once again, knock back some beers, stick on some INXS CDs and dance around the room miming like a teenager, there was another infamous hotel that I was longing to experience.

The Chelsea (in Manhattan, New York) is a relatively non-descript hulk of red brick squatting on Twenty-third Street near Seventh Avenue. It was constructed in 1883 as a co-operative apartment building, and in 1905 became a hotel, specialising in catering for long-stay tenants. This was New York's theatre district back then, so the hotel's guests were mainly creative types. There were musicians whose bodies ran almost entirely on a diet of heroin, whisky and junk food, actors and artists living life through an LSD whirl, playwrights, photographers, fashion models, beat poets, philosophers and their muses. They lived there with hell-raising writers, sex-crazed groupies, alcoholics and other assorted hedonists.

The Chelsea was home to Jimi Hendrix, Mark Twain, Tennessee Williams, Brendan Behan, Arthur Miller, Dylan

Thomas, William S. Burroughs and Arthur C. Clarke – who wrote part of his script for the sci-fi epic *2001: A Space Odyssey* while living in Room 322.

Notorious and admirable as these men were, one event stands out as the most infamous of all at the hotel. Everything changed at the Chelsea when one Simon John Ritchie (aka Sid Vicious) and his girlfriend, Nancy Spungen, checked in, as Mr and Mrs Ritchie in October 1978. Nancy never checked out, at least not in the usual manner.

Her involuntary departure from this hotel and this life happened on 12 October in Room 100, which she was sharing with her clearly devoted boyfriend.

A dull thud on the reinforced and virtually soundproof floor was the only thing that alerted the outside world that all was not well with the couple. An anonymous call from a neighbouring room came through to the front desk, followed by one from the room itself (presumably from Vicious) asking for help.

Nancy, aged 20, lay dead in the bathroom in her underwear. Blood was everywhere, smeared over her body and her peroxided hair, and over the mosaic tiles of the bathroom floor. Among the drug paraphernalia found in the room by the police was a blood-stained Jaguar K-11 folding knife, which had a five-inch blade and a black jaguar carved into the handle. This had caused Nancy's untimely end.

Sid was wandering the Chelsea's corridors, high on heroin and alternating between bouts of fury and sorrow, when the cops jumped on him and locked him in handcuffs. In a few hours he was charged with second-degree murder.

The courts never determined whether Sid was guilty of the killing, but according to both testimony and anecdote it was supposed to have been a murder-suicide. Sid later confessed he had not kept his side of the bargain, but his fellow band-member John Lydon (Johnny Rotten) maintains Sid's innocence to this day, as do his fans.

As one waggish guest at the Chelsea explained to me in the lobby, with the kind of black humour that thrives around Twenty-third Street and Seventh Avenue, 'People who love Sid and the Pistols say that Nancy kept running into Sid's knife over and over again, so it really wasn't his fault at all.'

By February 1979 Vicious was dead too, aged 21, having overdosed on heroin he had found in his mother's purse at a party in Greenwich Village. The Chelsea, meanwhile, rarely left the headlines, and skyrocketed into rock'n'roll infamy.

In the soft light of the New York spring day when I visited, the Chelsea's edifice and its wrought-iron balconies looked somewhat forlorn. With only a small sign over the lobby entrance, passers-by do not pay much attention to the hotel and scurry by without giving it a second glance.

I was hoping it would be a little on the grungy side, and I would have been disappointed if it had not lived up (or down) to those expectations. But what I found was something altogether more thrilling.

It is a shrine to the bohemian lifestyle. Apart from some immaculately renovated and furnished rooms, the place looked like it had hardly changed since Spungen's corpse was removed on a stretcher. The lobby looked like an after-gig party had just ended and I had missed the band only by minutes before they went up to their rooms to hand out the Valiums and sleep the day away. The soft grey armchairs were worn, and there was cigarette ash on their arms and on the brown carpet.

At the reception desk was a tall man in a beige overcoat and brown trilby hat who was trying to convince the desk staff that he had a reservation. His mid-Atlantic accent was that of an English-born frequent visitor to the USA. Momentarily he paused to help a silver-haired woman with a skinhead haircut who was carrying a small spaniel-mongrel cross. She had dropped a file of papers and was trying to pick them up without dropping the dog.

The papers were cuttings of hairstyles for dogs that she had clipped from magazines. The two giggled as they gathered them together, and the man suggested either 'punk spikes or a green Mohican would be perfect, just for fun'. The woman crouched there and thought for a second, then smiled and agreed, and rubbed the dog's head and told her she was about to look beautiful.

The dog bit the man's hat.

Here were two kindred spirits, people who looked at life on an angle, and sometimes upside-down and back-to-front. Real bohemians. The desk staff saw this too and checked the tall man and his trilby hat in with a smile. He was 'one of us', they could see.

His place at reception was soon taken by a short, stocky man with a limp, who had wandered in from the street and shuffled across the lobby floor. He wore dirty sneakers and black jeans which sagged around his arse; like their owner, the jeans were turning grey and frayed at the seams. His hair was dyed jet-black and was gelled into short, irregular hedgehog spikes, and the skin on his face looked like it might come in handy when sanding a hardwood floor.

From the side he vaguely resembled Lou Reed in the 1980s, after a big night out with Nico and the rest of the Velvet Underground. From the front he looked like a human train wreck, a former backing musician or roadie perhaps, so drug-addled that for every one year he lived he actually aged seven, like a dog. I was relieved he kept his Ray-Bans on when he glanced at me, because I feared the sight of his sunken, jaundiced eye sockets would return to haunt me in my sleep.

I was gripped with the sudden urge to ask him if he had been in a band, but then I realised that if there were one rule that the unruly Chelsea would religiously enforce, it would probably be: 'No asking the guests if they were backing musicians or roadies for Black Sabbath (or similar).'

I also realised he had not been glancing at me at all, but at a young woman sitting behind me dressed as a French schoolgirl – cute brunette pigtails, a revealing skirt and big black patent-leather shoes. She was pounding away at a laptop, her brow furrowed.

'Second novel,' she told me when she caught me staring at her knees. She had great knees. 'Twice as much of a head-fuck as the first. Head-fuck, head-fuck, head-fuck!' She said it so loudly that the limping ex-roadie and the reception desk staff heard her and paused momentarily. They have been hearing this kind of stuff for decades, I guess. It's when they stop hearing comments like this from nutty guests that they'll probably close the Chelsea – when the place loses its kooky edge and becomes too conservative.

To avoid this ever happening, the Chelsea's advertising should really carry a warning: 'If you have never listened to and got high on 'Lust for Life', or read 'Howl' and *On the Road* and surrendered your souls to the authors, allowing them to take you on those frightening, wonderful American journeys, then don't check in to the Chelsea. Stay safe and try the Waldorf=Astoria instead.'

The novelist with the great knees then looked bemused and angry as she wondered why she had announced her project so publicly, and to a stranger. I flicked my eyes away from her and my gaze landed on the largest pile of ash on the lobby's brown carpet. I imagined a record producer being there just a few hours before, flicking big grey nubs from his cigar. He had been cutting a deal with an unsigned outfit from New Jersey who had greasy hair and sniffed a lot so that people would think they were cocaine-heads, but in fact they were former choirboys who had only recently developed a rather innocent taste for beer.

Next to the record producer's cigar remains was a pile of something else, something off-white and flaky. It would have been no surprise at all to find someone had spilled their heroin bag on the floor and left it there for general consumption, but the answer was, sadly, more practical.

Directly above the centre of the lobby was a big patch of bare brick ceiling, from which plaster had, inexplicably, been peeling away, seemingly for some years. Maybe Brendan Behan in a first-floor room had been so caught up with a play that he had left the bath running and the water had seeped through the floor and begun this decay. Maybe a long-lost chandelier had freed itself and fallen to the floor in a theatrical crash.

Either way, its presence seemed to fit perfectly here at the Chelsea. The hotel is luxuriously scruffy. Decadently down at heel. Temptingly tired.

At least, that's the theme for the public areas. The rooms are stunning and designed with immaculate attention to detail. They are what I always wanted my university room to be like back in the 1980s – stylish, dramatic, edgy and a dead-cert shag-pad. I ended up with a cheap copy of an Arabian tent, with walls covered in Blu-Tack holding up swathes of psychedelic material from Afflecks Palace in Manchester, and some borrowed posters of Jean Shrimpton and Iggy Pop. Unlike me, the Chelsea actually spent money on its rooms and got the design right.

Today, they are a rich mix of stark monochrome patterns,

black-lacquered floors and vibrant coloured bedspreads and curtains. Many have wood-burning fireplaces and some boast kitchenettes – perfect for cooking a bowl of porridge or warming your dope ready to crumble into a fat joint. Rooms don't automatically come with televisions but they can be requested. Maybe the owners have realised that rock stars and televisions don't always mix.

Room 100, where Sid and Nancy had their little tête-à-tête, is, sadly, no longer. That part of the first floor was redesigned soon after the incident, and now four rooms take up parts of the original one. Guests wanting the Sid and Nancy experience have to request rooms 134, 138, 140 or 144 to ensure at least a quarter-share of the sordid punk past of the Chelsea and a chance of getting in touch with Nancy's bloody ghost.

No other celebrities who frequented the Chelsea matched the destructive genius of Sid and Nancy, but some came pretty close. The Welsh poet and author Dylan Thomas collapsed on 9 November 1953 at the White Horse Tavern in Greenwich Village, a short stumble down Seventh Avenue from the Chelsea. He was on a promotional tour and had been writing – and drinking swimming pools of booze – at the hotel and anywhere else that served alcohol. Thomas later died at St Vincent's Hospital, aged 39. A plaque at the front of the hotel is dedicated to his memory – it says he 'lived and labored last here at the Chelsea Hotel and from here sailed out to die'.

Brendan Behan, the Irish playwright and nationalist, also pushed himself to the edge with alcohol while staying at the hotel. He was struggling with largely unwanted fame and drank to mask it, although he famously maintained he was a 'drinker with a writing problem'.

During the mid-1960s the Chelsea became a hang-out for

Manhattan's artistic icon, Andy Warhol, and his band of doe-eyed young starlets, who became known as the Warhol Superstars. His favourite, at least for a while, was a wealthy, beautiful but troubled heiress called Edie Sedgwick, who modelled for *Vogue*, and became briefly the face of New York cool.

She starred in *Chelsea Girls*, Warhol's film shot at the hotel, which follows the lives of his 'Superstars' who were living there. After she and Warhol parted company she stayed on living at the hotel, finding its bohemian free spirit as addictive as the drugs she was enjoying. Bob Dylan was also living in the hotel at the time, and the two got involved. She tried LSD and inspired Dylan to write 'Just Like a Woman', which appeared on his album *Blonde on Blonde*.

I was hoping the recent biopic about Sedgwick, *Factory Girl*, had used some real interiors from the Chelsea but as far as I can gather the whole film was shot in a studio in Louisiana.

Jimi Hendrix lived at the hotel too and his ghost lives on in the hearts of some of the Chelsea's long-term residents. In the lift I met a German woman in her late sixties who gave me the bohemian once-over, a long stare from head to toe and back to eye level. Judging by her apparent lack of interest, I did not make the grade.

'I'm a writer,' I offered.

'Do you write songs or books?' she asked, doing her best Marlene Dietrich impersonation, which was not half bad.

'Oh, bit of both,' I lied.

'Aah, so many songs made here,' she sighed. 'I remember Hendrix, I remember Jimmy here. They were very good times. Everybody had parties and sang and played music. Real music!'

The Marlene Dietrich impersonator spat out the last two

words with so much passion that her eyes became moist and she felt the need to give me a light punch in the sternum. I could feel that one of her rings had made a tiny impression on my chest.

'Did you know Jimmy well?' I asked.

'Ha! Yes, everybody knew Jimmy well. He was part of the Chelsea. For a while he *was* the Chelsea,' she said.

And with that she was gone. The lift touched the ground floor. She did not say goodbye but walked briskly with small steps through the lobby and out into the blinding spring sunlight of Manhattan.

I wondered if she had known the not-quite-as outrageous but still certainly quirky Holly Woodlawn. Holly (born Harold Santiago Franceschi Rodriguez Danhakl in Puerto Rico) was another Warhol Superstar who frequented the hotel. If you have ever wondered who Lou Reed is singing about in his seminal song 'Walk on the Wild Side' – 'Holly came from Miami, FLA,' etc. – then wonder no more. It was little Harold Danhakl from Puerto Rico.

Another Velvet Underground member, the hauntingly beautiful and secretive German (or possibly Hungarian) singer Nico, was also at the hotel in the 1960s. In 1967 she was inspired by her surroundings and the Warhol Superstars to compile her debut solo album, *Chelsea Girl*. On this blissful record, she sang with a list of performers who now rank among rock 'n' roll royalty, including Bob Dylan, Jackson Browne, John Cale and, of course, Lou Reed.

Naturally for a hotel with this kind of artistic, hedonistic clientele, an awful lot of sex was going on. Most of it was consensual but not all of it was remembered clearly the next day. One union which became more public than at least one of its participants might have liked was between Leonard Cohen and Janis Joplin. Their one-night stand in Room 243 was later broadcast to the world, courtesy of the song Cohen wrote about it, 'Chelsea Hotel #2', from his 1974 album *New Skin for the Old Ceremony*.

It looked like a whole lot more sex had gone on there when Madonna's photographic book *Sex* was published in 1992. Tagged on to the back of each copy of the book was a small comic book-style pamphlet showing the sexual antics at a party meant to have taken place at the Chelsea. But then *Sex* should really have been called *Tease*, as there was a lot of nudging and winking but no actual shagging.

The most recent high-profile hedonist to check in was British pop singer Pete Doherty from the band Babyshambles (and formerly the Libertines), who took to the Chelsea like Dylan Thomas to an open pub door. In April 2003 Doherty recorded the original Babyshambles sessions there. Of more interest to the tabloid media, however, have been Doherty's addictions to heroin and crack cocaine, and his relationship with British supermodel Kate Moss. Not a bad effort for a 28-year-old former gravedigger from Liverpool.

Sadly, I fear the Chelsea might be maturing into a quieter period of its life. Admittedly the artworks are still there and still challenging to the eye – for many years the hotel has allowed artists, known and unknown, to hang their work for free, sometimes in lieu of rent. The walls flanking the oak staircase are covered with paintings, some sublime and dreamy, others tortured and full of pain; some vast and rambling, others neat and pocket-size. I walked past one that still had blood-red paint wet on the canvas, and I thought Sid and Nancy would have approved.

But paintings are not enough to maintain an image as an edgy, punky place. The raunchiest thing to happen at the Chelsea in the past few years was a photo shoot with Halle Berry for *The New York Times*. She posed, cute but clothed, in front of the raspberry-red walls of Room 309. The room is one of the hotel's best, with views south over Chelsea and on over the rooftops and a thousand air-conditioning units to Downtown and the Battery. Sunlight floods in and changes the hues of the walls hour by hour, as it arcs left to right across the city.

I scoured the hallways for signs of potential future scandal. A rock band vomiting into the corridor, or a poet high on crystal meth and reaching literary nirvana. Anything reminiscent of the hotel's past exploits. The best I could find was a young eccentric artist back in the lobby, furiously sketching scenes of tortured and malnourished African babies on sheets of white paper. 'It's my political statement and it's called Bushed, as in, like, President Bush, ya know,' he explained. 'I beena Africa, last year, um, and, um, it's like this – like what I am doing here in the picture but, um, worse, ya know, worse, but more colourful, but, um, worse. Ha, ha.' Not exactly Sid Vicious, but if he keeps taking the pills we'll see what happens.

On the stairs a few floors up from the lobby, I met another struggling novelist. I was beginning to wonder if these weren't just rich trust-fund kids having fun and struggling not with novels but with the guilt of having millions in the bank thanks to Mummy and Daddy and not really being any good at anything. Maybe that was merely spite on my part; no-one despises a rich struggling writer more than a poor struggling writer. This girl could have been a bestseller for all I knew. In a few years she might be the next big thing in publishing, doing the rounds of talk shows and celebrity readings and having her exotic prose and vivid characters made into Hollywood films. Or she may be dead from pneumonia caught on the cold stairs of the Chelsea.

She was blonde and dressed all in black, with skin that

had not seen sunlight since last August. She looked up and said hi but she was not wholly there; she was lost in some other space, seeking the answer to something that would finish her sentence. I knew how she felt so I left her alone, but as I passed I noticed she wore only one shoe. The other was propping open the door to the corridor to allow a cat to come and go with regal grace.

While the 1960s hell-raisers were ripping it up at the Chelsea, across the continent in sedate Seattle one hotel was developing its own infamous reputation. On the surface, you wouldn't think fishing off the shore of Elliott Bay on an innocent summer afternoon in 1969 would create anything other than a warm, fuzzy feeling. But when the fishermen are members of rock behemoth Led Zeppelin, and when one unsuspecting fish, fresh off the hook, is used to pleasure a female groupie in their hotel room, the scene shifts somewhat.

What actually happened – and memories are hazy, to say the least – became known as the Mudshark Incident, and it is one rather unsavoury hotel legend that has a thousand variations. The more it is told the more improvisation is used, like a Zeppelin jam session that has got way out of control after too much experimentation with pretty coloured pills.

It happened – or some of it happened, in one order or another – at the Edgewater Inn on Pier 67 in Seattle, probably during Led Zeppelin's July 1969 tour. The hotel had been built in 1962 for the World's Fair and was the only one right on the waterfront. One of its selling points was that guests could fish from their windows. To me this sounds about as exciting as watching paint dry on the ceiling, but apparently the guests loved it.

To cut a long and rambling story short, Zeppelin's drummer, John Bonham, and the group's road manager, Richard Cole, fished with abandon, dangling their lines and discussing the merits of coloured flies, skippers and other angling paraphernalia. It is rumoured one of their catches was later used to – how can I put this – entertain a naked groupie.

If you want the full fishy details, I suggest picking up a copy of Stephen Davis's highly entertaining biography of the band, *Hammer of the Gods – Led Zeppelin Unauthorized*.

While staying at the Edgewater, I spent some time trying to track the groupie down for an eye-opening interview, but to no avail. Even if I had found her, I imagine a now fifty-ish woman with a secret fish fetish and some rather scratched Led Zeppelin LPs might be somewhat reluctant to recount her afternoon of angling with England's rock gods.

I also managed to confirm that the hotel's new 'Nautical But Nice' package is absolutely nothing to do with the incident but rather a very generous way of enticing cruise ship passengers to get their land-legs again for a couple of nights.

By the time the hairy Zeppelin men checked in, the Edgewater already had a reputation as a rock hotel and was doing well from the publicity. It had taken the plunge five years earlier in the summer of 1964, when general manager Don Wright received a telex from a tour official for none other than the Beatles requesting accommodation for the boys during their tour in August.

All the other hotels in town had turned them down, terrified that the Liverpool mop-tops would pull the duckdown from the pillows and run off with the silver. If the city's hotels were worried about the well-mannered Beatles, God knows what defences they erected when Zeppelin and the Rolling Stones came to town a few years later.

According to the Edgewater's then director of advertising and public relations, Marty Murphy, Wright met with his staff to see if they could handle the onslaught of Beatles fans. Everyone gulped a little but went for it, and the hotel set about establishing the most elaborate security measures anyone in the city had seen.

'A 350-foot barricade of plywood and barbed wire was erected in front of the hotel around the parking lot,' said Ms Murphy. 'Police and hotel security were taking their stations at all entrances and all three floors of the hotel.'

The staff liaised closely with police to ensure the protection of the Beatles during every moment of their stay. Since the hotel was literally at the water's edge, Seattle's harbour police patrolled the bay to stop anyone approaching the hotel by boat or by breaststroke. As the Beatles' limousines arrived at the Edgewater, hundreds of fans pressed against the barricades, trying to get a glimpse of the band.

'The entire front end of the hotel was locked down to the public,' said Murphy. 'At that time there was an entrance to the coffee shop right next to the main door by the parking lot. That's where we took the Beatles in, then up the stairwell to the second floor, to room 272.'

That room served as the suite where the band met and swapped jokes. They slept in the adjacent Rooms 270 and 274, both of which were furnished with two double beds. Girls were crying on the hotel phone, while fan mail, full of lip-stick and 'I love you' written on envelopes, was delivered to the hotel, along with stuffed animals, cakes, cookies and jelly beans. One girl even sent her father's Masonic ring. In alarm, Marty Murphy contacted the girl's horrified parents and had the ring returned.

You could say celebrities, rock stars in particular, made the Edgewater what it is today. It's still there, a fine institution with a fabulous panorama over Puget Sound, at which guests sigh as they sip their Canadian Clubs in big armchairs with moose antlers for arms. All guest rooms are furnished with hand-crafted pine furniture, river rock fireplaces, overstuffed chairs and footrests. It has swapped the rather old-fashioned 'Inn' for 'Hotel' yet, thankfully, has retained its bright red rooftop neon 'E'.

The Edgewater has come a long way since its Mudshark days, but without them I wonder if it would have gained the scandal that some hotels undoubtedly need, if they're to be catapulted from moderate fame to immortal infamy.

Chapter 4

Your Teeth, Madam

WHILE SOME LUXURY hotel addicts crave infamy and association with fame, others do not care which rock star or screen idol stayed in which hotel, let alone in which room. Neither is it of the remotest importance to them what scandalous antics these famous people got up to while they were checked in, or what harm they did to themselves or others. Instead, their definition of luxury is focused entirely on service.

A taxi driver who picked me up one Friday evening in Sydney, Australia, explained this succinctly. He was mad on cruising – a luxury habit I confess I have never been drawn to, as I generally prefer my hotel room to stay still.

'Cruising is bloody ace, mate,' he told me enthusiastically, as he changed lanes like a man possessed and bombed through a red light and down Oxford Street, a rainbow of bars blurring by.

'I'm going this weekend. Soon as I finish my shift tomorrow night I'm off to Spain to pick up the boat for a two-week cruise around the Med. I've done the Caribbean – didn't like it much. Not enough ruins. I like ruins. You know, Roman stuff, Greek stuff. And the service wasn't crash-hot either. Bit lazy, I reckoned – mind you, I'm a tough customer.

'Every year I do this – take two weeks off in July. I tell the boss, go fuck yourself, I'm off to Europe on the ships. For those two weeks I'm *somebody*. I am not your driver, not someone's employee or money-maker. I am a person who is being waited on, pampered, whatever you want to call it. And I want it all. I want the Full Monty – butlers, silver service, flowers in my room … the best! I've even been to breakfast in my black tie, mate.

'If they say you get a free shoeshine if you leave your shoes out, I bloody leave my shoes out – I even left my running shoes out one night and they came back all cleaned and white. I thought they'd bought me a new pair.

'Then there's the food. I eat in a different place every night – I try every restaurant on board, and then room service. Sometimes I wake myself up in the middle of the night just to get someone to bring me a sandwich.

'Best of all is one night on each cruise I dine at the captain's table – that's the highlight. It's because I've been on so many cruises and they know me now, that's why I get invited. It makes me feel special.

'For the rest of the year I live in Sans Souci and drive this cab. I'm a slave to you mongrels. I clean puke off the doors, and drag people out and carry them to the kerb if they're so pissed they can't stand up. I've stopped a heap of fights. Saw one girl smack her bloke in the head so hard I had to take him to hospital. Later that night I found her wedding ring in the car, so I had to go back and return that as well.

'I do all this service for other people, so when I am cruising, that's when I get my turn – a couple of weeks when I am the boss and people are calling me Sir.'

I sat silently. This guy was a cruise-ship porter's nightmare. Every second he was on board was crucial to his self-worth. Sure, he wanted to see some ruins, but he placed far more importance on the quality of a 3 AM room service sandwich. One missed 'Good morning, Sir' or one seat at a table with a disappointing view of a pillar rather than the ocean could send him into a frenzy. Cross him at your peril, and God protect the shoeshine boy who does not do a top job on his runners.

But he was right about the service, and many of the world's highest ranking hotel managers would agree with him. Of the 50 or so I interviewed for this book, almost every one said it was the staff and the service that make a luxury hotel luxurious.

Jeff Klein, owner and manager of the Sunset Tower Hotel in Los Angeles and the City Club in New York, said, 'Putting a fax machine in a bedroom doesn't mean anything if your room service order took an hour and a half to reach your door. And there's nothing wrong with calling a guest and explaining what might have gone wrong and trying to find a solution. That makes guests feel like at least the staff are trying. Not calling a guest back is the worst thing.'

A former manager of the Ritz-Carlton, the only truly stylish hotel in Dubai, said his service philosophy was built on one set of unmovable foundations: 'The answer is yes – now, what was the question?'

I confess I winced a little when I first heard this as it smacked a little of PR-speak but the more I thought about it the more I agreed with the phrase. If you believe anything is possible, there is a good chance your guests will too. That's the kind of thing that breeds loyalty among us fickle luxury hotel addicts.

The Ritz-Carlton makes a very big deal out of service and it has a subtle and clever way of letting guests know that they have a role to play as well. At a recent and highly enjoyable stay at the Ritz-Carlton Bahrain Hotel and Spa I was trapped in my room one afternoon by gale-force winds and temperatures of 6°C – it was the coldest day Bahrain had experienced for some years.

I cranked up the heating and sat by the window wrapped in a full set of clothes and a bathrobe. Drinking my way through the Nespresso collection, I happened upon a letter from the management referring to etiquette in the hotel's VIP lounge.

'We request that our younger guests under the age of 12 are accompanied by an adult in the Lounge. Please be advised that in order to preserve the serenity of the Lounge, children are requested to observe proper etiquette befitting the young ladies and gentlemen of The Ritz-Carlton,' it said. It was a highly intelligent way of telling the little blighters to put a sock in it, while building brand loyalty from an early age. Had I stayed here under the age of twelve and seen this letter I would have made much of telling my richer friends at school that I was a 'young gentleman of The Ritz-Carlton'.

Managers also recognise it is becoming increasingly difficult to find people able or willing to provide really top-flight service. Klein said nowhere was that more apparent than in the USA.

'In America it is very challenging because to serve is considered demeaning,' he said, as I was served perfectly by the head bartender at the Sunset Tower's Tower Bar. 'It is especially hard for me because what I am trying to create is a collection of hotels that reclaim that high level of sophistication and subtle glamour.'

Klein also believes a luxury hotel has to run in a 'completely unscripted way, as if it is in-built'.

'When staff in hotels ask, "How may I enhance your experience?" it drives me crazy. There's no manual for running a luxury hotel – it has to be natural. The service has to come from the heart,' he said.

The unfailingly polite and congenial Edward Gray, former managing director of London's Coburg Hotel and now a consultant to the industry, believes that once you strip away the gloss and the hype, you can spot a genuinely luxurious hotel by the strength of its service.

'I really feel that you can have all the luxuries in the world, but what it really boils down to is the staff and the service,' he said.

'The sweetest voice that any guest could hope to hear is their name when they arrive at the hotel, and when they are addressed on the phone in their room. It is an immaculately trained staff and ingenious service that really make a true luxury hotel.'

'I could not agree more,' I thought, as I lolled in my hammock in the Honeymoon Suite at Yasawa Resort in the islands off the west coast of Fiji. Five minutes earlier I had been inspired by a glorious sunset to obtain a gin and tonic but could not quite muster the strength to walk the 100 yards up the beach to the bar. So I called room service.

'No problem, Mr Brace, gin and tonic coming up,' came the reply. The sunset blazed away and the surf crashed, and tiny, fluffy green acorns fell on my head when the breeze blew the trees softly. I kept my eyes fixed on the beach to spy the approach of my cocktail but instead heard the squeak of a four-wheel-drive's brakes.

The vehicle arrived and out stepped both driver and waiter. They were grinning from ear to ear and as they walked across the sand beneath the casuarina trees and up the steps to the huge deck, I noticed they were both carrying trays.

'We brought some snacks too. Just cheese and biscuit, and lobster salad. Still an hour till the dinner time,' said the waiter, as he handed me a tall and well-iced gin and tonic that had been kept cool inside a little padded jacket. 'The road is rough, so the gin is mixed just right for you,' he said.

I told him that if I had known he was going to go to so much trouble to serve me a cocktail, I would have asked them to bring the bottle – to save him having to come back in a few minutes with another one.

'No problem, Sir,' he said, and from a small picnic hamper bag slung over his shoulder he produced a perfectly chilled bottle of Bombay Sapphire and then another of Tanqueray. 'Which your favourite?'

When you pay several hundred pounds a night to stay in a place like Yasawa, where the lobster and the romantic sunsets are on-tap, then you expect the service to be pretty good, but this surpassed even my expectations. It is this sort of service that makes the difference, that makes a hotel stand out as genuinely luxurious. Going the extra mile, which can sometimes be a bumpy and dangerous one; not just serving the best gin and seafood, but serving them with fun and sincerity … and with speed, even in sleepy Fiji. Yasawa has it down to a fine art.

Receiving above-standard service when you ask for it is one thing, but it gets even better than that when it is predicted. In Bali, high up on the clifftops of the Bukit Peninsula, is a private villa called Istana that has to be experienced to be believed. As *Hotel Heaven* was going to press the ownership and management of the villa had changed hands so I hope it is still rentable.

My stay there was the only time in my career as a luxury

travel writer that I have experienced truly telepathic service. I don't know how they did it. I knew the guys who used to manage the place and they knew me well enough to know I like swimming pools and Veuve Clicquot and Barry White CDs, and a good spicy beef randang for supper. But they did not know me well enough to equip the Istana's staff with the information to satisfy my every craving.

The telepathy happened first one hot afternoon. This was hot even for Bali, and breathless, which is even rarer up on that clifftop. I walked to the edge and looked out at the silent ocean. Its swell was coming from the south and turning slightly north-west about 100 metres offshore, sending the breakers crashing into the rocky shoreline at an angle.

A large seabird was flying solo about 20 metres beneath the lip of the cliff, wheeling and gliding out to sea before using its wing tip as an apex on which to turn, whereupon it drifted back towards me again. It was a steel-grey bullet against the solar radiance of the afternoon.

'I wonder ...' My thought was interrupted by Wayan, a diminutive butler who was carrying a book that was almost as big as he was.

'I think, frigate,' he said, smiling an impossibly wide smile and showing me his dazzling teeth. He had somehow worked out what I was looking at – which could easily have been a ship or a fluffy cloud that looked like a chicken – found me a book on Bali's birds, and neatly inserted a little yellow card in the appropriate page.

He opened the book and he pointed – first at the coloured drawing of the bird, and then at the real thing flying over the waves. I was speechless. Not because he was right, which he was, but because he had known intuitively that I would want to find out what bird it was.

I put Wayan's powers of telepathy to the test again later

by sneaking out of my room and embarking on a commando exercise to see if he could guess my destination without seeing the direction I was heading. I ran through the foliage and hid behind frangipanis and banana plants to dodge his gaze and that of the rest of the superhuman staff. I finally made it to the other end of the Istana's grounds, rather hot but pleased with my skills in evading detection.

There is a private honeymoon villa and pool at this end of the resort … where Wayan was waiting for me with a cold towel infused with lavender oil. I saw all his teeth again.

Later Wayan passed his telepathy baton to a fellow Istana wonder, Ketut, who brought out martinis when I was by the pool at dusk just when I was thinking how pleasant it would be to wrap myself around one.

Just before we move on to the next round of tales from a luxury lifestyle, this might be a good point to raise a sticky issue.

You are probably wondering how realistic all this is. Do real-life paying guests get the same service in luxury hotels as travel writers and celebrities? Does everyone get the limo from the airport, or just when the hotel wants to appear in *Vogue* or when Pierce Brosnan is checking in?

Now that luxury hotels are being frequented more and more by a growing band of guests who are not famous and who are earning only modest salaries but who are willing to save and save and then spend to experience this new essential lifestyle choice, how are they treated?

Celebrity guests, and those with bottomless bank accounts who book out the Presidential Suite for ten days whether they intend to use it or not, are undoubtedly going to get superior service to the rest of the mere mortals who want to stay.

And yes, I must confess, hotels do turn on the charm when there is a travel writer in-house. They would be crazy not to. They have a golden opportunity to impress a writer for a magazine which they have identified as being read by the very people they want to come and stay there. It's far cheaper to give me a good room and a bottle of something nice and cold with a yellow label than it is to take out an advert in the same magazine – and who believes adverts anyway? Of course they are going to be nice to me.

So, you could ask how I can write a fair and honest review because I am getting tailored service, whereas my so-called 'truth in travel' colleagues, who check in without announcing they are travel writers, might get service which is closer to the real thing. It is a good point and one I get harangued about regularly, but it also assumes that I can be bought with a complimentary limo from the airport and a bottle of Veuve Clicquot in my penthouse suite. Even though I strongly encourage any hotel managers reading this book to continue giving me such luxuries – because I am, after all, a luxury hotel addict so it would be mean not to – these gifts are not in themselves enough to make me write a gushing account about my stay.

A truly good luxury hotel cannot hide its brilliance, no more than a fake one can mask its incompetence.

You would not believe the number of hotels masquerading as luxury establishments who still mess things up, are rude to me and are generally useless even when they are fully aware I am there to write a review. No amount of vintage champagne is going to make me write a good review about a luxury hotel that fails in the simplest tasks, like delivering a newspaper to my room on time in the morning after it has promised to do so the night before, or one that does not care about a leaking tap in my bathroom and leaves it unattended for the better part of a day, or one that allows its staff to call me 'mate' on first meeting. All three of these things have happened, and at expensive luxury hotels in Sydney. I shall spare them the blushes by not naming them, because even though I am a pedant for all things luxurious, I am also a jolly decent chap.

So, to ensure a fair and honest review, once the Veuve and strawberries are consumed, I set to work. I may have to creep about like a loon in the middle of the night seeing whether the carpets are suitably vacuumed and the lifts are polished, but it's the only way I can really tell how the place runs and whether it is deserving of a glowing report. I also make a point of asking as many of my fellow guests as I can for their take on the place. I collar them when they are least expecting it and ask them some quick-fire questions: Have you had good room service? Did you get your newspaper this morning? Is your tap leaking?

This got me into hot water once, at an only passable hotel in San José, Costa Rica. An over-friendly couple from Miami insisted I look around their room, which, although more expensive than mine, had an appalling view of the back of a bus station. The room looked as if an orgy had finished only minutes earlier. The floor was littered with their discarded underwear, through which I tip-toed sheepishly. As the husband showed me the view and I watched the buses coming and going in little puffs of exhaust fumes, his wife decided it might be a good time to strip off and make herself a cup of coffee in the nude.

I turned around precisely as she was bending over and peering into the fridge for the milk. Their silence and the rich, seductive smile she shot me as she turned her head towards me delivered a clear if unspoken invitation to stay and join them in whatever they had in mind, but I had seen this scene before in a film somewhere and I seemed to remember it hadn't ended well for the third party so I made a dash for the door.

It's never dull, this travel writing, I tell you.

Apart from the odd bad experience, generally non-VIP guests seem to get treatment equal to mine. I just get a few more perks. They get the icing but I get thrown a cherry as well now and then. Long may they be thrown.

Most hotels are not fortunate enough to have telepathic butlers and waiters, but they do have some handy tricks up their sleeves to give guests the illusion that magic is dancing through the air.

For example, there has been an explosion in specialist concierges. The Benjamin in New York has a 'sleep concierge' to help you choose from a menu of twelve pillows.

The Starwood group offers pet services at its W brand. At check-in guests receive a pet toy and treat, pet tags and clean-up bags. Up in the room there is a customised W pet bed, food and water bowls, a 'pet-in-room' door sign and a special canine or feline treat at turndown. Oh, and the hotels also provide designated dog and cat concierges who can instruct the pampered ones on where best to go for a walk. I think I would rather be a toilet-cleaner than a pet concierge – I'd get more tips.

And at the Four Seasons on Park Lane in London, younger guests are greeted by the hotel's full-time 'teen concierge', who hands out child-size bathrobes and lets the kids know all about fun things to do while visiting London.

The director of Sydney's InterContinental Hotel School, Peter Lewis, is a former Ritz-Carlton manager and another service fanatic who has gone to some lengths to please his guests.

'Once you have satisfied all the physical comforts by designing a space-age lobby and beautiful high-tech rooms, what's left? It's got to be the service,' he said.

'Luxury is all about guest recognition these days, and we imbue that fact in our hotel school graduates very seriously. We make sure they are aware that all staff must be engaged in that process. They must be trained to collect data from all quarters and feed it into a guest's profile.

'Return rates at luxury hotels are considerably lower these days, which shows there is less loyalty from guests, but the hotels that *do* get big return guest numbers are those which are recognising their guests and making them feel special.

'At a hotel I used to manage in England years ago I had an idea to start taking down car number plates. I asked the valet parking attendants and the doormen to start making surreptitious notes and matching them to guest names. About 50 per cent of the time, when those guests returned we were able to open the door and say, "Welcome back, Mr Brace." It used to freak them out a bit but they loved the fact that we had remembered them.

'It's great for customers and it's great for business because it's cheap. Why would hotels not want to adopt something like that?' said Lewis.

'Of course you have got to make sure it is flawlessly conducted, and be ready for the odd surprise, especially if the guest in question is travelling incognito with his secretary-cum-mistress. Then it might not be the best option to have his name publicly blurted out and echoing around the porte-cochere.'

Lewis was manager of the Ritz-Carlton in Double Bay before the Michael Hutchence incident. He says the chain perfected the practice of guest recognition.

I would argue, however, that the Ritz-Carlton Millennia in Singapore – my favourite in the city-state – may even have gone too far. One night, battling a bout of insomnia following my father's sudden death, I went on my customary nightime prowl, trying to find fault with the place. I was looking for unpolished antiques, cleaners picking their noses in the lift, and room service trays left outside doors with their food scraps congealing.

I found none of this at the Ritz-Carlton Millennia. Instead, the hotel's artworks – which include some Andy Warhol paintings and prints by Henry Moore – were being dusted and straightened, the carpets vacuumed by almost-silent machines, and the awkward corners of corridor ceilings cleaned vigorously.

The public spaces of the Ritz-Carlton Millennia are almost as heavenly as the rooms, and my nocturnal padding that night explained why – they are treated with the same loving care. I turned a corner at the far end of my corridor near the Presidential Suite where, just a few days earlier, Mariah Carey had disrobed, showered and slept. This was before her memorable MTV moment, so presumably she did all this without a camera crew in her room.

There, I met a man picking nano-size atoms of fluff from the carpet and placing them in a little bag. He stood to attention, hid the bag behind his back and said, 'Good morning, Mr Brace.' I smiled, said good morning and stepped around the patch of carpet he was so diligently de-fluffing.

It is no great surprise for me to be addressed by my name in luxury hotels, because any hotel manager with half a brain will circulate information to his staff that there is a travel writer in-house writing a review, and to give him VIP service, or else! If they have a photograph of me, they will distribute that too, or at the very least a visual description. The staff know which room I am staying in, which room I stayed in last time, what I like to eat and drink and when and where. Presumably, rather worryingly, they also know what colour my underwear is and if I leave my dirty socks on the floor for the maids to pick up. I do.

Whereas that information is usually only circulated to the staff who are likely to have contact with me – doormen, porters, the concierge, restaurant staff, and so on – at the Ritz-Carlton Millennia in Singapore the Matthew Brace personal dossier had clearly done the rounds of the entire hotel.

The de-fluffer knew me, as did the man polishing the buttons on the lift and the woman delivering a bowl of cereal to another insomniac on the eighth floor. A plumber making his way to the lobby toilet said it was nice to see me back at the hotel and he hoped I was enjoying my stay.

I was famous, but it is a slightly disconcerting kind of fame to know that upwards of 300 people may well be fully versed in my most intimate underwear habits.

For Jeremy Goring, the owner of what can only be described as London's paramount hotel, the Goring, service has become an art form: 'Luxury can manifest itself in many ways: beautiful silks, highly luxuriant beds and arresting chandeliers. All of these last but a moment. What remains is the memory of how one is looked after by human beings,' he said, as we sipped fizzy mineral water and ploughed through a plate of hors d'oeuvres in the hotel's bar one frosty London lunchtime.

For generations, the Goring's staff have been fine-tuning service in the hotel, often using cunning innovation to gauge the satisfaction level of guests. John Shepherd, the hotel's driver since 1977, who is known fondly as John Taxi, used to pick up all sorts of useful feedback from guests. He would casually ask, in his Cockney brogue, 'So how are you enjoying your stay?' Comments – good and bad – would find their way back to management and action was taken accordingly.

Such attention to guest happiness has been a mainstay of the Goring since its earliest days, when its first owner and manager, Otto Richard Goring ('O. R.' to all who knew him), invented the hotel's mantra: 'We make a profit while our guests sleep, so see that they sleep in peace.'

Today the Goring is the last privately owned luxury hotel in London and its service is as impeccable as ever. Ever keen to dote on its guests, the owners recently commissioned interior designer Nina Campbell to refurbish some of the guest suites.

A real test of service is maintaining harmony for all guests, both the law-abiding and the incorrigibly naughty. Sex, of course, is the ever-present antagonist. There can be no better examples of how this delicate balance is so professionally kept than the entries from 'The Goring's Night Porter's Report Book' from the 1980s, recounted in the hotel's official history book, *A Very Special Place: Tales from the Goring Hotel*, by Robin Rhoderick-Jones.

Thursday 22nd, 0300. Room 73 Mr Minsky rang down to ask me to fix him up with a Linda Lovelace type female. Explained to guest that we were a No-Go Area in this respect. Suggested we sent him up a do-it-yourself kit (a Playboy magazine and an empty Marmite bottle). Guest refused offer but I think he got the message.
Friday 9th, 0510. Stopped young male bearded and

be-jeaned person (who had come down the stairs) from leaving the hotel and inquired who he was. He informed me that he was not a guest but had been staying with Mrs Mackinson in Room 45. Checked this out before I let him depart. (Mrs Mackinson sounded very sleepy – not surprised, he looked a big lad!) She is paying double rate. Lucky old her.

I have better uses for an empty Marmite bottle – like refilling it with yummy Marmite – but I know where Mr Minsky was coming from. It is easy, when you are in the lap of ultimate luxury, to believe that the hotel staff are angels who can provide whatever your heart desires, no matter how illegal or immoral that might be.

Sometimes I have bedded down in hotels that are not five-star and that are not on my list to review. These are invariably the transit hotels at airports where I wash my smalls in the sink, re-charge my cameras, laptops, tape recorders, Ipods, and try to give myself at least a few hours off.

Mainly the transits are planned but sometimes they are involuntary. One such impromptu stay happened in Thailand. Despite the most valiant efforts of Bangkok's road engineers and the introduction of a light-rail system, the city's rush hour can still persist for most of the day, which makes getting to the airport a tense affair best embarked upon several days before your flight is due to depart.

I had given myself a good few hours to sit in traffic and inch along but on that afternoon Bangkok's gridlock had reached a new level of excellence. Nothing was moving. Forget sprinting through departures and immigration; I didn't even make it to the airport. Instead, I sat for almost an hour in my taxi, within sight of the terminals but jammed solid between cars and trucks.

I saw my Qantas jumbo lift off into the smog and make a graceful left turn towards Sydney. I paid my driver, got out in the middle of what had become a freeway car park, dragged my luggage from the boot and began weaving between the bumpers to the side of the road, where I had spied a large conference-style hotel called the Majestic.

I made it across the main freeway, then over a scrappy grass verge before having to throw my bag over an open drain and follow it with a leap. One more two-lane side-road lay between me and the hotel's lobby, and it was packed as solidly as the freeway. The cars were nose to tail, so I had to heave my suitcase onto my head, balance it there like an African water-carrier and side-shuffle between them. A smartly dressed porter from the hotel spotted me and ran to my rescue, lifting the case down and magicking it off into the cool, lofty reception hall.

I was without a reservation and the hotel staff were hectic dealing with a myriad of requests from groups of men all wearing ill-fitting suits and name tags, who were milling around after a day in various conference seminars and workshops. They were asking the reception staff to change rooms, or pick up messages or book cabs that would never show up because of the gridlock, while showing each other small brochures and exchanging business cards in the formal, two-handed fashion that is so popular in the Far East.

Amid the bustle and blur, a man bowed to me and invited me to sign a guest registration form. He was polite, efficient and quick, and within ten minutes I was checked in, changed and in the pool. The sun had passed over the hotel and was fast falling into the rice fields west of the city, so the pool was in shade. It was also deserted. I swam a few lengths and surfaced to find two white fluffy towels had been delivered to my white plastic lounger, along with a glass of iced water.

For once I was incognito – this hotel had no idea I was a travel writer. For all they knew I was another conference participant, and would be showering and slipping into a bad suit and gathering up my own brochures to join the rest of the conference participants.

When I returned to my room I found a message from the man at reception, saying he had called his friends at Qantas and they were holding me a seat on the next afternoon's flight to Sydney. He had also taken the liberty, he wrote, of reserving me a table for one at the hotel's lobby restaurant, which was Japanese, one of my favourites. I had to sit on the bed and take a moment to recover from this telepathic service.

I rang reception and got a female voice.

'Are you a four-star or five-star hotel?' I asked.

'No, only four-star, Sir,' she replied. 'Not luxury like Four Seasons.' And she giggled attractively.

'And how much is my room costing me?'

'Your room … let me see … $85, Sir, and that includes your breakfast tomorrow morning – you can have cooked breakfast or Japanese, whatever you want.' More infectious Thai giggling.

On the back of the mini-bar tick sheet I did some mathematics, which takes me a while at the best of times, and worked out that a week at the Majestic would not buy me a single night at most of the big luxury hotels I had stayed at over the previous year, yet this hotel had given me equally good service as I receive at the top end of the hotel scale. And, they had no idea I was a travel writer.

I felt a review coming on so I began to pick faults. The bed was hard, the air-conditioning was noisy, and the shower flooded the bathroom floor – but only because I was being particularly energetic with the soap. 'Surely the hotel's lobby restaurant cannot be that fabulous,' I thought. I approached it with some trepidation, but the table for one was reserved for me and was in a quiet corner – just where I like my tables for one to be.

I ordered sake and then made my way between the different counters, where four chefs hand-sliced my sashimi, prepared my miso soup, began to cook some wagyu beef and then taught me how to say 'please' and 'thank you' in Japanese. A pocket-size waitress brought me more sake and eagerly replenished my bowl of green tea. This was one of the best Japanese meals I had eaten, and it was made even more delicious and delightful as it was a slice of real unexpected luxury.

I wondered who was sitting in my economy seat on the plane, now somewhere over Borneo and halfway through the in-flight culinary delights, and I smiled to myself. I ordered a third round of hot sake, and with it toasted the Bangkok traffic planners and the Majestic Hotel, and made a mental note to return.

I pride myself on having only missed two flights in my life but both experiences have culminated in unexpected hotel excellence. A few months after basking in the joy of Majestic, I missed a flight in the United States, again due to the brilliance of traffic engineers – this time in Atlanta, Georgia.

The city, clearly for a wheeze, seemed to have hung only two signs to Atlanta's Hartsfield-Jackson Airport, both of them on gantries virtually at the edge of the runway. If you are driving south through the city, as I was, then finding the airport is guesswork. All you can do is look for planes in the sky and try to work out roughly where they are landing. I'll admit I haven't been back for eighteen months but I would dearly love Atlanta's mayor to explain this sign-less phenomenon to me, especially as the city prides itself on its airport, which is statistically the busiest in the world.

I hit Atlanta's northern freeways at rush hour and then proceeded to commit almost every traffic violation known to Georgia state law as I weaved and ducked and sped through the lines of four-wheel-drives and trucks.

I missed my flight to New York by ten minutes. Once I had spent a satisfactory length of time beating myself up in the departure lounge, I set about finding a bed for the night. Although I have the propensity for industrial-scale forgetfulness, I also have a bizarrely focused mind when I am travelling. From the depths of my brain I dragged the name of a B&B whose website I had visited weeks previously, when my original travel plans had included a stay in Atlanta: Maison LaVigne.

I found the number, and half an hour later I was having a Tennessee Williams moment. I sat on the porch of a large, green, early-1900s weatherboard house on South Fulton Avenue, with the warm sun setting behind the lime trees. Birds busied themselves in the branches and hopped up and down on the small gate into the B&B's pretty front garden.

The ebullient owner, Eileen Randman, produced a glass of chilled Chablis and some hors d'oeuvres, and we rocked on the wooden swing-seat together as if we were old friends.

She told me she was going to rustle up something fairly basic for dinner and hoped I would not mind its simplicity. What she did not tell me was that she is a fabulous chef, having studied in the pastry divisions of the kitchens of the Ritz in Paris, and that she was about to produce one of the best 'fairly basic' meals I have ever tasted.

From her kitchen, tucked away at the back of the house,

Eileen produced mouth-watering chicken and cream cheese crepes, Creole shrimps, home-baked bread, little patties of butter from Amish country in Pennsylvania, and lavender honey from Provence. She has brought a touch of France to her small corner of Atlanta, and has created a delightful home where guests can choose from a variety of superbly appointed, French-themed rooms.

During spring and summer she invites her 'new friends' to dine on the porch, southern style, and to sit talking late into the warm, enveloping night. Her proximity to the airport and a train line can make it a touch noisy, but the food and conversation are excellent distractions.

It is very tempting for luxury hotel reviewers to push the service envelope and see if top-flight hotels really can deliver the undeliverable. One night, during a stay at the Datai Hotel on Langkawi Island in Malaysia, I called up the front desk staff to say I had a particular craving for a midnight snack of braised pig's trotters, and would they be awfully kind and run out to a local village to procure some and then have the chef get to work.

After all, I reasoned, I was reviewing the hotel for a glossy magazine with a moneyed readership, so I needed to test the place a little. And I knew the island was awash with big fat pigs so I figured it wasn't completely outside the realms of possibility.

In less than a minute, the duty manager was on the phone declining my request but doing it so politely that I was almost as impressed as if the trotters had actually arrived at my door steaming in their own juices.

That's the key. Knowing when to go the extra mile with service and knowing the hotel's limits and when to tell a treasured guest, ever so politely and discreetly and with immaculate aplomb, to bugger off and go to bed.

I have experienced excellent service, such as that at the Datai, in numerous luxury hotels over my decade as a travel writer, starting with the waiters who picked up my spoons in unison at the Méditerranée in Cannes; they mirrored each other so perfectly they should have entered a synchronised swimming team at the Olympics.

However, I have only seen flawless service about half-a-dozen times.

The most memorable was in Bali, not at the telepathic Istana but by a Balinese woman called Tinmarisan, or Tin as her friends and loyal guests call her. Tin was found waiting tables in a nondescript café in downtown Kuta by Hans Meier, the engaging Swiss general manager of one of Bali's best hotels, the Legian. Hans has now moved on to the hotel's sister property, the Setai in Miami, where he is a roaring success.

He watched her intently and saw an unfulfilled excellence. When she came to deliver the bill, he asked her if she was interested in working at his hotel. She jumped at the chance and went into training with the English 'king of butlers' Robert Watson, who was busy imbuing his art into the Legian's staff, in the hope of making it into not just one of Bali's best luxury hotels but one of the top few in the world. He and his charges succeeded.

I met Tin at the open and breezy reception area of the Legian's exclusive Club section. The Club at the Legian is a private mini-hotel across the road from the main hotel. It comprises ten big, stand-alone villas, each within its own walled compound. Each compound comes complete with swimming pool, day beds, sunken bathtubs, and gardens painted with bird of paradise plants and scented with frangipanis.

Each villa is fully air-conditioned and boasts rainforest

showers, a CD and DVD library, free mini-bar as well as on-tap decanters of gin, vodka and whisky, enough cable channels to keep you entertained for a fortnight, and a bathroom big enough for a family of six. Centre-stage is a king-size teak bed, surrounded by white muslin drapes.

Tin spent a good 30 minutes showing my partner and me around our villa and acquainting us with what it and she could offer.

'Now, I unpack your luggage for you and do ironing. Then you will have everything nice for dinner this evening and for the beach tomorrow,' she said, her radiant smile not fading for a second.

'Okay,' we mumbled, still stunned at how high the luxury bar had suddenly been raised.

'Do your socks need sewing?' she asked. 'I can do that for you. Or maybe you have a button loose from a shirt, Mr Brace? And on your last night, let me know and I can come and pack your bags for you.'

Tin, we discovered, was not only the perfect butler, but she was also available 24 hours a day. Where and when she slept I never knew, but she was always fresh and smartly turned out, and ready with a polite bit of Balinese humour.

Each morning we slept late, and she would silently creep into the private kitchen situated in the separate dining pavilion and prepare what we had ordered for breakfast the night before. Even though we were slovenly and always emerged later than planned, Tin kept the food and coffee at the perfect temperature and condition.

As she served us Indonesian congee soup she explained its history and ingredients, and then told us what festivals were happening that day and where and when and what we could expect if we attended. If there was a ceremony at a temple, we should wear the correct sashes and headbands.

She had colleagues in the hotel who could lend them to us if we wished, and if not she was willing to run home and borrow some from her family.

On the rare occasion when she could not answer one of my incessant questions, Tin said she would find out. I wanted to know where the Balinese coffee had come from – where the beans had been grown – and within half an hour she was back with a full description of the beans and the history of the plantation up in the hills around Ubud. She had written it neatly on the hotel's parchment-style letterhead, rolled it up and tied it with a small bow.

We got to know Tin so well on that first visit and subsequent stays that she has become a friend. Tin teaches me Indonesian words and phrases, and I respond by fine-tuning her already good English grammar and vocabulary.

Secretly, I left her tips – a practice to which I have a pathological aversion, unless someone has gone above and beyond the call of duty – and swore her to secrecy as I wanted her to keep the money and distribute it only among her family.

But above all these qualities, there was one that Tin had mastered. She was like a perfectly balanced tide, knowing just how close to come to her guests, and then when to retreat once more. I know Tin and her fellow butlers had been trained to be expert in switching imperceptibly between laughing along with a chatty, ebullient American, and ensuring they did not look an austere Arabian businessman in the eye, which would be deemed an insult. But aside from the training she was a natural.

Tin, however, caused me one serious problem. Once you have experienced such immaculate service as hers, it is virtually impossible to expect anything less. Once that bar has been raised, you measure everything against it.

Even hotels whose service I would have previously considered excellent began to fall short of my new post-Tin expectations. I wanted the waiters who brought me my snails to know where they were from: a local farm or the local supermarket? They did not know, nor did they offer to find out, implying that merely the molluscs' elegant display on my plate and their tender quality should be enough to satisfy me and prompt a good review.

I wanted room service to leave four bottles of sparkling mineral water and a fresh lime in my room each afternoon; when I received just two and a couple of dry lime slices, my complaint was met with the excuse: 'Hotel policy is two, Sir, but you can buy more from the bar.'

Was I turning into a luxury hotel snob?

'Undoubtedly,' said my friend Alexander Walker, on the phone from Hollywood. 'You have reached the next stage in your induction into the world of luxury hotels. It happens to the best of us, but you'll get through it. Just don't go back to the places you don't like. Stick with the trusted favourites.'

For Alex and countless other luxury hotel aficionados, the 'next stage' is anti-service, that subtle and desperately elusive quality that so many hotels fail to master. I don't mean porters telling you, 'Carry your own bloody luggage, Sir.' Anti-service is all about knowing when to leave it alone, when to back off and let guests be.

It is about staff realising that a guest might be thinking: 'I have just got into this beautiful room in this drop-dead gorgeous city, I'm coming down from a big radiation hit at 35,000 feet and am consuming beer/drugs/nicotine/green tea (delete as applicable) as fast as my body can absorb them, and soon I shall be trying to entice my partner into having some spectacular new-hotel sex. SO GO AWAY!'

One hotel manager in Barbados told me it was 'incredibly difficult to get people who are trained to serve to stop buzzing around and trying to do everything for guests'. He said they could not get their heads around the concept that, in fact, some guests do not want fresh sheets every ten seconds, or more soaps, and they don't need their towels laundered every afternoon by some poor overworked peasant out in a sun-baked field somewhere.

'They feel if they don't give 110 per cent all the time they are failing and will be reported to the management, or – worse – they won't get any tips,' he said.

'So we tell them that part of what guests want is to be left alone. By all means carry their bags, run them a bath and invite them for cocktails at sundown, but let them get on with their stay.

'They might want to run around naked and pluck a live duck in the bathtub for all you know, and the last thing they want is you knocking on the door saying you have some chocolates you want to put on their pillow.'

Sometimes the over-attentive service comes in electronic form. Scores of luxury hotels are touting themselves as the most high-tech, Wi-Fi, inter-connected, intra-connected, voice-activated, remote-control, access-all-areas establishments in cyberspace, and reckon that's enough to tempt you to part with several thousand pounds to stay there. But stay there and do what? Spend all day on the super-fast broadband internet downloading rubbish that it takes too long to download at home, rather than switching off and getting horizontal by the pool?

Anti-service is about turning the service off, lowering the volume and de-teching yourself.

Tin, the Balinese Goddess of Butling, knew how to turn things on and off instinctively. She rapidly learned the times we woke and ate and swam and slept, and fitted in to our schedule effortlessly. If we had wanted to pluck live ducks in the sunken bathtub she would have made a mental note: 'Mr Brace and Ms Brady duck-plucking time: 6.00–6.45 PM. No disturb.'

Luckily, I prefer a pre-plucked duck in my bathtub, of the yellow rubber variety, so no such delay in service has ever had to occur at the Club at the Legian.

Although Tin reigns supreme in my list of best luxury hotel service, a close second must be the Four Seasons in Sydney. When my mother stayed there she spent her days staring at the addictive harbour view, watching the green and gold ferries pirouetting around each other as they chugged in and out of Circular Quay. She watched the sun rise out of the Pacific Ocean beyond the harbour's entrance, and then watched it set over the Blue Mountains. She explored the hotel, dining in its superb restaurant, taking tea at the lobby bar and treatments in the spa, and she rode up and down in the lifts.

She loved every second, and was so awestruck by the glittering beauty of Sydney and the majesty of the Four Seasons that, one night, her false teeth jumped clean out of her mouth and disappeared down the plug hole in her bathroom.

A call to reception prompted the arrival of a maintenance man carrying a tool kit and a long piece of wire. With not a glimmer of laughter nor impatience, he set to work extricating the gnashers and within minutes was reuniting them with their owner.

'Your teeth, Madam,' he said with a broad Aussie smile, and wished her a pleasant evening.

If you get such manners and service from a luxury hotel's maintenance staff, who rarely have contact with the guests, you know the hotel is up there with the best.

Several continents away in Buenos Aires, one hotel that had not yet heard of anti-service went a little too far.

It had taken me weeks to line up a stay at the Design Suites, a minimalist hotel near Santa Fe and Callao avenues. We had batted emails back and forth and played answer-machine tennis for some weeks. Finally, everything was set. New hotel, new city, New Year's Eve. Party time.

My British Airways 747 cruised in over the prolific sub-urbs of Buenos Aires shortly after dawn, banking obligingly to give us a town planner's view of the city's magnificent in-frastructure. Fat, snaking roads burrowed between masses of concrete structures, disappearing under glass skyscrap-ers and re-emerging to turn into big boulevards. The cars reflected the early sun's rays back up at the plane through the summer haze.

We skimmed the estuary of the River Plate and saw crew-members scurrying around like ants on the decks of their oil tankers and container ships.

The last few minutes of a long-haul flight can be the most rewarding. The films have ended, the headphones have been collected, everyone has been to the toilet and sat back down in their seats. The long night and the high-altitude jet-stream headwinds have passed, and a warm dawn is flood-ing in through the windows, bringing colour back to our air-conditioned cheeks.

Tiredness and hangovers have stupefied the passengers into quiet reverence. Even the babies are silent. We are looking forward to a taxi ride through an unfamiliar and thrilling city, and the chance to check in to a new and excit-ing hotel. The cabin crew are counting down the minutes to when they can send their uniforms off for dry cleaning and slip into a wet margarita by the pool.

I breezed through immigration and customs dressed in

what I thought was suitable Buenos Aires high-summer chic: white shirt, khaki pants, ochre leather shoes, Ray-Bans, pink velveteen jacket with lace cuffs. Okay, I am lying about the jacket. That was a flashback to my New Romantic days, brought on by too much in-flight champagne. It would have looked good, I feel sure, although maybe too much of a contrast to the austere lobby of the Design Suites, whose décor was more decontaminated deluxe than Duran Duran.

The hotel was cleaner than a hospital, and infinitely more ordered. Smartly dressed doormen made bags disappear with the raising of an eyebrow.

I felt as if I had entered a scene from a Fellini movie, circa 1974. A man with wild hair and big shades walked through the lobby with a tailored black and white check jacket draped over his shoulders. He had a black satin man-bag on one arm and a girl on the other who was young enough to have been at school with his daughter. An unlit cigarette was poised between the first two fingers of his right hand.

They spent some time looking me up and down, as if reviewing a poor art installation at a design college. As they passed me by I watched the girl's heavily mascara-ed eyelashes bat slowly like sea fans, and I swear they caused a small breeze which lifted my fringe momentarily and revealed a sweaty brow. But my real humiliation was to come.

The Design Suites was my third stop on a round-the-world tour of luxury hotels, interrupted only by Christmas with my parents in England. My mother had passed on to me a gift she had received free with a bottle of shampoo – a fluffy toy dog called Scampo. Being the sentimental type, I felt obliged to pack Scampo in my case and carry him back to Australia, where I could off-load him to a wide-eyed godchild and be the hero of the hour.

My partner and I settled in to our arctic-white room at the Design Suites, which felt as if we were living inside an ostrich egg. We drank strong coffee, sent off our finest shirts for ironing and hit the town. We went to San Telmo and danced tango in the street. We got caught up by an Argentinian marching band comprising lots of sweaty, overweight blokes with huge drums and whistles, and we shouted and sang along with them for a few blocks before peeling off and diving into a bar for a glass of wine.

We ate the best steaks we had ever tasted, and scores of tiny creamy potatoes. We walked along the harbour-front in the moonlight, and through the Recoleta Cemetery by day to visit Evita's tomb.

It was not until the second day that we realised something was dreadfully wrong. Scampo was missing. We tore the place apart, stripping the bed, shaking out the sheets, emptying all the cupboards and turning our suitcases inside-out, but to no avail. We sat for a moment, steadying ourselves with an early martini, and ran through the possible lost dog scenarios.

The first two were unlikely, to say the least: that he had run off and joined a pack of local nomadic Argentinian mongrels and was halfway to Patagonia by now; or, that a miserable excuse for a hotel chambermaid had stolen him and was busy wrapping him up as a present for her son.

We could not wait another day. The sudden loss of this recent arrival in our lives was having surprisingly depressive effects on us.

I reached for my Spanish dictionary and began piecing together what would turn out to be possibly the most embarrassing sentence I had ever spoken, and set off gingerly for reception.

I lurked behind pillars to make sure I did not bump into

the manager, who was my host and acutely aware that I was writing a review for a number of stylish magazines.

The Fellini couple were breezing through the lobby again. He still had not lit his cigarette. I quickly pretended to be highly interested in the ceiling. I smiled at them, pointed upwards and said feebly, '*Arquitectura ... excelente.*' They stared at me long enough for me to see his lip twitch and to feel the breeze from her eyelashes once more, but they said nothing. I made it to the reception desk and, taking a deep breath, asked if by any chance anyone had found, ahem, '*un perro velloso suave de juguete*', which actually translates as 'a smooth fluffy dog of toy', but they got the idea.

To their great credit, they stifled the considerable mirth attached to this question and took pity on me. I followed this with '*Soy muy importante*', which I thought meant 'it's very important' but then realised actually means 'I'm very important'.

The two reception staff were masterful in holding back their laughter, and I am quite sure that as soon as I had gone back to my room they both ran outside and collapsed in fits in the street. Once they had wiped the tears from their eyes, they put out an urgent APB, asking all staff to be on the look-out for a smooth fluffy dog of toy, because its owner was *muy importante*.

The manager was alerted immediately, and she contacted me to sympathise over the trauma that the missing hound must be causing me, and to ensure its swift capture and safe return. I wonder if she thought this was one of my travel writer's tests – to see if the hotel treated me with discretion and politeness even though my request was plainly bizarre and possibly a whopping big lie. Maybe the staff at the Datai had tipped her off about the pig's trotters.

On our last morning we were still dog-less. The manager

joined us for a working breakfast in the small and intimate lobby restaurant. She answered my questions about design and style and the *'arquitectura excelente'*, and told me how proud the hotel was to be appearing in my magazines. Scampo's name did not come up, and I could not face the further humiliation of asking once more if he had been found.

Just as we were finishing the breakfast interview and I was resigning myself to the dog being lost forever, I spied two chambermaids approaching and carrying a parcel that looked like a cushion.

Smiling, they walked through the lobby restaurant, their parcel catching the attention of every guest, including the Fellini couple, who looked at it intently and then giggled into their croissants.

As they approached our table the horrible truth became clear. The parcel was a see-through laundry bag, in which was sitting a sparkling clean 'smooth fluffy dog of toy'.

With regal ceremony, the chambermaids presented me with the parcel, placing it on the table between me and the hotel manager. Under the dog's nose was a small handwritten sign which read: *'Pequeño perro de peluche, Señor Brace'* ('Small fluffy dog, Mr Brace'). Scampo had been accidentally gathered up with our dirty sheets and subjected to a terrifying few hours being hurled around in washing machines and driers in the hotel's laundry.

The Design Suites' service had proved itself to be at the same time greatly impressive and painfully humiliating. Just as I was getting used to feeling pretty flash, flitting around the world and leading my luxury lifestyle and being the envy of my friends, I was utterly humbled by a small fluffy dog.

Never has a professional luxury travel writer on an official assignment blushed so deeply.

Chapter 5

Hot Peacocks

POSSIBLY THE MOST striking feature that will influence you when you are choosing a luxury hotel is what the place looks like: the interiors, the atmosphere and the sense of place. It is one half of the vital accommodation equation, the other being the way the hotel is run.

Are you a floral pattern, Laura Ashley, type, or someone for whom anything more than a spartan white box of a bedroom is an unnecessary clutter-dump?

Are you masculine or feminine in your choice of linens and drapes? Do you do doilies or deconstructivism? Soft curves or clean straight lines? Engraved teak day beds or tubular metal Bauhaus tables? Philippe Starck or Rococo Revival? Wi-Fi or No-Fi?

Do you want a cosy, miniature roomette filled almost entirely by one vast bed, or a suite big enough to play cricket in? Do you like big, bold rainbow-coloured carpets and shocking pink pillowcases, or matt black everything, including the light bulbs? You really can get matt black painted light bulbs, you know.

Our medieval travelling ancestors had no such style dilemmas to face – they simply found an inn that was standing upright and had a roof with no holes in it, and there they made their bed for the night, trying not to notice the vermin running around within its greasy walls. But for more than a century now, hotel guests have been acutely conscious of design.

As the various items and facilities that hotels originally introduced as luxuries – telephones, lifts, air-conditioning and the like – gradually lost their novelty value and became standard fare, guests looked elsewhere for the wow factor, and they found it increasingly in architecture, interior design and furniture.

They raved about streamlined art deco skyscraper hotels in New York, terracotta palazzi in Florence and Venice, and mahogany colonial piles in Singapore and Hong Kong. They flocked to see the latest and most outrageous designs around the world, wondering what César Ritz and the great hoteliers would dare to do next.

In Ritz's day, luxury hotels were a preserve of the wealthy, who began educating themselves in the disciplines of design, learning the names of architects and glassmakers, upholsterers and decorators. That passion for physical form and appearance has not dulled with time. In fact, it has blossomed, and the modern-day design elite – Philippe Starck, Ian Schrager, Marc Newson and the rest of the gang – have, like chefs, become celebrities.

For example, I have luxuriated at five hotels all designed by the flamboyantly named architects Wimberly Allison Tong & Goo (WATG): Emirates Palace in Abu Dhabi, Claridge's in London, the Venetian and the Mansion at MGM Grand in Las Vegas, and the heavenly Hotel Bora Bora in French Polynesia.

Design, more than any other single element, is what gets luxury hotels noticed and remembered. I group luxury hotels into two very different schools of design, both of which achieve this aim in their own unique way.

One is based on a peacock philosophy: painting yourself in bright colours and spreading your wings and feathers out loud and proud to attract as much notice as possible. This is favoured by hotels with serious exhibitionism issues and chronic attention-deficit disorders. They are unashamedly boisterous and ostentatious. If they were human beings they would be carnival queens in Rio or streakers at Test matches. If they were cocktails they would be big pink Shirley Temples with umbrellas and all the trimmings.

The other school of design follows the behaviour of the super-cool puss-cat, where subtlety and demureness are the ideal and everything is understated. These hotels delicately groom themselves without fuss, drama or fanfare. They know they are fabulous, so why flaunt it? They are stacked full of confidence and they know that anyone who comes close is going to want to stroke them. They go to great lengths to reduce visual clutter, stripping away any thoughts of floral wallpaper or psychedelic carpet. They will create a wide, white-walled reception area that feels more like a museum of modern art than a hotel lobby and decorate it with only a simple, black 3-metre earthenware pot standing sentinel in the corner. Less is more and more is less. Think Miles Davis, Bryan Ferry and Yoko Ono. Puss-cat cool.

There are some luxury hotels that, despite being noteworthy for other things such as service or location, are neither one nor the other when it comes to design. They are mainly the big chain hotel groups whose accountants and lawyers have taken over and surgically removed almost every last speck of creative evidence lest it adversely affect their profits by upsetting a single guest. They are neutral and neutered and monumentally boring to inhabit, so let's not worry about them here.

First, then, the peacocks. There can be few who have not seen a picture of the Burj Al Arab hotel in Dubai, even if they do not know it by name. It's the one that looks like a 300-metre dhow sailing in from the Persian Gulf; the sort of lavish, oversized, royal ship that a modern-day Cleopatra might use to make an entrance. I see Catherine Zeta-Jones in the starring role, resplendent in body armour.

It is also the hotel that, when launched in 1999, got almost as much publicity as Paris Hilton. For a press stunt, the PR department got Andre Agassi to put on his little white shorts and knock some tennis balls around on a platform which leans out vertiginously from the hotel's rooftop. A helicopter hovered overhead, filming him and his playing partner having a whale of a time on this aerial tennis court.

I was so impressed by this bit of pure escapism that when I visited the hotel I eagerly asked its spokesperson if I could see the sky-high tennis court – and maybe even have a game out there.

'It's so sci-fi, such a fun idea,' I said, giggling like a schoolboy. I even had my own little white shorts and tennis shoes at the ready, although I would have to blag a racquet and some balls.

But I was told that there is no tennis court – it's actually a working helipad, and it's strictly out of bounds. Agassi's game was a PR stunt to promote the hotel. I began to blush and quickly changed the subject, hoping she would instantly forget my naivety. Even for the most experienced VIP travel writers, humiliation is waiting to pounce around every luxury hotel corner.

The Burj Al Arab is undoubtedly the most swashbuckling hotel the world has seen for years. It is hard to get a sense of its size from photographs, because it stands on its own with only the ocean and blue desert sky as backdrops, so there are no neighbouring buildings with which to compare, but it is big. At 321 metres it is the world's second-tallest hotel building, after the Ryugyong Hotel in the North Korean capital Pyongyang (330 metres) but then North Korea has an awkward habit of not telling the truth, so without going there myself with a tape measure and a theodolite I cannot give you a clear winner in this race for the sky.

If the Burj Al Arab were temporarily displaced to Paris, it would look down on the Eiffel Tower; in Manhattan it would be only 60 metres shy of the Empire State Building; and it is just a metre lower than the Q1 apartment building on Queensland's Gold Coast. We are definitely in King Kong territory here.

You can see it from miles away. As my chauffeur drove me out of Dubai's airport shortly after dawn I saw it dominating the horizon, shimmering in the golden early light. Its graceful upward curve is the perfect antidote to the forest of new nondescript concrete and glass skyscrapers that you pass along Sheikh Zayed Road, the main road into town.

I could also see it clearly from the small breakfast balcony in the Club Lounge of the Ritz-Carlton Hotel, looking like a vast D sticking out of the ocean. I watched the D disappear into a sandstorm and then reappear again afterwards, as the dust cleared and it reflected the sun's rays once more. It looked invincible.

It reminded me of the images I had conjured up when reading Ray Bradbury's *The Martian Chronicles* as a kid. Back then, I was convinced that within my lifetime Earth would have exploded and we would all be living on Mars in buildings not unlike this: bold architectural sci-fi statements on a sandy landscape.

Everything would be pod-shaped and smooth with no

hard corners or jagged edges. It would be a soft, easy life on Mars, protected from the fierce heat and unrelenting sunlight by triple-thickness glass. There would be no more war because we would have learned our lesson when we watched our own planet blow up, and all our needs would be catered for through magical temperature controls, self-reproducing subterranean vegetable gardens and rapid transport in egg-shaped shuttles.

My vision resembled a heady, psychedelic blend of embryonic concept-car design and several Yes album covers, and that was before I had even heard the word marijuana.

At my junior school near Stratford-upon-Avon we did a kids' architecture project where we each had to draw a building we would like to see and live in when we were 50 years old. I had the artistic skills of a rhino, so my painting looked more like the result of a nuclear accident and was much-mocked, but in my mind I was thinking along the lines of the Burj. Big sweeping lines, solid and safe, and with futuristic elements like a special docking station for my private egg-shaped shuttle and a huge viewing deck so I could watch angry Martian storms rumble in across the red desert plains, and at night I could stare at the stars and the big black hole where the Earth had been.

More than 30 years later when I first saw an artist's impression of the hotel, I thought, 'Yep, that's almost what I was getting at back at Tiddington Junior School, circa 1974.'

Up close, it is one of those buildings, like the Sydney Opera House or the Guggenheim in Bilbao, that are so familiar from magazines and television that when we visit them we cannot really comprehend we are there, actually within touching distance. A fog comes over us, precipitated by the convergence of misty memory and bone-dry reality.

We become scared of disappointment – how could the real thing live up to the hype?

Luckily, like the Sydney Opera House and the Guggenheim, the unique, utopian architecture of the Burj Al Arab is far from disappointing. It is thrilling, beautiful and statuesque. How anyone can make such an exciting building from steel, glass and teflon I shall never know. Dreaming up such a design is one thing, but making sure the whole pile of rods and girders and nuts and bolts actually stands up and still looks fabulous is the real skill.

It is not an exaggeration to say the hotel is a work of art. Its tennis court – sorry, helipad – juts out like a small tray being balanced precariously by a waiter dressed in white and wading knee-deep into the Persian Gulf. I have not seen anything as fun and futuristic as that on a building since I watched *The Jetsons*. Perfect for egg-shaped shuttle craft.

On the other side of the hotel, looking north into the Persian Gulf, is the Al Muntaha restaurant, which from the ground resembles a rolled-up newspaper stuffed horizontally into the mouth of a letterbox. Back at Tiddington Junior School this would have been my Martian viewing deck, but here in Dubai – in real life – it serves hundreds of lucky sky-high diners each day.

But don't think you can just walk in and grab a table. The Burj Al Arab is about the toughest hotel to get into anywhere in the world. You don't have to be a guest to get through the big gold doors of the hotel but you must, at the very least, have a reservation for one of its six restaurants, or have an official appointment or be visiting a guest. The tight security sends a very definite message that this is as exclusive as a luxury hotel gets.

If you want to check out the Waldorf=Astoria in New York or the Beverly Wilshire in Los Angeles, just walk in.

As long as you are not dressed like a tramp or gibbering drunk, a smart-looking doorman will smile and open the huge brass door and voila, you're in Hotel Heaven. I have spent hours in luxury hotel lobbies without being a guest. They make very handy respites from a bitter Chicago winter (the Drake, 1997), a fierce Roman July (the St Regis, 2000) and the odd Florida hurricane (the Delano, 2003). You can usually get a cup of coffee (just say you'll pay cash), use the loo, have a nap in a leather armchair and even snag a free newspaper – all before some awfully pleasant junior manager asks if you are a guest and, if not, whether you would mind accompanying him to the front door and very politely and quietly buggering off.

Not at the Burj Al Arab.

In fact, you cannot even get close to it without one of these golden tickets, for the hotel is built out on a small man-made island. It is reached by means of a well-guarded causeway 280 metres long, from where the building takes on yet another appearance. It no longer resembles a huge D in gothic script, or an oversized dhow, but the kind of slightly podgy space rocket that Tintin and Snowy took when they went to the moon. From this angle it is more futuristic than ever.

Once you are past security and the fleet of sixteen white Rolls-Royces (on-call for any guest who feels the urge to pop down to the shops), you reach the revolving front doors and enter another world.

The lobby is not really a lobby at all but a showpiece entrance hall. Nobody does anything as mundane or crass as checking in here – that's all taken care of privately in your suite. Rather, it is an explosion of colour which serves no purpose other than to make guests' jaws drop and to convince them that the £1,000 they are about to fork out for each night's stay is worthwhile. It shows them that this place is going to be fun.

The entrance hall is a fusion of different set designs from celluloid fantasy. It is a bit *Wizard of Oz*, a bit *Willy Wonka and the Chocolate Factory* and a bit *The Little Mermaid*. Everything is curved and fluid, and there is little symmetry or order. It is light-hearted chaos.

The furniture is pure *Alice in Wonderland*, with red and blue chequerboard tables and legs that spiral to the floor like corkscrews. The edges of the coffee tables flow like meandering rivers. You know that in the depths of the night, in that secret hour between the last guest going to bed and the cleaners arriving to polish the door handles, these pieces of living design shake off their stiffness, come alive and run amok.

The floor is dominated by an elliptical rug, roughly twelve metres long and six metres wide, which in shape resembles a shield that a Norman knight might have taken into battle. Of course, no Norman knight with any pride, or any ambition for victory and power, would have been seen dead painting his shield in the hotel's carpet colours – red, blue and peach, with yellow and white squiggles all over it. He would have been laughed off the battlefield. But the psychedelic riot of hues works well here in fantasy hotel land.

The carpet's ellipse is mirrored by a gold and white ceiling with a blue-green 'eye' in its centre, which I half-expected would wink at me if I stared at it too long.

At either end of this space is a six-metre golden arch or half-shell. Inside each shell, resembling a very well-dressed crab welcoming visitors to its deep-sea home, stands a black-suited concierge.

The centrepiece of the entrance hall is a long red sofa whose back extends for twice the length of its seat. Had

Salvador Dali been hired to design the Burj Al Arab interior decoration and furniture – and it is hard to believe he was not – he would have come up with something like this, for it resembles the famous extended buttock which appears in his 1933 painting, *The Enigma of William Tell*.

I sat down on it but was immediately conscious of the all-seeing eye bearing down on me from the ceiling and the little concierge crabs watching me from their shells; maybe this was an artwork to be looked upon rather than sat upon. When I stood up the little concierge crabs went back to their relentless tidying of hidden items behind the desks in their half-shells.

The hotel is a fun palace in which you can expect the un-expected. The floors of the lifts are painted with yellow and white triangles that make you feel you are standing on top of an opened golf umbrella. At the top of the gold-plated escalators that lead from the entrance hall is a computerised fountain which squirts and flops and splashes in sequence. When it really gets going it shoots a single jet 42 metres up into the air and then begins a programme of aquatic gymnastics which sounds like many hands clapping. This is a clever homage to the delightful tradition of clapping songs, a practice found across the Arabian Peninsula.

The fountain is also a great place to lean back and look up, for above it is the world's tallest atrium. From this neck-straining position the interior's triangular design becomes clear, with the hotel's two ocean-facing sides made up of the suites, and the landward side made up of the huge sail.

The hotel's spokesperson told me that the sail really *is* a sail, woven from Teflon-coated fibres. It is the first time in the world that anyone has erected a sail to this height, and it extends up all the way to the roof. It is white by day, filling the atrium with natural light, and at night it acts as a canvas for light displays.

The atrium boasts fat pillars which are coated with gold leaf. A lot of luxury hotels boast they have gold leaf all over them when in fact it is gold paint slapped on rather roughly, but here it is the real deal. The hotel really does coat its pillars in 22-carat gold leaf. It is another reminder to guests that the price tag is worth every dirham.

There was more *Alice in Wonderland* topsy-turviness when I learned about the Burj Al Arab rooms and facilities. There are no rooms, only suites, and while there are 54 storeys there are only 27 floors, each with its own private concierge (or 'guest relations executive') and a small clutch of butlers. The undersea restaurant, Al Mahara, is not actually under the sea but certainly gives the impression that you are about to dine with Captain Nemo and his crew. It is built around a 300,000 litre subterranean aquarium. And, of course, we know about the tennis court which is actually a helipad. But fact does not really matter inside this hotel, because guests are happy to give themselves freely to the delightfully intoxicating nuttiness of the place.

They vegetate in the spa, which – as this is the United Arab Emirates – has large, separated, gender-specific areas. They walk around their floor, peering down to the clapping fountain below. They walk through the public areas, bemused and delighted to find a real kids' playground built just for adults.

They dine close to the clouds in the rolled-up-newspaper restaurant. Over risotto and ravioli they stare out at the Arabian Gulf and Dubai's two 'floating' cities, The World and The Palm. Here, in true Ray Bradbury style, islands have been made from land reclaimed from the sea, and on them have been built elaborate and high-tech homes for the UAE's rapidly expanding population. To the east, The World is a miniature version of a flat map of Earth, where you can choose to live in Europe, Asia or Australia. It's the closest any of us who are not lucky enough to be astronauts are ever going to get to looking down on the planet. To the west, The Palm comprises a central trunk island which is its main link to the mainland, and 'fronds' that sprout from it, on which will sit homes, shops and 20 new hotels when it is completed.

The Al Muntaha restaurant's ceiling is a series of waves, and between each are scores of small elliptical sections of bright primary coloured glass and lights, while the carpet is peppered with what look like small multicoloured planets from the edge of the solar system. A mobile cocktail cabinet moves between tables like a Dalek from *Doctor Who*, pushed by drinks waiters who insist on being called 'mixologists' and who can whip you up your own individually designed martini in seconds. You can even take the precise recipe home to impress your friends.

For the real design tour de force I had to take the express panoramic lifts and plunge back to earth at six metres per second into the bowels of the hotel, which is where *Alice in Wonderland* and *The Jetsons* give way to Jules Verne.

Guests descend in the hotel's 'submarine', which is actually a specially adapted lift with television portholes showing a diver's-eye view of the ocean, complete with fish and coral drifting by. The submarine comes to rest on what you easily believe to be the sea bed, and this is your cue to alight and enter the Al Mahara restaurant.

As if this wasn't thrilling enough on the excitement scale, you then get to walk through an entrance tunnel designed like a coral reef swim-through. For all you non-divers out there, a swim-through is a natural channel or tube in a reef or rocky wall through which you can float on the current. It is about the most exciting thing you can do in a wetsuit.

For diners at Al Mahara, the entrance is just as dramatic. The tunnel has a black, mirror-like floor and the ceiling is ribbed with corrugated gold and silver arches that glisten like moondust. As you progress through the tunnel, each arch magically lights up, announcing your arrival. You emerge into a mermaid's grotto: a restaurant with an aquarium as its centrepiece, within the foundations of a man-made island in the Persian Gulf.

It is beyond romantic; it is nothing short of breathtaking. Half the restaurant is blue and the other half red, accented by the colours of the chairs and the lights. Between them is the central part of the aquarium, which is shared by a multitude of fish and a few small blacktip reef sharks.

Because I am pathetic when it comes to sweet helpless-looking animals like tiny defenceless fish, I had to order a steak. In one of the most coveted seafood restaurants in the Middle East, I ordered steak – there was no way I could have sat there and let another fish watch me devour its cousin. There was one little fish that did look quite tasty as it swam close when I was choosing dessert. It was half white and half brown, and looked rather like it was made of a mix of milk and bitter chocolate. But all it had to do was peer at me mournfully through the glass and blow some feeble bubbles with its tiny mouth, and I got all maudlin again. I ordered cheese and biscuits and a large cognac, and went back to writing my notes.

The Burj Al Arab's dreamscape design has made it possibly the perfect example of how luxury hotels have become the new destinations. A Manchester couple I met in the lift standing on one of the yellow umbrellas told me they had saved for two years to come here.

'It's our golden wedding anniversary next week so this is our treat, before the rest of the family descend on us back home and we don't get a minute's peace,' they told me.

But had they come to see Dubai or the Burj Al Arab?

'Oh, the Burj, yes, definitely the Burj. We're not that fussed about Dubai, really. Just a lot of sand, in't it? We might do some shopping on the last day, but no, we don't want to leave the Burj. We've come here for the hotel.'

In the world of hotels, this is a seismic shift that has been felt around the world. Another good example is the Palazzo Versace on Australia's Gold Coast.

You don't go to the Versace to lie on Main Beach and get a tan. You go to walk around the hotel's marbled halls and purple shagpile-carpeted corridors, and strut your stuff out on the pool terrace. You have breakfast and lunch here, and, apart from maybe one skirmish into Tedder Avenue for some oysters at Shuck restaurant, you have supper here too. It is not that there are no alternatives for dining nearby. It is just that the Versace, like the Burj Al Arab, is the destination.

You tell your friends you are going 'for a long weekend at the Versace' and everyone knows what you mean – and everyone asks you to steal them a glass with the Versace head moulded into the base. Of all the souvenirs from all the luxury hotels around the world – Sandy Lane beach towels, Ritz-Carlton robes, and so on – the Versace glass is the one I see most often in people's homes.

Thankfully, no one has yet asked me to steal for them one of the gaudy Versace-designed cushions that sit around the circular sofas in the lobby, which is a relief, partly because I am sure they are guarded by remote-control attack dogs but also because if I had friends with such shockingly bad taste in cushions I might have to distance myself from them quite rapidly.

I must confess, however, that even though the Versace is a highly important peacock design hotel, I have only ever stayed there under some duress (see Chapter 9 for the gruesome details), and each time I have needed a packet of stomach quell tablets to stave off the sickly swirl of colours that assaults the eye.

It is unapologetically gaudy. The cobbled driveway is semi-circular and lined with faux Roman columns. There is always a Porsche 911 Carrera or Ferrari Testarossa parked by the front door to let guests know they are in good company and might spot a celebrity stretched out on a sun lounger by the pool.

The doormen all look like out-of-work male models (or strippers – this is the Gold Coast, after all) and wear jet-black suits with Nehru collars, and little headphones and mouthpieces so they can pretend they are in training for the FBI.

But don't let me put you off. Thousands upon thousands of guests adore the place and flock back for their special Versace weekends. I have never seen the hotel anything other than packed out.

One guest, an erudite Greek man from Sydney who told me his name was Tarquin, which I did not believe for a second, summed it up perfectly as we waited in the short queue at the breakfast buffet to pile our plates high with bacon.

'I work in an office,' he said. 'I have worked in an office for 40 years. The same office. I have made lots of money in that office, but my life is in black and white.

Every day is black and white, white and black, maybe a little grey. Your life – your travel writer luxury hotel life – you live in rainbow colour all the time. I come to Versace because this is my bit of rainbow colour.'

It was a little odd standing next to the unmistakeably

masculine physique of a giant-size Greek millionaire, whose body hair was so exuberant I could almost hear it growing, and listening to him talk so tenderly of 'rainbow colour'. Odd but touching.

He was right. I do live my unreal life in colour. I work bloody hard for it, the hours are long, it's a strain on your home and social life, and the pay is pretty average, but it is definitely always in full colour, and sometimes with the contrast turned right up high.

For Tarquin and thousands of other people who earn far more than I do yet live their lives in black and white, the Versace provides a big fat kaleidoscope in which to escape. I cannot fault it for that.

Nor can I criticise that undeniable monument to visual extravagance, the George V, just off the Champs-Élysées in Paris. The hotel reopened on 18 December 1999 after a monumental $125-million project to restore and renovate it, led by the French architect Richard Martinet and the interior designer Pierre-Yves Rochon.

The majority of hotel industry luminaries that I know consistently rate the George V as their number one. The very mention of the hotel sends their eyes spinning into the backs of their heads and they all but swoon with rapture.

'Darling, the flowers, the tapestries, that divine bar and … Le Cinq. Have you ever tasted anything like Le Cinq?' they gush, before having to sit down with a cold towel and take a moment to recover.

The flowers have become a big feature of the George V. American floral designer Jeff Leatham and his seven-strong team create a new theme each week, making the best use of the 15,000 blooms they have expressed in from Holland. The main 'flower sculpture' display is in the cavernous marble-floored lobby, but the theme is continued through more than 20 major arrangements in the other public areas, and then at least another 150 smaller bouquets. Each guest room and suite gets its own private display – at least a single stem or what Jeff describes as a 'leafy cluster'. He and his team check on the displays daily and sometimes hourly if they are dealing with particularly petulant blooms.

Jeff has had to teach himself everything about flower arranging. He grew up in the tough Rocky Mountains cowboy town of Ogden in Utah, where floral design was not exactly the mainstay of the economy. Instead, Ogden is famous for two things: being the spot where the two halves of the first transcontinental railway met in 1869, and being the birthplace of the Osmonds (Donny in 1957 and Marie two years later), neither of which lend themselves to the finer points of petal etiquette.

The wow factor of the floral sculptures is matched only by the original seventeenth-century Flanders tapestries that hang on the walls of the lobby, and in La Galerie, where guests can eat and enjoy music and martinis in the evenings.

'That divine bar' that my hotel friends tell me about goes by the inspired name of Le Bar. You have to love the French – they spend a good amount of their time pursing their lips and refusing to speak English, and maintaining that French is still a global language even though it is spoken as a primary tongue by roughly 1.15 per cent of the world (4.5 per cent if you add all those who speak it as a secondary language), and then they seem to adore using English words at every opportunity: *le weekend, le sandwich, Le Bar.*

Le Bar has sleek brown tables and burgundy chairs arranged over an inlaid parquetry floor. The wood-panelled walls are decorated with watercolours and oils. The main floor-to-ceiling window is framed by rich red theatrical curtains and offset by a towering palm tree. A wide, golden chandelier hangs centrally, and against the walls are sofas into which you sink and from which you feel you might need an industrial crane to extricate you. By the entrance is a slightly curved mini-sofa with art nouveau cushions, and tasselled fringes hanging down from the base of the seat. It is clearly designed for a spot of Parisian intimacy.

The luxuriance of the George V spreads to the spa, with its trompe-l'œil floral wall paintings and its chill-out room complete with muslin-draped cabanas and relaxation day beds. The guest rooms are inspired by Louis XVI design, with lemon-yellow and white striped fabrics and replica period furniture. There are enough Louis XVI gold trimmings to catapult the George V into the heart of hot peacock hotel territory. Whereas most luxury hotels have one Presidential Suite for passing dignitaries, the George V has three, and, as the hotel's PR director Caroline Mennetrier informed me, two Royal Suites for when world rulers – and presumably the owner, HRH Prince Al Waleed Bin Talal Bin Abdul Aziz Al Saud of Saudi Arabia – drop in for a night or two.

'And we have the Honeymoon Suite on the eighth floor, which features two private terraces with romantic views of the Eiffel Tower, the Panthéon, Notre Dame and St Louis des Invalides, just across the Seine,' said Caroline, looking more like a Parisian Audrey Hepburn every minute.

The extravagance turns to mouth-watering abandon in Le Cinq, the two-Michelin-starred restaurant, where gold, floral sculptures, diamond-spangled chandeliers and rich flavours swirl like a truffle soup. Sadly, I could only spend five minutes peering in jealously and did not get to dine at Le Cinq, for which reservations are required several lifetimes in advance. Nor did I meet its famous executive chef, Philippe Legendre, who was voted Chef of the Year in 2003 by his peers in the French magazine *Le Chef*, making him a Legendre in his own lunchtime. He was busy in his kitchen with his 70 staff, gutting line-caught turbot, preparing Brittany lobsters and roasting Pigeons du Pays de Racan. Nor did I get a chance to shake the fondant hand of Legendre's pastry chef, who goes by the beautifully appropriate name of Fabrice Lecleir, which according to my translation website is not a million miles away from 'Makes Cakes'.

But I did have a chance to savour the smell of luxury on a plate as a waiter passed by with a lemon and ginger soufflé with fresh raspberries, and I managed a quick read of the menu – enough for me to work out that the cheapest possible three-course meal I could have here would set me back about £110 before drinks and the tip. I decided I would wait until I can afford to book a table there, sometime around my ninety-fifth birthday.

Despite the wanton voluptuousness of the George V, for the ultimate in peacock hotels – the King Peacocks, if you like – we must set our sights on the USA, and in particular Las Vegas. In the time that elapses between me writing these words for you and you reading them, Las Vegas could easily have demolished three or four hotels and built the same number of new ones.

Its hotel habits are as promiscuous as the Serengeti lion in the mating season (who, in case you are wondering, has sex several times every day with a wide selection of lionesses and still goes to bed unsatisfied).

There are about a dozen contenders for the Las Vegas King Peacock crown, and each one is themed. The Venetian has canals with gondolas steered by gondoliers in authentic striped jumpers, straw hats and red ribbons. Tacky as this might seem, there are three major advantages of taking a gondola ride in Vegas rather than Venice: it is a lot cheaper, the canals do not carry the occasional pong of dead cat, and the gondoliers sing better. New York-New York is, as you might guess, a mini-Manhattan in the Nevada desert. You can chow down on a pastrami on rye sandwich in a Greenwich Village deli, walk through a Chelsea neighbourhood street, and take a ride on the Manhattan Express roller-coaster past a 100-metre replica of the Brooklyn Bridge and around the fake skyscrapers that make up the hotel's façade.

The Luxor is a vast 30-storey black pyramid down at the south-western end of the Las Vegas Strip and is the world's second-biggest hotel, with 4,408 rooms. It is one of the city's older hotels, a monument to everything Egyptian. It is impossibly cavernous inside and from its apex a beam of light shines so brightly it is visible from space. But for me, the most thrilling thing about it is the lifts. Sometimes I scare myself at how easily pleased I am.

Years ago I read somewhere that the lifts in the Luxor travelled diagonally up and down the sloping sides of the pyramid. 'Nonsense,' I thought. When I returned to Las Vegas shortly after 9/11, I sauntered in and pretended to play a one-armed bandit (or 'slot machine' in the local lingo) for half an hour before plucking up the courage to follow a guest to the lift and solve this riddle for myself. I knew you needed a hotel keycard to make the wretched things work.

I picked two of the fattest guests I could find, figuring that they would take longer to get into the lift and fumble for their hotel cards to operate it, which would allow me time to sneak in with them and hide behind their combined bulk. In Las Vegas, finding a fat person is about the only thing I would bet serious money on, for the city is a global magnet for the monstrously overweight who come here to gamble and eat even more fatty food than they do at home.

My targets were identified and I homed in on their wad-
dling backsides. One of them had the word Minnesota
printed on the arse of his tracksuit pants. On anyone of
normal size the 'Min' and the 'ota' would have disappeared
around their hips, but not on this guy – his girth ensured
that the entire state was proudly displayed. I made it as far
as the lift door but was stopped by a security guard who was
checking all hotel keys.

'I just want to see if the lifts go diagonally,' I pleaded.

'Hotel guests only,' he said, loudly enough for the fat couple to look at me down their broad, vaguely Neanderthal
noses.

In spite, I allowed myself to think a highly uncharitable
thought that involved the lift not moving in any direction
once they were inside it, but I checked myself and tried a
different approach with the automaton guard.

'It's to settle a bet. My friend bet me that the elevator
moved diagonally and I don't think they do.'

'I can't help you with that,' said the guard. 'Hotel guests
only inside the elevators.'

'Okay,' I said, 'I don't need to actually get in the elevator
but I just need to know if they travel diagonally, rather than
straight up and down. Can you just tell me that much?'

This time, silence.

I had been here before, trying to commune with the un-
dead; dealing with 40-watt brain security guards is, sadly,
the lot of most journalists. Trying to work out just what dim
and misty netherworld their plankton-like brains inhabited, so I could short-circuit them into giving me a vaguely
human answer. 'Even robots are being given consciousness
now,' I thought, but I also remembered that this was the
USA, just after its biggest ever terrorist attack. They were
ready to arrest squirrels for storing nuts in case they were

going to use them in an all-out bombardment on a bus stop.

I wished I had simply asked Minnesota's fattest couple if the lifts go diagonally but they were long gone, pounding around in their suite, distressing the mattresses and ripping into the Pringles in the mini-bar. So I retreated, with anger welling up inside me like a double dose of mainlined MSG, and with my riddle still unsolved. I only found out the truth very recently when I went back to the Luxor, this time with a room keycard. To my amazement, the lifts actually do travel diagonally. When they approach your floor and slow down, you end up leaning into the person standing next to you, which is fine if that person is a drop-dead gorgeous Latina casino host sporting an evening-wear bikini, but not cool if it is a track-suited mammoth from Minnesota.

Next door to the Luxor – which in Las Vegas means at least a 15-minute walk over bridges across huge traffic intersections – is another hot peacock: Excalibur, a hotel with a medieval theme of knights and dragons and damsels in distress. Along with the Luxor, it is probably the most recognisable of the Vegas hotels. Its castellated concrete structure is topped with red and blue turreted towers, and its huge casino halls are peppered with 'olde worlde' ways of relieving guests of their money.

Diagonally opposite is the monolithic MGM Grand, a giant of a hotel, which is the world's biggest with 5,034 rooms, and the resort which delivers, according to its PR department, 'Maximum Vegas'. It is famous for hosting big boxing matches, having a 14-metre bronze lion guarding its entrance (the largest bronze structure in the western hemisphere), being bathed in rather creepy green lights, and being clearly visible from distant galaxies. The lights are a rare hangover from the days when the hotel had a *Wizard of Oz* theme and the green was meant to depict the spooky allure of the Emerald City. Vegas regulars tell me they now call it the After-Dinner Mint.

The MGM Grand had better watch its back, however, because it faces being shoulder-charged into second place in the fat hotel stakes by the First World Hotel complex in Payang, Malaysia, which is promising an expansion to boast 6,300 rooms.

The first half of the hotel is operating and the rest of the rooms are now under construction. The lobby has 32 check-in counters, which is more than most airlines have at major international airports. There is an international convention centre covering 106,000 square feet, a ballroom that can accommodate 3,200 people, a two-screen Cineplex, a 30-lane bowling centre, 45,000 square feet of shops, and a truly massive indoor theme park with copies of icons from all around the world. You can walk between the Statue of Liberty and the canals in Venice. Sorry, Malaysia, but Vegas did all that years ago. Catch up. And enjoy your biggest hotel status while you can, because you will soon be dwarfed by a new hot peacock proposal in Dubai called the AsiaAsia.

It will have 6,500 rooms and will be operational by 2010. It is to be part of a massive tourism development called the Bawadi Project which will comprise a 10-kilometre strip of 51 hotels themed on ancient Egyptian palaces, the Wild West, London's Houses of Parliament and the moon. The initial investment alone is £27 billion but that might significantly increase. The Bawadi development will have more than 60,000 hotel rooms in all, more than three times the number currently available in Dubai, and will be able to host more than 3.5 million tourists annually by 2016. The new Emperor Peacock is about to land.

Until it does, my pick of the hot peacocks remains one

of the grandest 'grand dames' of Europe. The Ritz on Piccadilly in London could just be the most famous luxury hotel on the planet. It is certainly one of the most lavish and expensive. It was irredeemably immoderate when I checked in one wet winter's day in 2000, but now, after a thorough £30-million renovation and refurbishment, it is even more worthy of being credited as the pinnacle of extravagant design.

In his history of the hotel, Marcus Binney of *The Times* writes that César Ritz had a mission in life:

> ... to please and delight his guests. Spoiling, pampering and making people feel at home were his métier. His attention to detail, his determination to offer the very latest and best, his ability to set fashions rather than follow them, were qualities of a grand society host even more than those of a hotel manager.

The hotel should pop several bottles of the finest vintage Krug to congratulate itself for following Ritz's passionately held tenet to the letter. The Portland stone and Norwegian granite façade is as imposing and elegant as ever, and its French chateau-esque roof, dormer windows, and the bright, fizzy 'RITZ' signs make it instantly recognisable.

Binney writes that the great suite of ground-floor rooms:

> ... is one of the all-time masterpieces of hotel architecture. Here is a parade of spaces with the nobility of a succession of state apartments in a royal palace – grand vistas, lofty proportions and sparkling chandeliers.

The building is a perfect union of Ritz's grand schemes, the flamboyancy of the neoclassical Louis XVI style of decoration from the late eighteenth century, and the use of unusual shapes by the architect and design team who created the original building, French architect Charles Mewes and his English counterpart Arthur Davis. Today their circles, octagons and ovals play a major part in the décor. The main staircase arrives in a grand sweep in the hotel's lobby, following exactly César Ritz's direction that it should afford ladies the chance to make a dramatic entrance and show off their gowns to best effect.

The rooms and suites are nothing short of palatial. If you love the Louis XVI style, you will truly be in Hotel Heaven, for they drip with gold-leafed bas-relief urns overflowing with fruit and flowers, and draped with carved floral garlands. Heavy blue, white and gold curtains hang around the windows, and the original fireplaces are now marble and gold altars sporting carriage clocks and candlesticks. Only the plasma-screen televisions and the high-speed internet connections remind you this is a London hotel in the twenty-first century and not a private royal chateau in the French countryside circa 1784.

For every guest who stays at the Ritz, another hundred or more dress up and breeze in for afternoon tea in the Palm Court, with musical accompaniment from resident pianist Ian Gomes. So popular has the revived custom become that there are now five separate sittings daily, including – confusingly – one in the morning and an additional champagne tea in the evening. The revenue from the teas alone must considerably help the Ritz's coffers, as they cost £37 a head. There is also the added knowledge that you are having afternoon tea at the only hotel in the world which has been awarded a Royal Warrant for banquet and catering services by His Royal Highness The Prince of Wales.

But it's not just about the food. Guests are paying for an experience in unique surroundings, the chance to spend time in one of the world's most luxuriant hotel tearooms.

The ground-floor Palm Court was originally called the Winter Garden and was designed to greet people as they waltzed through the hotel's entrance on Piccadilly. Now that the celebrity–paparazzi sparring match has reached dizzy and dangerous heights and everybody is terrified of getting their pictures in the paper (apart from when they need to get their pictures in the paper to make some more millions), the Ritz has shifted its entrance to a more subtle welcome mat around the corner on Arlington Street. Three white marble steps take you from the carpeted hallway into the body of the Palm Court, where you are greeted by a waiter wearing a tail coat and bow tie and shown to your white and gold neoclassical chair.

Behind the vast floral display which takes centre stage is a statue known as 'La Source', depicting a nymph looking up at two Tritons blowing on conch shells. A dedicated team of people are employed by the Ritz to make sure the statue's 24-carat gold-leaf coating is kept immaculate year-round. When they are not working on keeping the nymph and her Tritons golden and beautiful, they are busy retouching the even more impressive statue ('The Thames and the Ocean') down the hall in the restaurant. These are the kind of people I long to meet in bars while I am travelling and whiling away a long and lonely evening.

'So what do you do?'

'I'm a gold-leaf toucher-upper at the Ritz Hotel.'

'No kidding! Fancy a drink?'

'Sure. A shandy would be tops, thanks.'

If you fancy a break from Louis XVI, then make your way across the hall and push open a nondescript white, mirrored door. On the other side is the Rivoli Bar, a tiny and intimate Aladdin's Cave of streamlined art deco, which has recently reopened after 29 years. During the past three decades this space has sported luxury shops, but believe me, the wait for the rebirth of the Rivoli has been worth it.

The interior designer who masterminded this transformation, Tessa Kennedy, said she wanted to 'create a magical effect, as if you are walking into a jewellery box'.

The bar is made from satinwood, and on it rests an alabaster top which is lit from beneath to make it glow. The cocktail waiters (in white tuxedos) appear and disappear through a curtain of shimmering crystal beads. The Rivoli's walls are coated with a wafer-thin veneer of camphor wood, and the floor is split bamboo, ash and dark brown wengé wood from West Africa and decorated with art deco rugs. The ceiling has large scallop-edged shell-like inlays, the chairs are covered in faux leopardskin, the sofas in gauffered velvet, and set into the pillars are Lalique panels displaying classical figures which have been taken from moulds originally used for decoration on the Orient Express.

There are mirrors on the walls engraved with hunting scenes full of stags, hounds and birds of the field and forest. To make the window curtains precisely what she wanted, Tessa Kennedy sent some semi-transparent art deco designs she found in Germany to India to be embroidered, and the only carpets she thought would be fitting for a peacock hotel bar such as the Rivoli were ones she had picked up in Tibet.

Kennedy had to go even further to find the cute little table lights. She tripped over these in an antique shop in the Melbourne suburb of St Kilda when on a design expedition a few years ago.

The drink of the moment is the Ritz 100, a blend of

champagne, vodka, Grand Marnier and peach liqueur garnished with flakes of 24-carat gold leaf.

Each night, after the last film star and Japanese banker have retired for the evening (possibly holding hands and heading for the lifts), the bar staff lovingly remove the Australian table lights and line them up next to each other to be recharged in special trays.

I could go on about the Rivoli but I think you get the picture. It's the richest, most sumptuous and genuinely elegant and cool hotel bar in the world. You can forget all the others you have read about – the Writers' Bar at Raffles in Singapore, the Horseshoe Bar at the Shelbourne in Dublin, the Skybar at Hollywood's Mondrian – the Rivoli is as extravagantly chic as it gets. It is also entirely fitting that it exists inside the most extravagant and genuinely lavish hot peacock hotel of them all, the incomparable Ritz.

Chapter 6

Cool Cats

IF ALL THE talk of the rich, creamy excess found in hot peacock hotels has made you feel a little queasy, then maybe you are not a peacock person after all. Perhaps you are a believer in the other school of luxury hotel design – the one that follows the behaviour of another admirable creature, the streamlined, self-assured puss-cat.

These hotels are just as luxurious as hot peacocks, and some fall into the most expensive range, but whereas a peacock puffs out its chest to show off its rainbow of coloured feathers, the super-cool puss-cat mocks such flamboyance and instead dilutes the bravura to leave a concentrated, stylish, minimalist shell. The luxury in this kind of hotel is its simplicity. The style is known as 'design hotel', but you could equally call it 'anti-design', for the emphasis is on stripping away the glitz and getting back to basics – plain white walls, black terrazzo fireplaces, functional furniture, exposed plumbing, and in some cases a lack of all obvious visual comforts save a bed and a chair. They appear beautifully basic and understated but still manage to offer a wide array of luxuries.

The first such 'design hotel' was the Royal in Hammerichsgade in Copenhagen. Construction was completed in 1960, under the direction of the legendary Danish architect and designer Arne Jacobsen.

Such was Jacobsen's reputation as a visionary that he was commissioned to design the entire hotel, from the superstructure to the interior and the finest of details on curtains, light fittings, ashtrays and knives and forks. Two of Jacobsen's trademark works, the Swan and Egg chairs, were created for the Royal. When the hotel was taken over by Radisson SAS, they quickly bought 450 additional copies of the chairs so they could be displayed throughout the building. Each room has at least one Swan. One of the best used to be in the lobby, sitting underneath the sweep of a spiral staircase as it gracefully makes its way down.

The hotel has managed to keep a lot of its 1960s jet-age feel, which is to its credit, but when you go – and you must – book way, way ahead for Room 606. It is the only room with the complete original Jacobsen décor from 1960, complete with radio and intercom system. The walls and furniture are a turquoise, sea-green colour. The dark, tropical wengé wood is still there too, bringing a touch of Africa to the otherwise white, northern-European ambience.

Nothing came close to the Royal for years, as luxury hotels went flamboyantly strutting down the hot peacock path. But then in the mid-1990s design hotels went through a renaissance and caught the attention of discerning guests desperate to escape floral wallpaper and the curse of the doily. They started popping up in Munich, Reykjavik, Glasgow and New York. As the style became more and more popular, word spread around the world, so you can now stay in minimalist luxury in Australia, Bali and Miami too. There is even a Berlin-based hotel marketing company called 'designhotels', which is dedicated to promoting these shrines to simplicity.

The key founders of the modern design hotels movement are Ian Schrager and Philippe Starck, names you probably already know. They might not have come up with all the elements of the style, but they brought it to the attention of luxury hotel addicts and showed that small, intimate alternatives to the big hot peacocks were possible. Hotels once more became not just places to bed down but places to meet people, to show off and to party – just as they had been back in the first few decades of the twentieth century.

I love these hotels. I'm more addicted to them than any other style, but that's probably because I am a modern design addict as well as a luxury hotel addict, although I cannot survive on a diet of purely design hotels all year. I have to indulge in a good hot peacock once in a while. However, I have also always suspected that some design hotels might be a little bit of a rip-off. I have stayed in some that were so lacking in furniture or decoration that I felt like I was sleeping in a room that had just been burgled.

The selling point, design hoteliers often tell me, is Zen-like calm, a tonic for our poor senses that are battered daily by media and advertising. The cynical old Fleet Street journalist in me has always thought this was a load of tosh, a bit like the 'nouvelle cuisine' craze during which hotels and restaurants made pots of money by serving one Polynesian lettuce leaf and a single baked bean stewed in Tibetan yak's semen and charging you £40 for the experience.

So I check in into the cool-cat Medusa Hotel in Sydney's funky Darlinghurst district, owned and created by Australia's design hotel visionary, Terry Schwamberg, in the hope she could reassure me that I was not addicted to a placebo and was in fact hooked on the real deal.

'Often when I visit luxury hotels (especially chain hotels) and it feels beige, too safe or too gaudy, I suspect that the general manager's wife or partner might have had something to do with the general design,' she said.

'A luxury hotel needs a good design aesthetic, and it will only achieve this by commissioning a high-profile designer or an interior architect. Credible design is crucial for the luxury market, and to have interior experts acknowledging your establishment is a fabulous marketing tool. Gone are the days of the doilies!'

Well, not quite, Terry. Unfortunately, doilies are still adorning the tables of B&Bs, boutique hotels and some five-star luxury hotels too, but it is true they are a dying breed. And good riddance. In New Zealand once, in an unbearably twee little B&B, one of these rotten doilies snagged the edge of my suitcase buckle as I dashed out to catch a taxi to the airport. I brought a table full of ghastly porcelain ornaments crashing to the floor. The owner of the B&B was so horrified when she saw the havoc I had wreaked that I thought she was going to expire in front of me. Her knees threatened to give way and her bottom lip started to tremble. On the floor, the remains of a menagerie of china animals were scattered liberally, and in the middle of them all sat the offending doily. The B&B had given me a free stay because I was writing a review, but I ended up with a substantial bill for damages which exceeded the fee my newspaper was paying me for the article. That's a lose-lose situation for me, so I have been passionately hateful of doilies ever since. Round up all remaining doilies, I say, leaving no lace-curtained mum-and-dad B&B unchecked, and burn them all.

Schwamberg also believes in what she calls 'credible design' and is convinced that the new generation of global travellers is far more discerning than its predecessors and can spot the genuine from the fake.

'They are well read, and they want design credibility and

luxury with good value,' she said. 'They are information junkies who are savvy on the internet and will often pay over the odds for a special luxurious experience.

'I suspect years ago guests went to luxury hotels for a treat but also to brag about how wealthy they were. Today more people can afford to go to them and I believe it's more about having an intellectual appreciation of design, as well as other aspects. Entry into a luxury hotel used to be like getting in to a secret nightclub. Now it's more about voyeurism of beautiful interiors than snob value.

'Most guests require a hotel experience and not a home experience. The fun, the vibe and the glamour are major factors guests look for, and they also love to find design ideas that can be used in their homes. A luxury hotel is where a guest might experiment for the first time with mood lighting, minimalist interiors or a Swan Chair, and then go home and think, "I'm going to consider that for the lounge room or the bedroom,"' said Schwamberg.

'Guests are more and more interested about where they can buy the hotel sheets and accessories. They want to know about the joinery in the rooms, and where the hotel got its glassware and china. They want to know where they can get the French lavender scent that was left on their pillows, and where they can buy the goose-down pillows themselves. They appreciate the fine detail in a way they never did before.'

Schwamberg said it is essential for hotels and their guests to understand what she calls the 'cool factor' and the 'fun factor' simultaneously.

'At the Standard Hotel on Sunset Boulevard in Hollywood, sparse minimalism compromises comfort. People love the cool factor and the fun factor, so the hotel, with its plastic swimming pool toys and fake blue grass, obviously has guests seduced because they rarely complain about the discomfort of the beds,' she said.

'At the Mondrian [Ian Schrager's white modernist monument, also on Sunset Boulevard], the cool factor makes guests realise that they cannot really moan about the fact that the noise from the Skybar below comes right up through the windows – it's all part of the package.

'Successful owners of design hotels have got to be able to recognise the youth lifestyle drivers: fashion, art, music, social and nightlife, sport (like the Nike fashion phenomenon) and new technology (iPod, Wi-Fi). If you understand that the lives of today's creative über-travellers are being dictated by these things, then it gives a wonderfully intellectual element to hospitality management and marketing.'

As well as loathing doilies, Schwamberg shares my passionate hatred for stunts and tricks.

'What is not good in luxury hotels are the gimmicks that seem fashionable at some chains, like the earpiece headphones that everyone wore at the W Hotel in Sydney. Thank goodness, the W has now gone and it is a "Blue" hotel. The forced corporate cool thing is, quite frankly, uncool,' she said.

There is nothing uncool about Schwamberg's Medusa, however, which is as sleek and stylish as a peacock-hating cool-cat hotel gets. It's not minimalist and is instead full of life, but it is restrained. The use of colour and patterns by interior architect Scott Weston makes you feel that a single brushstroke has taken place. Just when the richness of a palette is coming to the fore, the designer has stopped and said, 'Enough.' The result is a pleasing and relaxing subtlety. This is one reason why *Condé Nast Traveller* voted it one of the 21 cool hotels for the twenty-first century.

'In appreciation of the modern and the classic, the

design and building team pared away all the non-essential elements of a traditional hotel. Next was the introduction of vibrant colour and texture,' said Weston. He used a mixture of timbers, and clever joinery, to give the hotel a theatrical feel, and then gave each room a polished feature wall in an individual colour, allowing each its own identity.

A 90-minute flight south from the Medusa is another deliciously deconstructed design hotel. The Prince on the corner of Fitzroy and Acland streets in the trendy ocean-front Melbourne suburb of St Kilda looked fairly unassuming from the outside on my first visit. Behind me, the trams were rattling up and down the middle of the main road and a group of animated students in long stripy scarves were trying to draw attention to themselves by talking loudly. I took in the art deco façade, which was attractive enough but nothing to get overheated about. On the ground floor was a pub that was famous for live bands. Big deal. Melbourne is full of them.

It got more promising when I followed the students up Acland Street. They ran on ahead, no doubt having just remembered with glee that there was some cold pizza left back at the flat. Their scarves disappeared around the corner, and I found myself standing at the door of an inviting underground vodka bar called Mink. The bar is part of the same Prince complex, which also boasts a restaurant called Circa and a gourmet bakery called Il Fornaio. Food and cakes could wait; vodka sounded far more appealing.

Inside Mink, the crimson velvet curtains were tied together with gold sashes, and the terracotta-coloured banquettes were supporting the delicate frames of half-a-dozen models, who were drinking away the stresses and strains of Melbourne Fashion Week. An impressive and brightly lit vodka fridge stared at me from behind the bar, with 42 varieties from ten countries. Poland was responsible for 21 types on its own. On the wall the chiselled faces of Communist propaganda posters stared out, making me feel guilty for the avaricious thoughts that were whirring around my head. Far easier on the eye were the splashes of graffiti art and paintings of nude nymphs looking coy and coquettish all at the same time. The PR blurb says the design was influenced by the carriages of the Trans-Siberian Express, but to me it was a faithful rendition of an up-market Moscow brothel.

The real design masterpiece in this complex is the Prince Hotel itself, which the management now modestly calls 'Planet Prince'. The wow factor is there from the first step in the door. A pink-lit curtain behind a cantilevered, matt-black reception desk leads the eye soaring up fifteen metres to a distant ceiling. The pink swathe is made more dramatic by the fact that the rest of the lighting is minimal and there are dark brooding corners on either side. I felt like I had stumbled into a theatre on dress rehearsal night for an experimental version of Offenbach's *Orpheus in the Underworld*, in which Orpheus and Eurydice would be played by a couple of video installations and Pluto would be the big pink curtain.

Chairs by Australian wunderkind designer Marc Newson sit on the polished wooden floor, as isolated from each other as exhibits in a modern art museum. In the centre of the space a black staircase beckons upwards, to where a hot-pink Swan chair sits, flooded by a ceiling spotlight. Arne Jacobsen strikes again.

The rooms are the antithesis of the after-dark lobby. They are full of natural light and white linens, and the beds are on raised platforms, which makes clambering into them an adventure. I could not wait to play with the Bose WAVE radios and Loewe televisions, and flick through endless channels of nonsense.

I equally loathe and love watching television in hotel rooms. Massive procrastination takes hold, and I find myself getting engrossed in awful soaps and sentimental docudramas about who invented particular tanks and submarines which killed thousands of people in World War II. And then there are interminable hours of drivel about people who lost their legs in gruesome combine-harvester accidents but still went on to become world-famous footballers by running on their hands and scoring goals with their heads.

Okay, I made that last one up, but you get the picture. Television in hotel rooms makes me feel like I'm really ill and off work for weeks and propped up at home with nothing but *Oprah* and *Days of Our Lives* to keep me sane. But somehow it is as addictive to me as the very hotels I am staying in, and I hate myself for being so easily sucked in. Once, in a hotel in Amsterdam, when I should have been working on an article, I watched a documentary about penguins regurgitating fish for their young. It was in Dutch so I could not understand a thing, but I knew how the little penguins felt. Most of my hotel televisions do something quite similar – throw up dead programmes for me to swallow whole.

The Prince is so achingly hip, however, that it actually feels as if you are insulting the furniture and décor if you watch television in the room. It's much more fun to walk around the corridors and experience the hotel. Book for dinner in the beautifully theatrical Circa, taking a moment to sit on an aubergine chaise longue and spin around in a Swan chair. It feels like you are backstage at Studio 54 circa 1981, and around any corner you could meet KC and the Sunshine Band in psychedelic spangly stage outfits and rollerskates.

Another groovy little number is The Hotel in Lucerne, Switzerland, where scenes from a series of films are projected onto the ceilings of the guest rooms. You can choose between the Spanish surrealist Luis Buñuel, his countryman Pedro Almodóvar, British painter and film director Peter Greenaway, and others. It might sound like a pretentious idea dreamed up by art-school students having love affairs with existentialism, but it's also a real piece of escapism for guests. It makes the rooms look pretty and colourful, and it's great fun.

Such design elements can work well in sleek modern hotels, but there is one property that needs no added extras. The Sunset Tower Hotel on Sunset Boulevard in West Hollywood is a stylish masterpiece; it is the most superb example of art deco on the West Coast of the USA, and it even gives some New York and Miami deco edifices a run for their money.

It was built in 1929 as an apartment block, but has had several reincarnations as a hotel and a private club since then. However, the original and elaborate exterior has hardly changed in almost 80 years. Windows climb in continuous columns up the height of the building, on the rounded corners as well as on the main façades. Most are filled with clear glass for superb views up to the Hollywood Hills, along Sunset Boulevard and down across the flat, brown plain of the Los Angeles basin. At 5-metre intervals there are striking black and grey chevron panels.

Three-quarters of the way up, the grey-pink building is broken by a white concrete cornice on the east side and by a full masonry frieze on the balcony facing north. The cornice has a naked woman balancing its centre, flashing her

breasts to the drivers along Sunset. She is flanked by mythical creatures with the heads of rams and the bodies and tails
of rainforest tree ferns. These creatures scamper around to
the north-facing balcony as well, and above them, on the
ribbed and ribbony lip of the balcony, are two male stone
heads, facing each other.

Another frieze higher up boasts standing eagles spreading their wings, stately ibis looking wise and wonderful, and
the occasional flower displaying its petals. And at the very
top, around the edge of a square rooftop block, are palm
trees, planets and bright stars shining their light down on
the Earth.

The balcony of one suite has odd additions that resemble
two anvils placed one on top of the other. I only realised
what these were when I walked back across the street for a
long view of the place. They are the tops of some very clever
deep crimson painted trompes-l'œil. From across the street
they look like heavy industrial springs rescued from some
giant machine down at the docks at Long Beach and hauled
north to Hollywood to support the top storey of the hotel.
They provide a wonderful final flourish of deco, this time
a throwback to the industrial age, and offset the mild, soft
colours of the building's exterior.

Admittedly, I first saw the Sunset Tower at dawn after
a large night out on the town with a long-lost cousin, but
I swear I returned later that same day after a good sleep
and several aspirin and examined these details soberly, so
they are not figments of a drunken imagination. The hotel's
owner, Jeff Klein, told me he has also seen on the friezes
'airplanes and zeppelins flying over what look like they
might be pagodas', so I can only imagine what kind of a
night out he must have had.

The rooms have chocolate-coloured 1930s low-backed

sofas, light aubergine bedspreads, easy chairs and long flowing drapes. The walnut coffee tables and writing desks are
nut-brown with smart brass trim along the edges. Exquisite
standard lamps stand to attention with candy-pink shades
and brass bases. Klein has kept the original art deco lifts
with their wooden, inlaid fan designs, and he has placed
more chocolate-coloured sofas next to the lift doors on each
floor, in case you fancy a quick sit-down before boarding.

Known for some years as the Argyle, it was listed in the
National Register of Historic Places and by the Historic
Preservation Commission of West Hollywood, and because
the heritage preservationists in Los Angeles are vociferous
about not letting any more of their buildings be bulldozed
or yuppified, Klein had to tread carefully when renovating
the exterior. Yet he has managed to blend the new with the
old as well.

'What I am doing is a throwback to a more elegant era,
but not so much that it's weird,' he said. 'You know, you
walk into some hotels that are trying to be retro and they
have gas lights, and you're like, "Why would you have gas
lights? We have electricity now, you know." At the Sunset Tower we're modern, we're clean, we're Wi-Fi, we have
iPods in every room, and we have flat-screen televisions in
every room. It's important to embrace modernity. Just because you are an old-school hotel does not mean you have
to have a big old television stuck in there from 1972.'

The lobby is cool and uncluttered, with dark brown walls
acting as a relief from the fierce Hollywood sunlight outside. Small and well-spaced clusters of chairs and sofas
encircle small round walnut tables and the floor is a collection of marble flagstones. In the Tower Bar, diners slink
into smoky grey suede banquettes and order from impeccably mannered and mercifully attitude-free staff. One or

two regulars prop up the long bar near the piano and order martinis and Bloody Marys and, with virtually no effort at all, end up looking very LA and very fabulous.

Apart from the beady eyes of the Historic Preservation Commission of West Hollywood, Klein found himself in a rare position. If you own the hotel, you can sculpt it in your own image. Of course, you have to shell out the millions as well, but at least you can do things your way, design the place to the specifications you know your clientele will appreciate.

A small but perfectly formed hotel in Paris has recently done just this. Edouard VII does not have a fleet of Rolls-Royces or a helicopter pad. It does not have a small battalion of laptops for use by guests, or floral designers doing magical things with 15,000 blooms per week. Instead it offers guests a discreet and charming stay in a uniquely designed and decorated townhouse hotel with views up the grand boulevard to the neo-baroque façade of L'Opéra.

The hotel was built and opened in 1877. It was one of many buildings in the city designed by Parisian-born town planner Baron Georges-Eugène Haussmann, who was responsible for so much of Paris's rebuilding in the mid-nineteenth century under the patronage of Napoleon III. Many of the open spaces and sweeping 30-metre-wide boulevards that visitors enjoy today were the work of Haussmann, including the graceful Boulevard Saint-Germain on the Left Bank and the Avenue de l'Opéra on which the hotel stands.

In the later nineteenth century Europe was entering an era of decadence known as La Belle Époque, and Paris was at its heart, so the hotel soon became the haunt of the wealthy and fashionable. One of the most famous residents was the Prince of Wales, a bon viveur soon to become Edward VII, and in deference to him the hotel adopted his name.

That is where the history lesson ends and modern design makes a dramatic entrance. Today, the small irregular-shaped lobby sports a floor of Sainte Croix de Mareuil marble from the Dordogne region of south-west France, mahogany reception and concierge desks, an orange and white floral chandelier from Italy, and a collection of modern wooden artworks by French sculptor Nicolas Cesbron which mimic flowing natural forms. There are opium poppy lights perched on the end of bowed, wooden, willowy stems, some of them three metres tall. Two shorter ones are made from darker wood and hold white orchids instead of light bulbs. Near the entrance stands a chocolate-coloured sculpture with three flowing wooden legs and a cut-away bowl at the top, which doubles as a writing station – perfect for making a quick scrawled note when you are charging off to do some shopping and the concierge yells out the address of a must-see boutique.

The central feature is a two-metre flowing wooden sculpture which either resembles the swirling skirt of a flamenco dancer or a very large field mushroom, depending on your point of view. I found a fellow guest standing next to me and staring at it too. 'What do you reckon – flamenco or mushroom?' I asked.

'No, no, no, it looks like pizza dough that is being thrown up in the air by a chef. King-size pizza dough. You must have seen them do that, throw those big circles of dough in the air and catch them again to make them bigger. That's what it is.'

He had a point, but I am going to stick with my large mushroom theory. Anyway, it is smooth and looks alarmingly comfortable, but it is strictly not for sitting, unless you are younger than five (when, in Paris, you can do anything you like and get away with it).

The Edouard VII is a good deal more lush than the Medusa, the Prince and the Sunset Tower, but it follows the same philosophy: take risks with design and décor and then pull back. The hotel recently changed hands I met the owner, Marie-Ange Corbel, for lunch in the hotel's Angl'Opéra restaurant (I had a delicious fillet of sea bass, in case you're interested) and she gave me her definition of hotel luxury.

'For us, it is the personal touch. We cannot offer what a Four Seasons can offer but the personal touch is really our strength,' she said. 'We wanted a typical Parisian hotel, but from today, not from the past. There are lots of old-fashioned palaces here so we were determined to produce something different, something contemporary. Guests can see clearly they are in Paris because the base of the building is classical Haussmann, but at the same time we want them to be surprised when they walk through the door.'

The biggest surprise awaits guests in the sexy rooms and suites, which are sleek and modern with cute white-shaded box lamps, plum velvet sofas, black-and-white-tiled bathrooms, and big, low and heavenly comfortable beds. It is one of the best hotels in Paris. It is not the most exclusive, nor the most lavish, there is no Michelin-starred restaurant or a Mercedes limo on hand to ferry you to and from the Musée d'Orsay or the Arc de Triomphe, and it is certainly neither the most starred or expensive, but for me this is one of the most genuinely Parisian of Paris's hotels. Marie-Ange and her architect husband designed the hotel not to give visitors a taste of what they think Paris should be like, or what it felt like 100 years ago, but what it really feels like today: chic, cool, confident, modish and just slightly pleased with itself. The ancient influences are all around, but this is a living interpretation of what Paris has learned and absorbed over its many centuries of existence.

I love the Edouard VII and the Sunset Tower and the Prince and the Medusa, but I only dip in and out of each for small baby-luxe fixes, for the true engine room of my addiction lies elsewhere. There is one small chain that delivers my luxury design hotel mainline every time. Only the most addicted luxury hotel junkies have heard of the blandly named General Hotel Management (or GHM), but we love the group's hotels with such a passion that we have been nicknamed GHM junkies.

It is incredibly difficult to describe what it is about these hotels that is so special, especially as the design luminaries behind the brand – the chairman Adrian Zecha and his style guru Ralf Ohletz – rarely grant interviews, and they made no exception for me.

The overwhelming philosophy seems to be one that combines Zen-like symmetry with bold, strong yet simple architectural styles. Wood and stone are used side by side to create an earthy, natural feel. There are strong Asian touches, using dark-stained wood, circular doors and windows, grey volcanic stepping-stones that make their way through emerald gardens, and single-stemmed hibiscus flowers in slender earthenware vases. Then the focus turns Moorish, with palatial square ponds, dead-straight watercourses and divine rectangular swimming pools (public and private). GHM's property in Chiang Mai in northern Thailand, the Chedi, has a distinctly Nordic look, with liberal use of blond wood and white walls.

What the properties (sixteen in all, in nine countries) share is a deft ability to produce sublime luxury from the simplest of designs. At the Chedi Chiang Mai, the turquoise-tiled infinity pool sits within an infinity lotus pond. In each beach bungalow at the Chedi Phuket is a hollowed-out coconut, in which, at various times of the day, little treats arrive secretly, like sticky cakes and small fragrant frangipani biscuits. At the Heritage House in Mendocino in northern California, warm brick floors meet floor-to-ceiling windows that frame glorious panoramas of the Pacific Ocean. And at the Datai on the island of Langkawi in Malaysia, huge banks of layered grey slate and stone pathways are the perfect backdrop for the lush green of the surrounding rainforest.

GHM rooms are big and sexy, with polished wooden and terrazzo floors, rich brown and ochre fabrics, and sparingly and dramatically placed ornaments and flowers. The architecture of the hotels is so neat and uncluttered that guests get a good look at the craftsmanship, which means architects and designers have not been able to cut corners. No aspect of a GHM property is left undesigned. All the joinery, stonemasonry, parquetry and woodturning are very much on display and thus become a major element of each property. Design gurus would no doubt say GHM properties were the epitome of 'clean lines', but I've never really understood how a line can be clean, so let us just say they are impeccably smart and orderly, and as a result they induce an enormous feeling of calm and wellbeing.

The GHM properties are a more affordable version of the Aman hotels, of which luxury hotelier Adrian Zecha is also the chairman and a creative force. The Amans are delightfully over the top, but they are aimed more at supermodels, movie stars and big CEOs. Rupert Murdoch booked out the entire Amanjena in the Atlas Mountains of Morocco for a family party. The GHM properties are cooler and more subtle than that. They are hotels you or I might save up to go to, for a week of blissful relaxation and to achieve luxe by design.

Whichever design hotel you decide to jet off to, it pays to do your fashion homework. There are few experiences more sobering for the luxury hotel addict than to be standing in your underwear in your suite, late for your restaurant reservation and in the midst of a wardrobe malfunction. At most hot peacocks men can get away with a suit and tie and women look fine in a black cocktail number or a floral Missoni kaftan, but design hotels are much harder to dress for. The edgy city properties, like the Prince, really need a lot of black and then some striking primary-coloured statements: polo-neck jumpers, fitted T-shirts, trim jackets and big shoes for the boys, and something avante garde and possibly Asian-inspired for the girls. Less is more. At places like the Datai and the Chedi Chiang Mai, you can let loose and wear a glowing gown or go baggy with huge flares and billowing white cotton shirts.

In a decade of luxury travel I have seen more than my fair share of fashion crimes, and some experiences have left me feeling quite unwell, so I have a bit of an issue with guests who check in to luxury design hotels and think it is okay to waddle around in cut-off shorts and flip-flops. It is not, not even in Bali; in fact, especially not in Bali, where most locals dress smartly and with good colour co-ordination even when they are picking rice in their bare feet.

A frighteningly large number of guests believe that as they are paying top dollar they can wear what they want. It's the same philosophy that results in the very worst-dressed people on any given international flight almost always being in first class. Next time you are flying overseas, hang out near the first-class lounge and see the truly abominable fashion disasters stumbling around like delegates at a computer game convention. There are £2.50 flip-flops, cut-off shorts that have seen far too many summers, baggy T-shirts, ill-fitting everything, and all in the same washed-out, cheap colours that they use to paint the outsides of bargain-basement supermarkets and charity shops. I'm sure you can get swatches of these colours in paint shops called 'Poverty-Line Puce' or 'Lower-Class Lime'. And if you ever wondered what happened to the shellsuit – that rustling, static electricity-inducing piece of haute couture – it's alive and well in the first-class lounges and cabins of the world's airlines, and in some of the most fabulous hotels.

This philosophy – that rich travellers and hotel guests somehow remain above style laws and immune from fashion crimes – never held water during the first Golden Age of luxury hotels at the beginning of the last century, and it should not be accepted now. No self-respecting luxury hotel addict would be seen dead approaching a check-in desk without being kitted out in something smart and funky. Staying at a luxury hotel has progressed way beyond being merely a bed for the night. It's an event, a special moment, and every guest – no matter which thousand-pound suite they might have reserved – bears some responsibility for maintaining that stylish accent.

Some luxury hotels maintain dress codes – notably the Ritz in London: no jeans or trainers in public areas, please – which they advertise to prospective guests, and which they enforce. Not only is this entirely suitable but it is also a fascinating piece of social behaviour: as hotels have become more and more exclusive, the dress codes are actually excellent ways of offering an inclusive experience. The Ritz says no trainers and jeans because it wants all its guests to get the genuine classy Ritz experience, not just the high-rollers. The last thing they want is for a smartly dressed couple from Sydney or Long Island to go home after a stay and tell their friends it was great apart from the shell-suited, trainer-wearing, first-class-flying scruffbags hanging out at reception and lowering the tone of the place.

Thankfully, guests – at least at design hotels – seem to be getting the message that from the moment they step in the door they become part of the design ethic, a living, breathing installation. And apart from being respectful of the hotel and your fellow guests, it's jolly good fun. How often do you get a chance to wear all your posh outfits in one week, night after night? Take them, wear them and be design-fabulous.

Chapter 7

Eco-luxe

TRAVEL TIP: IF you want a surefire way to stay awake on a long flight try working out your annual carbon footprint at 35,000 feet. I recently attempted this somewhere over the Hindu Kush en route to Singapore, scribbling down lots of sums and notes on scraps of paper.

I am notoriously bad at mathematics and at one stage discovered to my horror that I was thousands of pounds in debt to the planet, a fee that was accelerating by about a pound for every second in the air.

I ordered an emergency gin and tonic from the stewardess and realised that by the time it took me to drink it – two-and-a-half minutes – I was another £150 worse off.

My next set of calculations revealed that I had overcompensated and that my debt was, in fact, growing at more like a pound for every few hours aloft rather than every few minutes, which looked a lot better on my pen and paper abacus. This came as a great relief but still did not hide the fact that being a travel writer is among the most polluting of all professions; up there with coal-fired power station owners and Formula One racing drivers.

The most sustainable kind of tourism is to stay at home but the human race is simply never going to do that. We are going to travel more and more and further and faster. We're addicted to it. So how do we do it while minimising the impact on the environment. Well, not by being chauffeured between hotels in BMWs and Rolls-Royces, I admit.

To soothe my conscience I have, throughout my career, tried to seek out and promote the sustainable side of tourism, even in luxury properties. I have tried to find truly ecologically-friendly hotels and resorts, those which are preserving coral reefs, or funnelling profits into regenerating fish stocks or building schools for local communities.

And I am appalled to say that the vast majority of operations promoting themselves as clean and green have been anything but. I cannot begin to tell you the number of times I have been told by hotels or their PR agencies that they have 'embraced sustainability' or are now part of the 'eco-generation'. They might recycle their bottles and the odd scrap of paper here and there but putting in rainwater tanks and grey-water systems are too much like hard work.

I believe this unsavoury habit of fibbing is called 'greenwash': hotels doing next to nothing to save the environment yet painting their walls green, calling their rooms after rare tropical birds and claiming to be eco-warriors. What is even worse is that a lot of them get accredited by incomplete and ad-hoc green schemes and can then boast their dubious sustainable credentials, which amount to nothing more than audacious spin and marketing. They are lying to us and getting away with it.

It is both sad and exciting to announce that really only now, more than fifteen years after the Rio Earth Summit in 1992, is the hotel industry beginning to adopt meaningful sustainable tourism.

Only now are hotels and resorts putting genuine sustainable tourism practices into operation. Recycling, low-energy use, water restrictions and emissions caps are no longer considered huge leaps worthy of fanfares and gushing press releases but basic, standard parts of daily operations.

They are the bare minimum that sustainable properties should be implementing, and should ideally be supplemented by a second tier of more ambitious and innovative measures.

The ideas that hotels are coming up with are beautifully practical. The Trident Hotel in San Francisco has eco-suites where everything in the room is organically made. The glorious Bel-Air in Los Angeles uses the California sunshine to drive a solar heater for its swimming pool. The Taimo Resort on Andros Island in The Bahamas has developed an entire solar field for its electricity, and it offers solar-heated rainwater showers. The run-off from showers and sinks is filtered and used to water the resort's kitchen garden.

All well and good but where is the sustainable tourism Holy Grail I have been searching for during the past fifteen years? Where is the genuine super-sustainable luxury resort? Does it even exist? Should my ambitions be lower?

I had almost given up hope of finding it when I took a chance and checked into a place called Whitepod, which consists of a collection of what look like domed tents halfway up a Swiss Alp.

Camping in mid-summer in the Dordogne might sound attractive, romantic even, but camping in the Swiss Alps in January does not. For someone who has grown far too attached to heated towel rails, soft carpets, 500+ thread-count cotton, ginseng steam baths and multi-directional touch-sensitive temperature controls, the very idea of juxtaposing canvas and sub-zero temperatures makes me shiver.

But I had been reliably informed by an eco-savvy mate in London that Whitepod was as green as they come and that it was far more luxurious than it at first appeared. When booking my stay I comforted myself with the hope that these would be super-tents with radiators or maybe hot springs and a free mini-bar full of Aquavit and glühwein. Perhaps there would be a butler to bring toasted slippers and a cognac and a Mozart concertante CD at bedtime, to ease me into a deep Alpine sleep.

Whitepod's website had some alarming news for me. The domes, or pods, offered neither electricity nor running water so a slipper-bearing butler was most unlikely.

So, on the evening of 1 January, wrapped up for the Arctic and nursing formidable New Year's Eve hangovers we had carried on a bumpy flight from Venice, my wife and I slithered precariously to the door of Whitepod's main chalet.

Icicles hung like daggers from the eaves and glistened in the moonlight. Below, down in the valley, the lights of Aigle shone silently, and on the far peaks were dustings of snow. Snowfall had been poor and skiers had only been able to get action on the uppermost slopes.

Through the steamed windows we saw a table of a dozen people laughing, chatting, drinking wine and endeavouring not to lose their bread in the fondue. Two seats were untaken, their napkins still folded neatly and tied up with coloured ribbons. A log fire roared on an open stone hearth, warming a large rust-brown dog. We opened the door and slid in.

'Hi, you must be Matthew and Erin,' said the petite blonde woman serving wine. 'I'm Sofia. Lovely to see you. Come in, warm yourself, have a glass of wine. I'll get Eric to show you to your pod. He should have lit the fire by now.'

And so began one of the most memorable hotel stays of my career. Luxurious? In the sense of a five-star Peacock like the Ritz or the Waldorf=Astoria, no. But expand the definition to include experiential luxury and Whitepod's star rating is incalculable.

Filled with raclette and fuelled by Swiss red wine – I didn't know the Swiss made wine but it's really rather good – we handed our bags to Eric and tottered over the iced asphalt of a mountain road which ended at the foot of a hillside. Ahead of us, standing proud and firm across the hillside, were the pods, ghostly white in the moonlight.

Fingers of wood smoke rose from the pods' chimneys into the still crystal air. The firmament had all its lights on, moon and stars dazzling like diamonds and making the hardening frost gleam around our feet.

'Maybe you 'ave brought snow,' Eric said, telepathically. 'The TV says cloudy for tomorrow. We need snow.'

We wished for snow on one of the billion or so stars above us and tip-toed on up the hillside, still not sure exactly what awaited us in our pod.

Despite the canvas element, the pods are not really tents at all but semi-permanent homes on wooden platforms. They are geodesic domes, which for the non-geometrically minded, means they resemble oversized golf balls sliced in half horizontally.

Imagine these giant's golf balls sealed against the elements by a canvas coating and fitted out with double beds, double duvets, sheepskin rugs, hurricane lamps, velveteen armchairs and a pot-bellied wood-burning stove which can take the temperature from a frigid 4°C to a sensual, sultry 24°C in about a quarter of an hour.

The ceiling is high enough to walk about inside.

Eric unzipped the flap door and in we bundled. The fire was blazing, the hurricane lamp burning brightly on a table, and the bed looking every inch a luxury. We stripped off our many layers and propped our frozen boots by the stove where they melted and fizzed satisfyingly.

Eric left us with a basket of wood and a promise to be back in the morning with a flask of tea and one of coffee.

In the minute after he left we were speechless. All we could offer each other was a widening smile and a mutual feeling of immeasurable cosiness.

We munched the in-flight cookies we had not been able to stomach on the plane and watched the night gleam and freeze on the other side of the pod's plastic half-moon window. Inside our little pod there was warmth and comfort and a welcome snow-white bed in which to curl up and dream. It was as close to hibernation as I have ever come … and I relished it.

In the morning we woke slowly and languidly, reluctant to move and unanimous in our decision to spend the entire day in bed, regardless of how many flasks of tea and coffee Eric delivered. Hibernation was good. The bears have had it right all along.

For the first time in months we had slept through a night without waking. No pressures niggled at our nerves, no feelings of dread loomed, nor the dull panic that can strike first thing in the morning when you remember the thousand tasks that must be completed before the day is over and your head can sink into the pillow once more.

Life felt soft and oddly muted.

We were lying in a snow-white bed with snow-white sheets, duvets and fluffy sheepskin rugs. Even the plastic half-moon window, which had been transparent the night before, was a white wall. I hadn't felt this blanched since my mother tipped a bowl of lukewarm porridge over my head during what my family have dubbed the Tantrum Years.

Chivalrously I agreed to make the fire, sliding out from

under the duvets, shoving logs into the stove space and holding matches to fire lighters. In minutes the fire was crackling contentedly and heat was seeping luxuriantly around the pod.

A rustling broke the hush somewhere above our heads on the top of the pod – more a sweep than a rustle. It started quietly but grew into a considerable swish as something slid off the dome and knocked the white coating clean off the plastic half-moon window. The pod trembled. We sat bolt upright in bed and looked out the window over a winter wonderland. In the hours we had slept, deep and snug in our cave halfway up an Alp, snow had been busy falling. Lots of snow.

When snow fell on my childhood home in Stratford-upon-Avon, it was a vast gossamer blanket softening life's rough and painful edges. It hushed traffic from a roar to a gentle purr. It absorbed the plethora of ambient noises that rattle our ears. It felted down a welcome dormancy over the land, making it safe and padded.

That feeling, which I had not had since childhood, when winters were winters, came flooding back.

We leapt from the covers, pulling on thermal long johns, T-shirts and several pairs of trousers, and pushing our ski-socked feet into crisp and perfectly dry boots. We tugged open the door flaps and fell out into the blinding sunlight of this new white land. Two serious men in very expensive salopettes were skiing past our dome, en route to the small private piste nearby. They slowed to stare at us as we stage-dived off the dome's wooden platform and sunk up to our waists in the drifts.

We laughed and screeched and threw snowballs at each other and pushed each other's heads into the drifts. It had been a decade since either of us had seen snow.

A snowmobile made its way up the mountainside towards us. 'Bonjour,' said Eric. 'I 'ave brought wood for your fire and some tea. And you, you 'ave brought snow. Thank you.'

Our faces were flushed and our eyes glimmered with the prospect of a perfect day ahead. Snowman construction was of paramount importance, followed by snowshoeing up our mountain – for it was now definitely *our* mountain. We had brought the snow so it was our mountain – seemed a fair exchange. We planned to snow-shoe along a trail through the forests, then back home to cosy up in our pod under sheepskin blankets and in front of the roaring logs.

Whitepod is the creation of Sofia de Meyer, who grew up just across the valley. Her childhood sounds perfectly Heidi-esque: running free over the hills and among the summer edelweiss, tending her father's chalets and eating chunks of cheese while listening to his stories about the landscape.

'He meant everything that matters to me. He taught me patience and respect for nature,' Sofia said as we crunched through the snow after breakfast. Life drew Sofia elsewhere, to London and a job with a City law firm, but she never lost her love for the mountains and a few years ago she made a life-changing decision.

'I was 30 years old and had to decide whether to become a partner in the firm or follow my heart and my passion for nature,' she said. 'I came back here to the valley and spent three days in the forest for inspiration. My decision was made. I decided I wanted to create something. What was most important was for me to live according to the philosophy

I respect most and that means respect for nature.'

Whitepod was born.

Virtually every element of the resort is environmentally sensitive. It is what I have been looking for during the past fifteen years of travel writing – the sustainable tourism Holy Grail. At long last I had found a genuinely sustainable tourist resort that not only gives the body a fabulous holiday but treats the soul too.

Sofia and her team wait for the first frosts in November and then rush out to bang the wooden stilts of the platforms into the ground. As the ground freezes it locks the posts in place, solid until the spring melt. Then, up go the pods and in go the beds, pot-bellied stoves, floor rugs, hurricane lamps, torches and armchairs.

So minimal is the imprint the pods leave on the landscape that a passing walker crossing this wild-flowered hillside in summer would never know that they had been there through the previous winter.

'We do not have any electricity or running water in the pods, which is a deliberate attempt to reduce energy use and pollution. There is a shared toilet cabin in the middle of the pod area. This is one thing that some guests are concerned about: the idea of a freezing-cold toilet on a hillside that you have to share with other people, but really it is very good.'

Really, it is. When it comes to ablutions, there are few people as fussy as a luxury-hotel reviewer. I like my bathrooms big, warm and very private. I trembled at the prospect of a visit to the shared toilet cabin, or snow loo, and the thought of having to hear someone else going about their business and then meeting them afterwards. Why is it that people always feel the need to shake hands while coming out of a hotel loo cubicle, or any public loo cubicle for that matter, before washing them?

I am forever making up excuses to avoid contact: 'Hi, sorry, dodgy wrist.'

I have also had a lifelong hatred of cold toilet seats and the unnerving experience of seeing your breath while in a rural public convenience.

Whitepod's snow loo was infinitely more accommodating. It turned out to be a warm and cosy wooden mini chalet complete with a washbasin and three cubicles, each with a flush toilet. It was more than adequately warmed by a radiator and was altogether a huge success. And nobody tried to touch me with an unwashed hand. I came blustering back in through the flap of my pod in a gleeful mood.

One equally fussy English guest approached the snow loo with trepidation through a blizzard one morning but within 20 minutes was bounding out, calling to his wife, 'It's better than the loos at Camilla's school.'

By now you'll be thinking, okay, the loo sounds OK but where exactly do we shower? Well, you have to take a short walk but then this is sustainable tourism, so there is an onus on the guest to do his or her bit.

The walk takes you down the hillside past big fir trees meringued with inches of snow, to the chalet where we stumbled in on our first evening. The chalet is the nerve centre of the Whitepod operation. The showers are downstairs, while the top floor is where all meals are served, where activities are organised and where you can take a day off from playing in the snow and curl up in a woolly jumper and thick cosy socks in front of the log fire in the open lounge and read a book, drink wine and doze.

I spent one day doing precisely that and was intrigued by occasional screeches and screams and flurries of snow outside. I braved the elements and discovered that the downstairs floor of the chalet houses not just the piping-hot showers but an even hotter sauna and a spa area where a visiting masseur will come and knead your ski-worn muscles back into shape.

The screamers were a couple of frisky Germans taking great delight in running from the sauna through the spa area in their Euro swimwear (bright colours, snug fit) out into the snow and pounding each other with snowballs.

The heating for the showers and the electricity for the sauna and spa area – in fact *all* the chalet's electricity – is solar powered, and the water is collected straight off the mountain. The greenery continues: there's no gas-guzzling limousine making the half-hour drive trip up and down the mountain between Whitepod and the nearest train station at the town of Aigle. Instead you are encouraged to find your own way there, again making guests think about the power used and pollution caused by transport.

At least 95 per cent of the resort's food and drink comes from within a three-hour drive of the pods. This means that each evening before supper Sofia wanders through the living room with a bottle of Swiss wine and a plate of delicious cold meats 'from a little man just down the valley. He cures them all himself by hand.' And, all the resort's produce arrives in wooden crates, reducing the use of plastic and Whitepod's waste.

The only things Whitepod has to import are oranges and dried fruit, and because no pesticides are allowed in Swiss farming, everything you eat here is virtually fully organic.

This makes sitting down to Sofia's famous raclette and a bottle of Chateau Suisse even more appetising.

Crucially, Whitepod busts three myths about sustainable luxury tourism. First, it turns a profit, proving it can be economically viable. Also, despite the fact that the pods have no electricity or running water, they are luxurious and comfortable – two descriptions that are rarely associated with sustainable tourism.

And, third, never let anyone say that sustainable tourism cannot be romantic. All you need to do is book one of Whitepod's special activities involving the Refuge. This is a chalet an hour or two's snow-shoe walk further up the mountain. You and your beloved can ascend at your leisure during the afternoon and find a fondue supper and bottle of wine awaiting you. Then, just when you think it cannot get any more romantic than being alone halfway up an Alp, you can wrap up warm again, don your skis, light flaming torches and swish down the mountain in the moonlight.

I would willingly trade a month in some of the world's finest five-star hotels for a week in one of Sofia's pods. Judging by her booking sheets I am not the only one.

'Last year by mid-November we were completely full for the entire season – right through until March,' she said. 'Thousands of travellers and tourists are now demanding luxury, quality, comfort and sustainability. For years hotels and tourism companies thought it simply could not be done – but it can.

'When guests leave they do two things. First they re-book for next year, which is good, but they also feel inspired to demand more places like Whitepod from their travel agents and from the travel industry.'

Sofia may not have started the sustainable-tourism movement but she can be credited as a pioneer in making it economically viable, which is a huge step. She has helped to set a new benchmark for travel and it is one that I am sure will be replicated all over the world.

It was invigorating to walk through the snow with her and hear her story. I felt like I was present at the dawn of seriously sustainable tourism, not just the 'greenwash' that has blighted the industry for years.

Whitepod is the real deal.

'What is frustrating is that it has always been easier to be non-ecological and that will continue until we reach some critical mass of true sustainable tourism,' Sofia said.

'Look at most consumerism and tourism. One advert I saw here in Switzerland offers free car parking for the ski pistes that are covered in artificial snow. This is all wrong. This laziness makes it more difficult for tourists to be environmentally ecological in their decisions.

'The business world has also been keen to perpetuate myths about eco-tourism, such as ecology equals failure and bad quality. I think we can turn this around. At Whitepod you can sleep in a pod that requires no power and leaves virtually no impact on this landscape or any other, yet it is warm, comfortable and luxurious.

'Guests are responsible for lighting their own fires and keeping an eye on how much wood they are using. There's plenty available, you just need to ask for it. This gives guests a real sense of how much fuel they need to keep warm, a thing many of us don't even pay attention to because we are so used to turning on electricity.

'And we even have Eric to bring you tea and coffee each morning. It's a real travel experience.'

Enjoying this real travel experience with me was an equally real variety of tourists. The Germans wanted a fairy-tale anniversary holiday in the snow – and the sauna. An Italian couple wanted to go on a dogsled run, which they did as soon as the husky truck showed up and the yelping snapping scramble of dogs was finally pulled into line and harnessed. Off they sped, between the pods and over the brow of the hillside, dressed in skin-tight, luminous, mouthwash-green trousers – the Italians, not the dogs.

What all the guests told me was that the Whitepod experience changed them. This had not been just a holiday; it had been a meaningful pause in life. They had luxuriated, eaten great food, skied and sledged, all the while learning about the pressures on the environment and how easy it is to reduce them while still having a jolly good time.

'I call up my secretary in Rome yesterday,' one of the green-trousered Italians told me as they were checking out, 'and told her to buy the panel solar for my company's office. No delay. Tomorrow? No. Do it today.'

If everyone who stayed at Whitepod called their secretaries to buy the 'panel solar' for their offices and homes, then Sofia de Meyer could be halfway to reducing emissions of greenhouse gases in Europe. And how about this for karma? Sofia's brain was on overload one day when she thought how wonderful it would be in this not always sunny part of Switzerland to have another source of energy: geothermal. She commissioned her first investigation of the hot rocks beneath Whitepod. It revealed a geothermal source right under the sauna.

Until recently Sofia was a clear front-runner in sustainable tourism, but she now has a rival on the other side of the world in Australia. Having spent fifteen years trying to find one genuine sustainable tourist resort, I ended up with two in the same year.

You can't stage-dive into snow drifts or ski by moonlight down a mountain at the Great Ocean Ecolodge, on the Cape Otway peninsula, west of Apollo Bay in Victoria, but you can walk with wallabies in native forests, stroll along deserted Southern Ocean beaches and reconnect with the natural world.

A few years ago eco-pioneers and all-round good eggs Lizzie Corke and Shayne Neal got a bank loan, stretched their finances to the limit and bought 165 acres of former dairy land which had been extensively cleared of native trees and shrubs.

'Back then we wondered if we were crazy but we have pretty much everything in place now and we think it's looking all right,' said Shayne as we sipped strong beer and toasted our feet in front of the pot-bellied stove on my first night at the lodge.

Lizzie and Shayne are masters of Australian modesty. Their 165 acres of Victorian paradise looks far more than 'all right'; it looks superb and is an internationally recognised model of sustainable tourism.

The lodge is a large building reached by a sweeping gravel driveway and bordered by wild grassy paddocks and a landscaped pond.

The building's walls are made of bricks baked in the sun, which means no power was used in their creation and no pollution generated. The bricks also make superb insulators, keeping the lodge warm in winter and cool in summer. The eaves have been positioned differently around the lodge, dictated by the angle and path of the sun at different times of the year. This allows light in when the sun is lower in the sky in winter to warm the place up but shades the interior areas from the fierce summer rays, so power use for heating and cooling is kept to a minimum. All power is solar – and I mean all power, not just one low-energy light bulb in the loo but all light and heat, including for the hot showers.

In the interests of fair travel writing I tried to pick holes in Lizzie and Shayne's Ecolodge.

I imagined the showers were only hot at useless times like

between 3.34 and 4.21 in the morning and the rest of the time guests had to shiver under drops of cold water.

No, the showers are hot and available 24 hours a day. I set my alarm for 3 AM to test out the theory – and had a hot shower and one with great pressure too.

Surely you cannot get good shower pressure from a solar power pump? There must be a secret generator somewhere running on bad fossil-fuel electricity and pumping out filthy emissions into the clear Cape Otway night. Wrong again.

Shayne has constructed an ingenious piping system that pumps (using solar electricity, of course) the 370,000 litres of rainwater that is collected by the lodge's roof space each year 500m up to the header tanks at the highest point on the land.

The water rushes back down to the lodge creating about 20–25 psi in the shower and lots of very happy clean guests. And while we're talking water, the Ecolodge has the local water authorities a little stumped. 'We have good filtration systems built into the water system,' said Lizzie.

'We also get the water tested very regularly by the council and we always come in better than their own mains water. When they measure, some minerals or impurities are allowed to make up a small proportion of a sample but in our water they cannot even find a trace of them. It's so pure I don't think they know quite how we do it.'

In the privacy of my room on my first night I schemed some more, determined to catch Lizzie and Shayne out. After all this was no holiday for me. I was on a mission to determine whether the Ecolodge deserved its title. I could not have raved about it to you unless I had road-tested it and found that it ticked at least 90 per cent of the sustainable-tourism boxes.

I bet the ducted heating gets turned off at night to save

using up the solar energy and icicles start to form on the bed head, I thought. But no, my room stayed at a perfectly respectable 18°C and I was there through a wild windy and bitterly cold July weekend when even the wallabies were getting knocked over by the gusts.

I couldn't pick holes in their use of timber either. Most of the timber framework of the lodge is recycled and was dragged out of piles of rubble by Lizzie and Shayne in demolition yards in the town of Geelong, about an hour's drive east.

The lodge's main pillars are felled cypress, which came from a nearby farm, where they had served as a windbreak before the farmer decided he needed to give his chainsaw a bit of an airing and replace them with indigenous species.

Up in the roof the next evening the sustainable ticks kept coming.

'We used polyester for the insulation, which is a lot less toxic than fibreglass. You don't even have to use a mask when you're laying it,' said Shayne.

'All the cleaning products are made from natural ingredients,' added Lizzie. 'A small business in Geelong makes all these things and when we run out of them we send all our bottles back there for refilling.'

Roughly half of the food is organic and the vast majority comes from within an hour's drive of the lodge, which means far less pesticide and insecticide use, less fossil-fuel pollution generated by carting carrots several hundred miles. It also means that Lizzie and Shayne are helping to support the local economy, which ticks yet another box in the 'how to be ever so sustainable' start-up guide.

Beyond the kitchen is a totally organic vegetable and herb garden, which they planted recently but which is already going great guns. 'We will be doing our own root vegetables and beans in time and setting up an orchard using propagated trees from a registered organic orchard,' Lizzie said.

'Okay, I'm convinced. Enough with the ecological marvels already,' I said.

'Ooh, one more thing,' said Lizzie. 'We're also working on a few research projects: insect biodiversity in revegetated areas, koala ranging behaviour and a study of the social structure of the kangaroo mob. The wool in our blankets is all Australian and from natural fibres, and the beer you are drinking is from a local brewery.'

'That's three more things,' I said.

'Sorry, I keep remembering other things we have done. Oh, and of course we run the Cape Otway Centre for Conservation Ecology here too.'

The centre is an ecological research centre and a fully equipped rehab base for injured and orphaned wild animals. On the weekend I came to stay, the patients included two orphaned swamp wallabies and one of the redneck variety, as well as a couple of fire-damaged koalas. Lizzie's job is to care for whatever animals turn up on her doorstep, usually those injured or traumatised by road accidents. There's a nursery for the little ones and a larger enclosure for adolescents. Once they are fit and well, she returns them to the wild.

The couple's dedication to the centre won Lizzie the Prime Minister's Environmentalist of the Year award in 2005 and the two of them were presented with the Australian Geographic Society's Conservation Award in 2007.

One freezing morning, more reminiscent of Austria than Australia, Lizzie allowed me to accompany her on her daily rounds to the nursery and the sanctuary. 'This is not something we let guests do, because these animals are in quite a traumatised state, so they need calm and safety.'

In the nursery Roger the Swamp Wallaby took an unnatural interest in my bootlaces and did more damage to
them in under a minute than they have endured in several
years of serious globetrotting. Neither the whipping searing
sands of the Sahara nor the icy grasp of the Cairngorms had
anywhere near the destructive power of this wallaby's young
teeth. The laces I could replace but the boots themselves are
like family, so I had to have a word with Roger when he
turned to the waterproof lining for his main course.

An elderly female koala was not doing so well.

She was already getting on a bit in years when she was
badly damaged by bushfires. Lizzie's concern was clear as
she carried her to her favourite branch and fed her specially
prepared milk from a bottle and spoke to her gently. In the
skies above us olive whistlers whistled, fantails fanned and
superb blue wrens wrenned, and somewhere, sleeping off a
long night of rodent hunting, was a Powerful Owl, Australia's biggest owl.

Slowly the entire 165 acres is being turned back into a nature reserve and already kangaroos, wallabies and numerous other species are moving back in. It's a huge draw for
families. Lizzie and Shayne are living their dream.

'Sharing a sighting of an endangered bird or an unusual
flower, someone's first koala or examining kangaroo poo
with children: we honestly get as much pleasure out of the
experience as our guests do,' said Shayne.

Lizzie added, 'By sharing amazing experiences with
our guests, we give them something real to take away – a
wonderful memory of a unique interaction or observation
that they will never forget.'

'One of the big things that the kids like when they come
here with their parents and grandparents is getting to know
an animal,' said Shayne. 'On the first day they are here,

they are usually a bit bored and a bit miffed that there is no television and no computer games.

'I go out with them on a nature walk and get them involved and before you know it they have become regular wildlife detectives, looking for pellets and feathers, bones and anything else that might identify what's about.

'At first the kids don't really want to get their hands dirty but they soon see the fun in getting a bit grubby. By the end of the stay they are picking everything up and putting it in their pockets. They want to take it home and put it under the microscope.'

This youth market is crucial for any sustainable development project. Most kids, whether from Australia or Aldershot, are already aware of recycling and climate change – maybe more so than their parents – but to see them transformed from computer couch potatoes into avid dung collectors in just a few days is a sign that the future of the planet might be safe after all.

Chapter 8

Luxe on Location

Very occasionally, on a perfect, sandy beach on the tiny islet of Akaiami, in the atoll of Aitutaki, in the middle of the South Pacific Ocean, the locals don grass skirts and perform a fire dance. If you are one of the few people on the planet lucky enough to witness this, the visions will remain happily branded onto your memory for ever.

Many hotels in the South Pacific arrange fire dances for their guests. Some are fun and include award-winning Polynesian pyromaniacs gyrating athletically to an authentic tribal beat. Others are cringingly bad – particularly when performed to songs from *Grease* or by the Backstreet Boys. They invariably demand audience participation and are to be avoided at all costs.

There is only one fire dance that leaves you speechless with awe and that is the one on Akaiami. It is also a perfect example of how some hotels can be fabulous purely because of their location.

I was on an organised press trip – a rare event for me – and was staying at the Pearl Beach Resort. Neither I nor my small band of fellow travel writers knew where we were going when the hotel's manager said he had planned something special and asked us to board a small launch at the jetty shortly before sunset. The hotel had kept the secret well. I feared the worst and fully expected that within the hour we would be forced to participate in some dreadfully humiliating game with the locals, like having to do impressions or learn embarrassing dances or put crabs down our pants. I cursed myself for going against my convictions in accepting a place on the trip, and I was frantically generating excuses for not participating in whatever publicly demeaning horrors lay ahead of us in the ominous darkness. Sore foot, bad back, have to take pictures, allergic to crabs – that kind of thing. 'Failing that,' I thought, 'I could always swim for it back to the hotel.'

My fellow writers were more relaxed. They drank beers and gnawed on chicken legs that the hotel staff had laid out on tables on the deck. The sun set with speed and a colourful flourish, looking like a fat slice of orange being dropped into a sea of Campari and soda.

And we chugged on slowly over the still, darkening waters of the lagoon. The moon did not rise, which allowed the stars to show off their full glory. I found a spare bit of deck and lay down to watch the heavens come alive. Maybe everyone would forget about me here and I could escape the embarrassment of whatever appalling staged event was about to happen.

I knew the lagoon was enclosed by numerous tiny sandy islets that make up the ring of the atoll, but they had disappeared into the inky, moonless night. We were going night diving? No, there were no tanks on board. Night fishing? Not that either, because there are strict rules on the catch that can be taken within the lagoon.

I felt the boat's engines slow suddenly and two of the crew stepped over me and made their way to the prow to grab ropes. Wherever we were going, we were there. I stood up and stared out into the velvety blackness.

A drum began beating, slowly at first and then with more rapid strokes. A second drum joined in. The beat was deep and booming and it came straight at us across the tiny lapping wavelets. It was 30 metres away, maybe more, I thought. I had lost my bearings in the darkness and was relying on hearing alone.

A woman screamed; a man hollered. I could smell the unmistakeable scent of frangipani flowers, cooling and moistening after a day in the hot sun and releasing their perfume. We were getting closer to land. My heart raced as I strained for some vision. The drums stopped, and two seconds later four violent bursts of flame ripped the black curtain of the night, and died back again.

That one second of brilliant light was enough to reveal that ahead of us lay a beach, backed by palm trees, and inhabited by semi-naked men with large muscles, even larger tom-tom drums and more than a passing familiarity with fire.

'Oh, God,' I thought. 'They're going to bloody well sacrifice us.'

Fire roared into the warm night once more, but this time the torches stayed lit and the drums began increasing their pace. Four men leapt from the dark line of palm trees and ran to the water's edge, and began to stamp their feet and shout at us. Their grass skirts did nothing to detract from their terrifying masculinity.

Their dance was a series of aggressive postures accompanied by wide eyes and wider mouths. It made the All Blacks' pre-match haka look like a rather camp hornpipe.

We were within fifteen metres of the beach now and the boat was dragging its keel on the sand. If they wanted to attack we were sitting ducks.

The dancers ran back into the palms and then reappeared, each holding a two-metre pole lit at both ends with spitting balls of fire. They twirled them in perfect synchronicity and with such speed that the poles became wheels of flame, spinning like comets. They threw them up into the night sky, illuminating the green fronds of the palm trees. The poles were still spinning when they came back down to earth and were caught dexterously by the men.

From what looked like single poles the men miraculously made replicas and proceeded to spin one in each hand. The fire flew high over their heads, shot between their legs and then blurred from hand to hand as they hurled the torches between each other.

They were as one, perfectly poised, perfectly in sync. If fire dancing was an Olympic sport – and God knows the Olympics needs something vaguely more exciting than dressage and a walking race – then Aitutaki would most certainly take Gold.

Four girls joined the men, dancing between them and the ricocheting fireballs. They were lithe and warm and wore coconut-shell bikinis which barely covered their breasts. I fell in love with all of them instantly, mesmerised by their gyrations and their smiles and their coconut bikinis. They were sirens, magical semi-human creatures who were effortlessly casting spells over me and the other two male journalists in the group, reducing us to schoolboys and making us giggle with delight. If those girls had asked us to swim out into the middle of the lagoon, dive down two fathoms and find them a rare black pearl we would have done it.

The dance built to its climax, with flames everywhere and drums being bashed so hard we thought they would rip their skins. As suddenly and dramatically as it had begun, so it ended – in darkness and silence. We burst into applause and as it died all we could hear were the beautiful sirens giggling and whooping with delight as the troupe retreated into the palm trees.

This must be a war dance, I observed to the boat's captain. He laughed and said: 'No, Matthew, this is a welcome dance. Whenever strangers used to come to Aitutaki, we would do this dance.'

If this magnificent, terrifying display of ferocity and strength was the Aitutaki way of saying hello then I would hate to see what they do when they are angry.

'Matthew,' said the captain slowly and seriously, 'you do not ever want to see that.' His eyes stared at me, and I could see the torches reflected in them. Flames danced over his dark pupils and he did not smile.

That night on the perfect, sandy beach on the tiny islet of Akaiami, in the atoll of Aitutaki, in the middle of the South Pacific Ocean, changed my life. If we can superimpose a scale onto the luxury hotel wow factor, then this was somewhere off its top end. Surely this was as good as it gets.

But I could easily have passed up this opportunity had I not made a significant shift in my behaviour. I have always been an independent travel writer, thinking up my own ideas, doing my own research and dealing with my own logistics. I pitch my articles to travel editors and seal commissions. I book flights at my own expense, for long gone are the days when airlines were willing to offer complimentary flights in return for a mention of their phone number and website in the fact box at the end of the article. I choose my luxury hotels with great care and beg some free nights from hotel managers, saying I am coming to stay to review the property for a glamorous newspaper or magazine.

What I have consistently shied away from is the dreaded press trip, a group tour organised by tourism authorities, airlines and hotels, where a small clutch of travel writers are herded around like a little flock of sheep. These trips are invariably exhausting and unsatisfying, and from an exclusivity point of view are utterly useless. My editors have always welcomed the fact that I unearth unique and newsworthy stories in my travels rather than merely turning in copy which tells readers that 'the hotel was nice, you should stay there'.

At the impeccably presented Sandy Lane Hotel in Barbados, I ate the most delicious fish I had tasted and discovered it was caught just offshore from Oistins, a fishing village on the south coast. Next morning, I passed up possibly the most luxurious beachside breakfast I have ever been offered so I could take a pushbike and cycle a sweaty two hours down potholed roads to Oistins to meet the locals and add a few paragraphs of unique colour to the article.

You cannot do this on a press trip. Living in the pockets of fellow travel writers every minute of your waking day means it is virtually impossible to keep anything to yourself. If you discover that the tropical paradise island on which you are staying is where bits of a burnt-out satellite once fell and are still stuck in the reef, or that the Bavarian castle you are touring was a Nazi spy factory in World War II, the chances are that your fellow journalists will be scribbling the same facts down. And anyway, there is an agenda, a strict itinerary and a usually stern host to whip you into line if you start wandering off and trying to do your own thing. The result is terrific for the island and the castle and their associated PR companies, but pretty useless for any travel writer hoping for a unique story.

However, when my friend Sarah at Air New Zealand came on the line and started trying to persuade me to join a 'small, select group going to the South Pacific', she broke through my press trip aversion in seconds.

The itinerary was full of locations to which even the likes of Bill Gates and Elle Macpherson might say 'wow': one of Fiji's smaller and less visited islands, Vanua Levu, the remote atoll of Aitutaki in the Cook Islands, and then on to Tahiti and Bora Bora. All five-star, all business class, all paid for by someone else. All good.

The schedule was tight and tough, and included one bizarre night in a hotel in Tahiti where we checked in just before midnight and left before dawn. Being dutiful to my profession and my loyal readers, I went for a midnight swim to check out the pool, whose waters were dark and foreboding as the lights had been turned out hours ago. And I woke myself at 3 AM, two hours after I had gone to bed, to order a sandwich and see if room service was up to scratch. It wasn't.

The flights drained us too, because almost all flights in the South Pacific arrive and leave at the least godly hours – that little window between 3 and 5 AM when even nightclubbers and early risers find solace in sleep. So our little band of gallant writers, my fellow luxury hotel junkies, saw an awful lot of each other at the wrong hours of the day. Hours when bags under eyes were at their darkest and puffiest. Hours when breath was at its stalest, and tempers were at their least patient. Hours that we normally reserve for privacy, rest and recharging.

All those pressures on mind, body and ego were worth enduring for the hour we spent on the beach at Akaiami watching the fire dancers.

It did not matter that the rooms of the five-star Pearl Beach Resort in which we were staying were explosions of rattan, with little to commend them to a luxury hotel addict. Nor did I care that the food was no better than passable and certainly not five-star, and was eaten in a strange canteen area that brought back memories of a United Nations outpost in Zambia where I had stayed on a foreign news assignment a few years earlier. (I hear it has been spruced up since.)

The location was enough to wow me. The location was everything: being there on the edge of Aitutaki's wide cerulean lagoon under a brilliant sun and rustling palm trees, and with a fresh Pacific breeze at my back. That was priceless. Being able to walk less than ten metres from my little rattan hut and sink my feet into sand which felt like moisturising cream, and then dive into warm water so clear that if I dived too deep towards the blue-white sandy bottom I had trouble knowing which way was up.

All the usual trappings of luxury hotel addiction, such as soft cotton sheets, chilled champagne and air-conditioning, meant nothing to me here. The luxury was the fact that I was standing on a tiny patch of sand in the middle of the Pacific Ocean.

I did not care if I ate boring old taro root for days in the canteen or on the beach out of a banana leaf. I did not care if I drank nothing but the fresh milk of the coconuts that occasionally fell to the sand near me with a satisfying thud. There was nobody to telephone or email. There were no postcards to be sent.

One morning I got up early and from the base of my suitcase retrieved my little tin of watercolour paints and tried to recreate a crimson hibiscus flower which had sailed onto the deck of my bungalow on a night-time breeze. My masterpiece soon resembled a squashed tomato, so I made a paper aeroplane out of it which nose-dived on its maiden flight. I did not get depressed at my complete lack of arts and crafts skills, but smiled to myself and decided to stick to something at which I knew I was a consummate expert – floating listlessly in a tropical lagoon and waiting for the next sentence of my article to arrive in my head or the next margarita to land in my hand, whichever came first.

Aitutaki was once part of the most luxurious travel excursion on the planet, the Coral Route. In the 1950s, Tasman Empire Airways Limited (TEAL) began flying seaplanes between Auckland and French Polynesia, splashing down for sojourns in Fiji, Western Samoa and the Cook Islands. Word spread to Hollywood, and the Coral Route quickly became a favourite jaunt of the well-heeled. Gary Cooper flew it, so did Cary Grant, John Wayne and Graham Greene. Noel Coward was once grounded (or beached, to be more accurate) due to technical problems on Akaiami. He and his fellow Coral Routers were forced to loiter for several days on a deserted beach with little to do but beachcomb, swim, and enjoy French claret and New Zealand brie by candlelight.

No doubt Coward drummed up a little ditty or a scene for a play as he watched the fish plop in the lagoon and smelled the frangipani perfume of an evening.

The fire dance is performed near the very same jetty where the TEAL seaplanes used to moor. There even used to be a small wooden hut terminal here, with a grass-skirted Aitutaki local who greeted the visitors.

Since I last visited – that famous night of the coconut bikinis – a new lodge has been built there. Akaiami Lodge was built from local timber and brass fittings to reflect the original design of the TEAL terminal. The place runs on solar power, although electricity needs are reduced to a bare minimum by not having television or radio. I cannot give you a personal recommendation on the accommodation, as I have not stayed there, but quite frankly, who cares what it's like? This is possibly the most idyllic location on Earth.

Aitutaki is also blissful because there is virtually no risk. No snakes, no crime, no ferocious wild animals. There's plenty of water, plenty of food and you can swim safely in the lagoon to your heart's content. Of course, the atoll would not stand much of a chance in a tidal wave, but the only real day-to-day concern is trying to make sure you back the fastest crab in a beach race.

A similar sense of bliss and security can be found in the amazing Sultanate of Oman, one of my favourite destinations. Oman forms most of the southern fringe of the Arabian peninsula and has historically been one of the most stable and progressive countries in the region. It is a traveller's delight, a mystical and magical place full of towering sand dunes, turquoise coasts and romantic forts. It has a long and prosperous maritime and trading tradition and is home to the frankincense tree, the sap of which is still burned across the Arab world.

In the western extremes of the capital, Muscat, stands a hotel that brilliantly reflects the beauty, splendour and openness of Oman. The Chedi (one of the more recent GHM properties) is more oasis than hotel. Guests arrive at a palatial entrance and are ushered into a central atrium whose centrepiece is a large cushioned area overhung by a carousel of white and red silk lanterns.

Doors open onto majestic Moorish grounds which have been designed to celebrate the falaj system of irrigation which oases have used for centuries. Water spits from fountains into large shallow pools and along narrow channels which trace the white flagstone walkways.

Where the water ends the grass begins, in sweeping lawns which guide the eye through glades of palm trees to the beach. The northern end of the hotel's beachfront is dominated by the Chedi Pool and adjacent dining area. A two-minute stroll down the sand is the Beach Restaurant near the Serai Pool.

If you find yourself kid-free at the Chedi Muscat don't believe people when they say you may have a more relaxing time at the Chedi Pool rather than its Serai sister which is more suitable for families. The Serai Pool is the go, mainly because the loungers are more generously spaced and you can find a secluded spot among the small bushy hedges and under the palm trees.

After dark the white-shirted staff flick switches secreted under rocks and behind bushes and transform the blissful peace of afternoon to the magical romance of evening. Guests emerge from rooms and villas to find the fountains sparkling and bowls of dramatically flaming coals reflecting in the still dark pools.

It's a photographer's dream. Never has it taken me so long to walk from a hotel room to the restaurant.

Such gentility is not everybody's cup of tea, however. For some travellers luxury means taking a lavish sojourn in a remote and dangerous place. In the world's driest desert, for example – a landscape boasting the tallest sand dunes on Earth, some of which drone haunting, mournful tunes when you slide down them, and secretive inhabitants who paint themselves with an ochre paste made from animal fat mixed with red sand. In a place where the desert floor is ruled by such strange creatures as tok-tokkies and sun spiders, and where dense fogs roll in from the ocean in the late afternoon, engulfing everything in spectral brume.

The world does not get much more challenging and dangerous than the Namib Desert, which stretches down the south-west coast of Africa like a second Sahara. Its shore is called the Skeleton Coast and is the graveyard of thousands of travellers. The waters just offshore are dominated by the cold Benguela Current, which streams north from Antarctica and takes ice-shelf meltwater to the tropics. Here, the South Atlantic is at its merciless best, and has dashed to pieces countless vessels. Their rotting carcasses litter the hundreds of kilometres of desolate beaches, giving the Skeleton Coast its name.

Those souls who perished at sea, drowned by tumultuous waves or taken by the white pointer sharks that favour the Benguela Current, were the lucky ones. At least their deaths were quick. Those who landed on this barren and unforgiving shore faced a slow, wretched demise. There is simply nothing here. No fresh water, no edible vegetation, nothing to sustain human life.

Shipwrecked here, the poor unfortunates sat among the giant whale ribs and vertebrae that litter the beach, picked clean by the gulls and bleached by sun and salt. They wrapped themselves in the clothes they were wearing the day their ship met her doom, and painfully, pitiably died.

Their deaths were watched studiously by the jackals and desert lions which inhabited the seaward dunes of this coast. The lions were always rare and have gone now, dying in much the same way as their former carrion – by starvation – but the hardy jackals are still there. You can see their tracks in the sand. They rely on stealth, cunning and a sprinter's speed to grab young seals from the colony at Cape Frio, at the northern end of the Skeleton Coast on the way to the Angolan border.

The ocean passengers who ended up on this shore were expecting to make landfall in Cape Town and not Cape Frio, so they had no knowledge of the geography. Some tried to walk away from the coast, not aware that inland from the morbid shore lies a sand sea 200 kilometres broad, where not even the jackals can survive. The only species known to relish the Martian conditions of the inland is the Onymacris beetle, whose sole water supply is provided by moisture droplets from the afternoon sea fogs that roll in like tidal waves of cold, clammy cotton wool, swallowing the mighty dunes as if they were plankton being vacuumed into the mouth of a whale shark. The beetle clearly descends from an age of chivalry, for the male of the species spends most of the day riding on the female's back to shield her from the sun so she can retain moisture. He, poor fellow, is left gasping for a drink by nightfall.

Even if, by some divine intervention, the desperate shipwrecked survivors had made it through the interminable sand sea, they would then have been faced with a rocky desert not dissimilar to great swathes of the Sahara. Wicked winds barrel down wide canyons, where balls of spinifex grass bounce along over the red and ochre stones, and big black eagles soar across the sun.

Surely this godforsaken outpost, beyond all humanity, is the last place you would expect to find air-conditioning, hot showers, bacon and eggs, and a jolly good wine cellar. Yet, against the odds, two select luxury hotels exist here.

I'll admit I gave them some points for sheer bravado. The pure logistics of getting several hundred bottles of far-from-shabby French claret and South African Klein Constantia pinot out there in one piece, and then keeping them cellared and decent to drink, is a feat in itself.

The first hotel is the Skeleton Coast Camp, a series of glamorous permanent tents next to a rough airstrip in the middle of absolutely nowhere. The lodge is an hour's flight by small plane from Namibia's capital, Windhoek, yet you feel like you have travelled to another world.

When I came to stay they were having a few engineering

problems. One of the Land Rovers kept getting flat tyres in the most unfortunate of places – like 40 miles from the camp and halfway to the coastline, in the middle of the Namib Sand Sea – which was inviting a little more adventure than most of my fellow guests were after.

We got one on the beach itself. This would have been fine had it been during the bright afternoon when we were having fun crawling on our bellies towards the Cape Frio seal population, trying to get close enough to take some pictures without them all freaking out and flip-flopping back into the waves. The Skeleton Coast was a puss-cat in the warm sunshine, and we were all smiles and laughter.

Our flat tyre came at about 5 PM, when we were getting ready to turn for home, a two-hour drive away over the sand and rocks. We had spent the past hour standing respectfully at the pile of stones that serves as a headstone for Captain Matthias Koraseb and the crew of the *Sir Charles Elliott*, lost in 1942. Captain Koraseb's is the loneliest grave in the world.

The fog bank had waited ominously just offshore since lunchtime, but then it began to advance. Jack and Fran, my two new friends from New York, noticed it first.

'It's moving. It's coming in,' said Fran.

'They said it would. It's really moving fast. Can you feel the chill? That's amazing,' said Jack.

Fran: 'We should go. Shall we go?'

Jack: 'Don't you want to see what it feels like to be inside it?'

Fran: 'Erm, no. Well, yes, but no.'

Jack and Fran: 'What do you think, Matthew? You're the travel writer. Do you want to know what it's like inside the fog?'

It was too late. It was wrapping its icy tentacles around us as we stood there debating on the beach. I felt the heat being sucked from my body. My eyes began to sting in the salty air. We were silent and we huddled closer together.

The fog rushed in, its white wisps passing between us like strings of gossamer. The ocean disappeared. We could only hear its angry waves crashing nearby, desperate to drag another victim down with their ankle-grabbing rips.

'Come a little bit closer,' I felt the waves calling. 'Dip your toe in. We want you.'

I shivered with fear, from my neck to my tailbone. Around me, dashing and spiralling now, were the silvery ghosts of the thousands of sailors lost in this terrible place.

It was then that somebody noticed the flat tyre. Never in the history of motor mechanics has a tyre been changed so speedily. Forget Ferrari's pit stops at Imola. We were quicker.

The little picnic table our guide had laid out with red wine and crackers was decamped and shoved in to the Land Rover in seconds. We pushed our way in to the vehicle, our anoraks drenched with the wet spectres of the drowned sailors. None of us said a word until we were clear of the suffocating fog and the stars began to appear above us once more. Even then we did not dare look back.

We established radio contact with the camp to say we were running late and to ask if they could save us some kudu steaks. When we arrived back we were cheered as returning adventurers. A fire was burning in the communal area near the main lodge, which was set aside for after-dinner drinks and conversation. Our fellow guests had eaten and chatted and were now heading for bed. They had waited up to see us safely home. A waiter brought us a bottle of port, and we fell on it, knocking it back as if it were lemonade on a hot summer afternoon.

Though the night was cold, Jack and Fran and I chose to eat under the stars by the comfort of the fire, in a bid to banish the remains of the ghosts we were sure we had brought back from the Skeleton Coast.

We reminisced about our camping days as youngsters, having adventures by day and then, after a bowl of baked beans and soggy wheat biscuits, happily crawling into musty sleeping bags and using our T-shirts for pillows. Not anymore. Now we were luxury hotel junkies and we needed as much comfort as possible, even out here in the backblocks of the wild world.

I unzipped my tent door and found someone had made my bed, turned down the sheets, and given me a hurricane lamp by which to read. In the bathroom was a full complement of solar-heated water for a thawing shower. A hot-water bottle was waiting for me between the sheets, and a pitcher of drinking water stood on a bedside table with a small glass resting on a coaster. The curtains were drawn against the chill of the night, and my carelessly discarded underwear had been neatly folded and my shoes lined up with the laces tucked inside.

There was a rolled-up piece of parchment at the foot of the bed telling me what weather we could expect in the morning, and what activities were available. I decided to go for the desert elephant safari.

Such comfort and care after so raw and cheerless an afternoon. Everything I wanted at that precise moment was before me. Warmth, light, security, softness and peace. It is the sort of reward that the contestants on *Survivor* win when they complete a challenge like balancing on one finger in the blazing sun for ten hours without blinking.

Maybe it was the port, or maybe the cosiness of my permanent tent, but I shed a couple of tears as I wrapped myself up in the freshly laundered sheets and let my head sink into the pillow.

As you fly inland from the Skeleton Coast Camp, the landscape beneath the wings of your little plane turns from orange sand (including the world's highest dunes at Sossusvlei) to red rocky outcrops, and eventually to a series of black and tan valleys which bear some resemblance to the iron ore ranges of the Pilbara in Western Australia.

Down there somewhere lies one of the most isolated hotels in the world, and one of my firm favourites: Sossusvlei Mountain Lodge.

The lodge is tucked halfway up a slope at the end of a huge canyon that does not look as if it belongs anywhere on Earth. Approaching by plane during the winter months (high season), the twisting winds that rifle down the valley tug and push at the wings, forcing the horizon to rise and fall and then swing left and right. There is a second or two of clear air before the wheels crash down on the rocky runway and passengers release their white-knuckle grips on the seats.

It is almost impossible to see the lodge until you are about to hit the dirt, as it has been sculpted from the same rocks as the landscape and so blends in perfectly. It is, perhaps, the most sensitively designed hotel in the world.

Each of the ten 'desert suites' is built from stone and has a curved wall shielding it. If you have ever toured the Hebrides off Scotland's north-west coast, or the Orkney Islands further north, you will have seen the 'brochs' or 'Atlantic roundhouses', double-walled dry-stone towers whose purpose is contested among archaeologists. Could they have been strategic defences to ward off marauding invaders? Could they have been really useful places to store things? Or could the rich landowners have been doing some chest-beating and saying, 'My broch's bigger than your broch'?

No such confusion at the Sossusvlei Mountain Lodge, where the stand-alone 'desert suite' brochs are most definitely built to house mini-palaces in the wilderness. Where the woolly men of the Scottish isles might have had just straw and salted fish to excite them, guests at Sossusvlei enjoy temperature control, CD players, log fires and panoramic views over the valley. There is even a personal telescope to watch for game trotting across the valley floors and tip-toeing along the rocky mountain ridge lines.

Each suite is built as a split-level abode, with its bed in the top section. The suites are shielded from their neighbours by sloping, curving walls. The showers have floor-to-ceiling glass walls looking straight out to the valley and are placed so that you can game-spot while you shower; the only living things that will see you naked are the eagles and an occasional passing oryx.

I spent a lot of my time at Sossusvlei game-spotting in the nude after a hot shower – not because I am an exhibitionist, but just because I could. 'I might never get the chance to admire springboks and hartebeest while standing stark-naked in the middle of a desert,' I thought. You have to take these opportunities when they present themselves. I just hoped the maintenance staff did not choose those moments to come and start cleaning the windows, but I was told later they have strict instructions that all areas to the rear of the suites are out of bounds while guests are staying.

This means that if you are an exhibitionist you could spend your entire day in the nude, walking from your living quarters to the patio, reading the newspaper, sipping coffee and taking peeks through the telescope when you see something move in the distance.

The only time you'd need to throw on a robe is when your butler comes to call. Yep, each suite has a designated butler.

He will prepare crispy bacon and fluffy scrambled eggs around the clock. He will bring you brandy and sodas if you feel slightly under the weather. And he is a walking authority on the local environment. What he does not know, he willingly and speedily finds out for you.

On my first night, after dinner, when I was warming my toes by the pot-bellied stove, letting the brandy rush warmly through my veins and thinking that the Sossusvlei's luxe might be peaking, my butler knocked on the door and invited me to attend a stargazing session at the hotel's observatory.

Small glasses of whisky and other liqueurs were served and we each had a go squinting through the telescope at the heavens. We saw Mars as clearly as if it were a second moon. I lingered on the Pleiades, my favourite constellation. I can be the most almighty nerd when it comes to stars and planets and all things geographical. I watched the cluster flicker like a church full of Easter candles through the miles and miles of empty night sky between us.

My fellow guests mingled around me in the observatory, which was housed in a smaller stone broch set back from the guest suites. We wrapped up against the chill and sipped our drinks for extra warmth. Our necks were craned upwards at this unsurpassed star display.

The nearest electric lights to Sossusvlei are back in Windhoek, a few hundred kilometres away, so a moonless night at the lodge is about as black and natural as you will see anywhere in the world.

Stargazing is possibly the best leveller known to mankind. It can make even an international company president or a self-made millionaire feel humble and small.

We knew we were in the presence of greater forces here, and certainly a greater beauty, for we talked in reverential whispers. Even when we saw shooting stars our gasps were hushed and at the backs of our throats. The husbands kept telling their wives what they were looking at. The wives politely ignored them and kept staring up, in awe of the magnitude of the experience.

Those hard-hearted souls who had still not fallen in love with the Sossusvlei Mountain Lodge by this time certainly did once they got some whisky inside them and began tracing the outline of the Southern Cross in the sky. For the rest of us who were already hooked, this simple but brilliant hotel activity, making use of a romantic, bewitching natural resource, was another of the magical hotel's tours de force.

My butler appeared again to escort me along the dark, dusty path to my broch. He asked if I had enjoyed the stargazing, to which I replied with a string of superlatives.

'If you like, when you go to bed, Mr Matthew, you can do some more,' he said.

I figured he just meant I could go out on my patio and stare upwards again but it was only after he had said goodnight and retired for the evening and I had leapt into bed that I understood his comment.

Above each huge bed in each stone desert suite at Sossusvlei is a skylight, through which the starlight streams at night. In my rush to explore the rest of the suite and enjoy its comforts, I had not even noticed it. I lay there letting my eyes adjust to the darkness once more. My white sheets were washed stellar blue by the combined light of a million planets, supernovae and red dwarfs that cascaded in through the skylight.

All my life I had wanted to fall asleep under a sky where, from horizon to horizon, all that was visible were stars. Sossusvlei granted me that wish. Heavenly hotel, out-of-this-world service, whisky-infused interstellar entertainment, and a private, in-bed observatory. It doesn't get much better than that.

I had come to Sossusvlei not just for some clothing-optional hartebeest observation but also to track bat-eared foxes while fully dressed. Bat-eared foxes are the most remarkable of creatures. I had been doing some research on them and had developed something of an obsession. I have always been a bit partial to a fox – despite growing up in good farming country in the heart of England where they are commonly hated – but these guys are freaks with ears the size of baseball mitts. As a result, their hearing is unparalleled in the animal kingdom – well, maybe only by the bats whose ears the foxes have clearly stolen. The bat-eared fox can pick up the click of a distant barking gecko, the otherwise inaudible squeak of a terrified ground mole at 50 metres, and, very probably, the blips of one of Rupert Murdoch's satellites passing several kilometres overhead in space.

Sossusvlei Mountain Lodge is one of the few places in Africa where you can track the foxes on the ground. The Lodge is run by Conservation Corporation Africa (or CCAfrica as it is known by its devotees) who manage a small selection of exquisite safari resorts all of which masterfully blend environmentally conscious tourism with big-budget comfort. To this end the group has engaged some of the continent's best wildlife guides to complete the experience.

At some of CCAfrica's properties, Sossusvlei included, guests can take ranger courses to earn a basic certificate in guiding. You get to identify tracks in the sand, learn the difference between a hartebeest and a wildebeest, and what to do if an elephant tries to charge you. On one elephant safari in Botswana, I joked that the obvious answer to the elephant dilemma was 'don't pay him', a quip that guaranteed that I was treated like a leper for the rest of the day.

At Sossusvlei I was in no mood for jokes. My ranger, the encyclopaedic Vernon, was an expert on bat-eared foxes. In fact, he was an expert on everything that ran, hopped, crawled, slithered and flew. He took me for evening game drives to listen to the jackals howling, and introduced me to barking geckos that called from their holes with an insistent 'ping, ping'. He met me minutes before dawn for a nature walk where we counted 25 different sets of tracks crossing the path just below the lodge's main house. During the night there had been a silent motorway of wildlife beetling past our brochs. Rabbits had run through, springboks had followed, and possibly an African wildcat looking for scraps from the kitchens. There were impressions left by the tails of scorpions, skinks and geckos. Vernon said he thought he might have found evidence of tok-tokkies and sun spiders, and I said he was not allowed to play God and make up new species.

But both are real, if surreal, creatures. Tok-tokkies are scavenging beetles that are so unattractive they feel the need to impress potential mates by slapping their stomachs on something hard, like a rock. Amazingly, it works. Females find the noise irresistible and reply with their own knock. Mind you, as the females have also been hit with the big-ugly-beetle stick, they are far from fussy when it comes to finding a mate. They come scurrying along to find their Prince Charming tok-tokkie and his big rock-slapping abdomen, and the species thrives.

Sun spiders, on the other hand, are far more elegant. They are light orange in colour, non-poisonous and extremely fast on their feet. When it comes to mating, they beat the crude tok-tokkies hands down by putting on a stylish display of dancing and stroking. Then the male flips the female onto her back and away they go. This may ring some bells for anyone who went night-clubbing recently and woke up the next morning with someone they only vaguely recognised.

Vernon's real magic touch came when, from the corner of his eye as we were bird-spotting one afternoon, he spied the tips of the ears of a fox. It must have been 100 metres away but he saw it clearly. I struggled to find it even with binoculars. Vernon held my shoulders and twisted me around slowly.

'There. You got them?'

I got them. Through a miniature forest of long grass travelled the ears, unmistakeably bat-like but definitely not attached to a bat. It was a family of foxes, with one adult at the head and another bringing up the rear and between them several young who were all but invisible in the grass.

I watched them make their way across the valley floor, into and out of grass clumps and over stony dry riverbeds, until they disappeared from view behind a rock buttress.

It is moments like this that change travellers' lives. Luxury hotels with unique locations like the Sossusvlei Mountain Lodge and the Skeleton Coast Camp give their guests the opportunity to alter their perspective and reassess their definitions of luxury. Now, when I am swamped with gloom or riddled with stress, I breathe deeply and imagine I am back with Vernon watching my family of bat-eared foxes cross the Sossusvlei valley floor silently and intently in the Namib Desert.

My article about Namibia was one of the hardest I have had to write, because what words can describe such intense personal feelings? How can a hotel – essentially a pile of bricks and glass – make the heart sing? I know I am a helpless luxury hotel addict, but I challenge anybody to go to these resorts and not be deeply moved by their surroundings. You might be wooed by the animals or awestruck by the landscape, but either way you will check out of there a different and more complete person.

The only thing these two hotels cannot provide is really big game. Most safari nerds will bang on about 'the Big Five', by which they are referring to their checklists of animals they must see ... or die trying.

The Big Five are the lion, elephant, wildebeest, rhino and leopard. If you take the Big Five Gang at their word, then no other animal is worth a toss. The graceful springbok? Wimpy. The noble giraffe? Long-necked freak. And the wallowing hippo is reduced to little more than a mud-dwelling bath toy.

Almost every safari lodge in Africa will swear blind they can show you the Big Five. Some even offer 'guarantees' that you will get your checklist ticked off, which is as solid a promise as a precise weather prediction for June in Stornoway.

So how do you pick through the charlatans and find the genuine gentlemen in this merry dance around the national parks? In my view, there is only one real gem that has it all – style, finesse, fun and the Big Five.

Stanley's Camp sits discreetly in a quiet corner of Botswana's Okavango Delta – the world's largest inland delta. Nights in the Okavango are not broken merely by the scratching of an insect at your screen door but by the meaty growl of man-eating mammals. A pride of lions lives and roams within roaring distance of the camp, so guests can fall asleep with the noises of wild Africa as a soundtrack to their dreams.

Where lions hunt, scavenging hyenas follow, so Stanley's is also a great spot for ticking them off your safari checklist.

Add to this hippos romping in the mud of the shallow lake-beds, cheetahs and zebras sprinting across the savannah, wild dogs terrorising antelopes, stately giraffes running in slow motion across the plains, and roughly 400 bird species, and you begin to get an idea of the wealth of wildlife on offer here.

Like the Skeleton Coast Camp and Sossusvlei Mountain Lodge, Stanley's picked its location expertly. Finding any high ground in the vast Okavango Delta is crucial, for by August each year this natural depression (an ancient lake that dried up about 10,000 years ago) floods spectacularly. The wadis and lakes that have lain barren and dusty through the waterless winter are once more knee-deep. The hillocks become islands and some can disappear completely before the waters subside.

Most of the water has fallen as rain months earlier in the tropical forests of Angola to the north, from where it embarks on an annual migration, trickling hundreds of kilometres south and inland to the mighty Okavango. In a good year eleven cubic kilometres of water can reach the delta, turning desert savannah into a world of lakes, ponds and connecting waterways.

Stanley's Camp is high enough to escape the floods and to afford its visitors wide and long vistas across this magical landscape. The camp has a communal meeting area on a raised platform built around a big sausage tree, with a large canvas roof that wraps neatly around the trunk.

There are permanent tents built on concrete platforms. Each has a stone deck at the front and two wooden garden chairs for lounging about in while you scour the terrain with binoculars. The only things you cannot see from the deck are your neighbours, as the tents are spaced well away from each other.

Inside are two beds, tables and chairs, and a fully equipped bathroom and shower. So reminiscent is it of drawings and early photographs of African expeditions that I half-expected to find a moustachioed, pith-helmeted Victorian explorer to be camping out in my tent, poring over some parchment maps of the Okavango lent to him by the Royal Geographical Society in London.

Maybe I could be his gofer, boiling him endless kettles of tea and making sure his jodhpurs were well starched in case he had to engage in diplomatic relations with the local chief.

But, as so often happens in my job, I found myself alone in my hotel room (or tent, in this case), miles away from home. 'It's luxurious but lonely, this life,' I thought as I tucked in to some biscuits which had been left for me on a table.

So why pick Stanley's? What makes it so luxurious? What gives it the edge over the hundreds of fabulous African safari lodges and camps? There is great wildlife, but then loads of places in Africa have great wildlife. Dining outdoors in the evenings on ostrich fillet, roast kudu and sweet potato mash, listening to the roar of the lions and the hearty chortles of the hippos, is wonderfully atmospheric, and the fine wines add to the sensual pleasure, but there is nothing unique about that. The camp is small and intimate but so are plenty of other 'boutique' safari establishments.

I was drawn to it partly because it is involved in a concerted conservation effort that maintains strict and thoughtful wildlife viewing policies drawn up in conjunction with local communities; but again, this is not a novel approach.

Above and beyond all of these factors are three stand-out reasons for picking Stanley's. First, the camp is in a 260,000-acre private concession, which means you won't see guests from any other lodges or camps turning up and scaring away the game. For real location luxe, the private reserves are definitely the go. So popular has the African safari now become that it is bordering on mass tourism. Some lodges and camps conduct game drives on shared reserves, which means that as soon as one scout spots a pregnant cheetah lying down in the grass to give birth, word ricochets around to the other scouts, and before you know it there are eight Land Rovers surrounding the poor bewildered thing.

Secondly, Stanley's is one of the few camps to offer what must be the most exhilarating of all experiences in the African bush – a walking safari. On walking safaris there are no steel Land Rover doors to protect you, and no driver to whisk you away from a sticky situation with an elephant or a baboon. It's just you, your wits and your armed guide.

And Stanley's earns its third luxury hotel addict gold star because it is truly wild. Safari camps tend to fence their guest areas for safety reasons – because visitors like to stroll about on warm evenings after a candlelit alfresco dinner and not have to worry about coming face-to-face with a large, hungry lion. In an adventurous and inspired move, Stanley's is unfenced. The wildlife that guests travel thousands of miles to see has as much right to pad about camp as they do. Such a bold move guarantees that a stay here is thrilling and memorable. You can go out and find the wildlife on game drives, or simply sit in your spacious and luxurious tent, sip mugs of rooibos tea and wait for it to find you. At night, after dinner, tall Botswanan guides carrying rifles are on hand to escort guests to their tents safely, lest they discover a lioness sitting on their deck sniffing their sandals.

One night I lingered a little later than my fellow guests and eventually was left alone staring at the dying embers of the fire, nursing a glass of Klein Constantia and keeping at least one eye on something slithering and twitching in the grass nearby. There was no-one in my tent to go home to. No warm wife to snuggle up to under the covers. Not even a moustachioed Victorian explorer with whom to share a nightcap snifter, toast the Queen and the Royal Geographical Society, and discuss the plan of action for the morning.

I could have stayed there until dawn, sipping my wine and listening to the busy night rustling, scurrying and flapping all around me, but there was the small issue of what to do if a lion arrived and fancied a nibble on my ankles.

So, reluctantly, I gathered up the bottle, kicked some sand on the fire and found the last Botswanan guard still awake to escort me back to my tent. Our shoes made soft squeaking noises in the sand as we walked along the path. A fat moon had risen over the Okavango and was now flooding the camp with light, allowing the acacia trees to cast playful shadows on the ground. A crash in the undergrowth broke the serenity and startled us. The guard lowered his rifle and I inched slightly behind him.

'Lion,' he said, his polar-white teeth reflecting the moonglow and appearing to float on their own in front of his night-black face.

'How do you know?' I whispered.

'They live here,' said the guard.

'Fair enough,' I said.

The managers of Stanley's had cleverly put me in the tent furthest away from the communal areas. It is considered the best, probably because it is the first to receive visits from wandering wildlife.

When we arrived at the front deck I thanked my guard, who bowed and began his lonely walk back. I dashed into my tent, eagerly checking under the beds for any wild animals which had managed to unzip the door and get in. I wanted to find them before my armed guard was out of screaming distance.

I was alone. The only visitation I had had was from a maid who had turned down my bed, fluffed my pillows and slotted a hot-water bottle between the sheets. Stanley's has a sense of humour – the hot-water bottles are tucked inside fluffy leopard-print jackets, so it is like having your very own leopard cub to keep your feet warm.

This delightful touch temporarily backfired a few years ago. A highly strung guest was putting his kids to bed and threw back the covers to reveal a bottle in its jacket. Fearing a real leopard cub had snuck in and was waiting to attack his children, he grabbed a large umbrella and beat the living daylights out of the poor, inoffensive bag. Hot water sprayed everywhere, the children burst into tears and the story sped around the African safari community like a summer bushfire.

But for me – and, I imagine, for thousands of other happy visitors to Stanley's Camp – this was bliss. I had been awake since before dawn and was ready for one of those deep luxury hotel sleeps I crave. I fell into bed, and was soon diving deeply into a cavernous and enveloping anaesthesia.

My only thought, as I tumbled down and down towards my bottomless sleep, was: 'Where else in the world can you tuck yourself in to such safety and comfort in the middle of a pride of lions?' All that was keeping me safe and them outside was a common metal zipper, yet until Africa's wild animals work out how to use these tricky devices, it is all the safari guest needs for peace of mind.

Or so I thought. Just a couple of hours later, far too soon for comfort, I came soaring back to consciousness to find my heart racing. The lions were roaring louder now, and more insistently. They were closer, too. The moonlight was so bright that I initially thought dawn had come. Sometimes the best luxury hotel sleeps only seem to last a minute, but you are refreshed as if you have slept a full week. But it was not dawn; it was the dead of night and the delta was alive with activity. An unidentified small creature was ferociously scratching at the base of the canvas tent wall behind my head, seemingly eager to join me inside.

Outside, beyond the deck, something much larger was crashing around. It was silent for a while and then there came another crash, with twigs breaking and small birds scattering. My Victorian explorer would have been out there by now in his cotton long johns, with a butterfly net and a hurricane lamp, making a groundbreaking discovery. It sounded to me like some very clever hippos had learnt to climb trees and were taking their first few leaps from branch to branch, devastating the local flora while they were at it.

Did I really zip up the tent door? Blimey, maybe I didn't.

I drew back the covers and felt the chill of the winter night on my thighs. I had one foot on the bedside carpet when I froze solid. Onto my front deck, not five metres away, leapt a hyena. It was the size of a St Bernard but nimble as a gazelle. It sniffed at the vapours from the kerosene lantern I had left burning on the table. It nudged my binoculars, which I had forgotten to bring inside.

And then, it levelled its head and, in a heart-stopping second, its eyes met mine through the mosquito-screened canvas door. We both held our breath. On my bedside table stood an emergency radio, standard issue with each of Stanley's tents in case of close animal encounters – like this one!

Fear fought with exhilaration. Adrenaline coursed through my body. My heart pumped faster and I slowly slid back under the covers. The hyena's stare did not falter. It did not blink, nor turn away. Instead it sniffed the air, no doubt receiving from inside the tent and from under the covers a waft of red wine, digested ostrich fillet and abject terror.

This heady scent was obviously attractive. The hyena padded closer and rested its snout against the mosquito mesh, pushing it inwards by a few inches until it drew taut.

What now? Claws and howls and slavering teeth? A fight to the death? A deadly shot to the creature's head from my Botswanan guard?

A tree-climbing hippo chose that moment to make another leap, this time in the sausage tree next to my tent. The hyena broke its drooling gaze, crouched for a split second, and then sprang off the deck and was away, lolloping through the grass.

I breathed for the first time in what had seemed like an hour, and ran to the tent door. It was still zipped firm, and all that remained of my visitor was a small patch of phlegm from its nose on the mosquito mesh.

I arrived at breakfast looking like a man possessed. My hair was even more disorderly than normal, and my eyes had the strung-out, staring, twitchy appearance that people get when they have come within a few metres of sharing their bedchamber with a large and peckish hyena.

I recounted my night of terror at the mercy of the dreadful beast in true schoolboy fashion, rushing my words and finding only the weakest of adjectives, like 'amazing', 'awesome' and 'incredible'. My small band of fellow guests was agog and increasingly jealous the more I told. An American woman said 'Oh my God!' a lot, and 'You lucky thing – that's, like, you know, a real sighting.'

The men were less enthused; it had not happened to them and they couldn't boast about it. They busied themselves finding bits of mud to flick off their boots, just to let me know I was not impressing them.

But I did not care what they thought, and I did not care what we saw or did not see on our game drives and walks that day. All I wanted to do was stay here at Stanley's for a year, spend evenings by the fire, get on first-name terms with my tent hyena and watch the magical landscape turn from desert to lake and back to desert again.

It is one of the very few luxury hotels to which I must return before I die or life will not be complete.

Another fabulous location hotel where people have had epiphanies while watching the world outside their window live and breathe is in Australia, in the continent's most powerful landscape. At Uluru stands the stylish Longitude 131, a series of striking white tents raised up on stilts above the burnt-ochre desert floor of the Red Centre. There has been hotel accommodation of one sort or another out there for years, but nothing as design-oriented and environmentally sensitive as this.

Longitude 131's design maximises the use of the landscape, affording every guest an unbridled view of 'the Rock' and reminding them at every turn that they are somewhere intrinsically special.

The resort grew from a concept developed by its owners and creators, Voyages Hotels and Resorts, who were looking to recapture the original elements of why people went on holiday. The group was acutely aware of the big changes in luxury tourism over the past decade, and as a spokesperson told me it wanted to carve its own niche.

'We looked hard at what everybody else was doing and saw that there was a lack of luxury experiential tourism product in Australia. People were getting very functional and sometimes very good service but were not coming away with a real sense of place or wonder. That is what we went after, and what we are still going after, and Longitude 131 is a perfect example of where to get a good dose of both those things,' he said.

Most luxury hotels in dramatic locations come with a host of activities – safaris, snorkelling adventures, midnight hyena heart-stoppers. But every now and then you want to go somewhere where there is virtually nothing to do, and for that you need to catch a plane to the Seychelles in the middle of the Indian Ocean.

An hour's flight in a small jet from the main group of islands is Desroches, little more than a speck on the map. It is a coral island about two kilometres from north to south and barely one kilometre east–west. It is ringed by some of the most romantic beaches I have ever seen, and there is no-one fussier about tropical beaches than me. I have categories for sand colour and texture, amount of rubbish washed up, warmth and swimmability of water, and prevalence of coconuts (too few and it is not tropical enough; too many and it looks fake).

On Desroches, apart from the odd dive trip, there is nothing to do. The resort is tiny, which means there are hardly any people here and you get the beaches pretty much to yourself. The equation is simple: number of beaches > number of people = privacy + luxury.

It is one of only two islands in the world where I have spent a day on a beach and only seen my own footprints. The other one is a small resort island on the other side of the world whose luxurious qualities are, sadly, being polluted by the mad, ageing fascist who owns it, and who seems to be conducting some twisted human experiment with his staff and guests. I hate the place with a passion, and refuse to even breathe its name.

Desroches, on the other hand, is delightful. The less there is to do, the more strenuous simple activities seem, like getting to breakfast on time or choosing a cocktail at the bar in the evening.

One afternoon I borrowed some old and rather worn golf clubs and some battered balls from the manager and spent the most blissfully wasteful afternoon hitting shots up and down the airstrip in the middle of the island. You can only do this for six days of the week as the jet plops down on the seventh, which could put you off your stroke a little.

Desroches is a honeymooners' idyll, and you would think the only real exercise guests get here is sex, but my guess is that such is the catatonia of the place that even that is a struggle. So my advice is to give in, order a picnic hamper, find your empty beach and tune out. Locations like this do not come along often, so drink it in.

Destinations such as Aitutaki, Sossusvlei and Desroches are deeply fortunate in being ravishing to look at and peaceful and tranquil to visit, but a recent phenomenon is the emergence from strife and turmoil of places that, a few years ago, we would not have dared venture to.

The most striking example is Northern Ireland. Until very recently no one in their right mind would have sat down to plan a romantic getaway and thought: 'I know, forget Paris and Rome, let's go to Belfast for the weekend.'

How times change. The once violence-ravaged city is now being tipped (by the tourism industry and me) as one of Europe's hot destinations. What convinced me on a recent visit was the presence of a truly luxurious hotel right in the city centre, The Merchant. Belfast has craved a place like

The Merchant for years but the success of such a venture could only have been possible after the signing in May 2007 of the peace accord between former sworn enemies Reverend Ian Paisley, leader of the Protestant Democratic Unionist Party (DUP), and Martin McGuinness of the Catholic and Nationalist Sinn Fein party, which signified the end of the Troubles.

Suddenly Belfast was alive. Pubs, clubs, restaurants, galleries ... life and liberty throughout the streets once more. What better way to celebrate than with a luxury weekend at The Merchant.

Tom Hanks had clearly had the same idea because he was sitting just a few tables away from me in the hotel's restaurant one lunchtime. When I say lunchtime I am using a bit of journalistic licence. It was gone noon but I was recovering from a long night of travel writer research in the fabulous pubs of Belfast and was still savouring a superb breakfast. I was also being extremely nice to the waiters in the hope that they would bring me another helping of The Merchant's porridge. Forget everything you know about porridge – this stuff was whipped with double cream and infused with whisky.

The Merchant has inherited its vastly thick stone walls and the high domed glass ceiling of its restaurant from the building's former inhabitant – the Ulster Bank. It is sophisticated, elegant. The rooms have followed a sexy and vaguely Gothic theme, with black walls softened by the hotel's signature sky-blue hue.

It's one of those hotels which are such a nightmare for the travel writer. I knew I should be out there, pounding the streets, gathering local anecdotes, checking facts and taking pictures of parks and buildings and smiling taxi drivers and Van Morrison's birthplace but I found myself inventing hundreds of reasons to stay holed up in The Merchant. Maybe Tom Hanks is in the room next door and wants to have a game of snooker. Maybe Van Morrison will show up unannounced and give us a song in the bar.

Maybe the staff will forget about me and I can stay here forever, sneaking down for whisky-infused porridge every morning.

Chapter 9

Privacy

THERE IS SOMETHING else I must own up to, apart from being a luxury hotel addict. Occasionally, in the past, when I have not been wearing my hat as a frightfully posh luxury travel writer and dining on foie gras and Bollinger at five-star resorts, or working as a foreign correspondent for the serious broadsheet press, I have taken a walk on the wild side. I have swallowed my pride, put on a heavy disguise, followed several Hail Marys with several Bloody Marys, and joined the ranks of unwashed tabloid journalism.

These desperate measures were taken for one reason only – to avoid defaulting on my rent – but having done a few ghastly, if lucrative, tours of duty swimming along in the media gutter, I realised these experiences have given me an extremely useful insight into how luxury hotels handle celebrity guests.

Almost all luxury hotels will swear they never reveal the identities of the famous faces that grace their spas and trash their rooms, for losing their trust and the huge wads of money they leave behind would be too dreadful a scenario to contemplate. In purely financial terms, each one is worth several mortal, non-VIP guests.

But there is a conflicting factor at work here. Where

celebrities go, tabloid journalists follow. And tabloid publications sell many millions of copies worldwide, reaching a global audience many hotel PR directors would sell their grandmothers to reach. So the rather simple equation is: celebrity guests = free worldwide PR. The reality is that while luxury hotels vociferously build their reputations by not disclosing the names of famous guests, they are in fact more than willing to make discreet phone calls from private mobile phones and from inside broom cupboards to the right journalists at the right publications at the right time, which later they will flatly deny.

In many ways, luxury hotels are just like you and me. Even though they may have limited interest in Britney Spears as a performer, they cannot resist taking a sneaky peek at a couple of paparazzi pictures of her shopping in her tracksuit. And poor old Rolling Stone Keith Richards could not even fall out of his hammock in peace at the ultra-exclusive Wakaya Club resort in Fiji without the world knowing about it.

There are some exceptions, of course: hotels that are so well endowed with reputation and rolling in money that they really do not need the publicity. But they are rare and probably all within the über-luxurious Aman group.

At the other end of the privacy scale, there are hotels which openly invite the paparazzi to hang out by virtually dangling celebrity guest lists in front of their faces. Some are so blatant they might as well put up a banner saying: 'The Hopelessly Indiscreet Hotel welcomes Tom Cruise and family – at 5 PM on Thursday at the side entrance. Fans and paparazzi welcome. Free coffee and doughnuts.'

In fact, some luxury hotels have a hotline to the local newspaper editor to tip them off when A-list celebs check in under pseudonyms. These hotels do not even mind if there is a bit of a dispute in the honeymoon suite between a rap star and his bitches; in fact, they would love nothing better as it spices the place up.

Even if a hotel is true to its privacy claims, there are two factors which are completely beyond the control of management. First, there is nothing to stop greedy fellow guests taking sneaky shots of celebrities picking their noses and emailing them to newspaper editors in return for several thousand pounds. And second, some celebrities are so desperate to get publicity that they are willing to invade their own privacy, and there is little the hotel can do once the celebrity or their agent has made their own phone calls to the media.

Australia attracts a healthy amount of celebrity glamour to its shores, which is why privacy has become a major aspect of luxury hotels here. Nowhere is this better demonstrated than on Queensland's Gold Coast. It is hardly Hollywood, but for three weeks each year the Palazzo Versace plays host to a gaggle of Z-list celebrities for nearby is the filming location for *I'm A Celebrity … Get Me Out Of Here!*

They arrive at Brisbane and Gold Coast airports, dressed head-to-toe in pink fluffy tracksuits, adidas T-shirts and Lacoste trainers, and sporting foul-mouthed Cockney accents, and are escorted to waiting limousines which take them to the hotel.

They usually bring with them their chain-smoking, shopaholic mothers, their vile and even less talented brothers who drink lager-top for breakfast, or the seven children they have acquired from seven failed marriages. It is a non-stop cavalcade of trashiness.

What the viewers don't see is what happens once the celebrities are voted out of the terrifying 'jungle', which – by the way – is more like a vaguely overgrown wood. Some departures are ignominious because they are the result of failing to complete some inane challenge such as eating 100 green ants in 30 seconds. Once the tears and furies have subsided and the cameras are turned off, the celebrities are helicoptered back to the Palazzo Versace, where they are hosed down, debriefed and let loose on the Gold Coast to spend their vast appearance fees.

This is where my tabloid journalism confession comes in. I reported on three series of the show and spent many hours squatting in the bushes outside the Palazzo Versace, dealing with my own green-ant challenges and waiting for the celebrities to do something newsworthy. I was always outside because for the duration of the show the Versace is in lock-down mode. Tight security is trained to spot, intimidate and eject anyone who looks or smells even faintly like a journalist.

From my camouflaged position I could have told you the names, heights, habits and shift-hours of virtually every front-of-house employee of the hotel. I knew the number plates of all the limousines, the names of most of the drivers, and who were the ones you could slip £30 for a celebrity story, true or otherwise: celebrities getting legless in the Versace bar, causing disturbances in restaurants on Tedder Avenue, spending £1,000 on a shirt and throwing a cocktail over it, snogging waitresses and falling off their surfboards.

Alas, many celebrities were crushingly boring. They bought postcards and went to McDonald's for £2.50 salads, and they didn't snog anyone.

When I finally managed to penetrate the celebrity force-field around the Palazzo Versace I pretended to be an estate agent on holiday from England. I told the celebrities I met that I was a huge fan of the show, and that I remembered them from when I was a kid. I could not shut them up. They banged on about rivalries and who washed the least and who did not clean their teeth and who swore like a pirate, and which one of the burly sportsmen cried himself to sleep every night.

Sadly, I am the worst tabloid journalist Fleet Street has ever known so few of these tales became news.

While the Gold Coast is about as glitzy and celebrity-tastic as Australia gets, the best examples of hotel privacy or the complete lack of it are to be found in Celebrity Central: Hollywood. If you are famous or rich – or both – and you want to disappear in Hollywood, there is only one address you should know: 701 Stone Canyon Road, Los Angeles, California 90077. Stone Canyon Road is in Bel-Air, Los Angeles's most exclusive and expensive pocket of wealth.

This is the discreet part of northern, semi-rural Los Angeles. It's where movie stars go when they are bored with living in the Hollywood Hills, their twelve-bedroom mansion is getting a little cramped, and they have just banked a cheque for $23 million for their last film.

Bel-Air is even more exclusive than its neighbour Beverly Hills, and it's infinitely more private. The further you drive up Stone Canyon Road, the bigger the houses get and the steeper the sides of the valley become. After a few minutes' cruising around the sweeping bends, past high leylandii hedges and metal gates and arrays of Rapid Response security warning signs, a car park appears on your left-hand side behind some low bushes. It contains a collection of vehicles that must be worth almost as much as one of the mansions clinging to the hillside.

When I showed up, in the middle of an April rainstorm that had already washed away whole hillsides in northern California before unleashing itself on Los Angeles, I spotted a midnight-blue Ferrari Testarossa, a new Maybach, a gaudy gold Rolls-Royce Phantom, and a sleek silver-grey Aston Martin (which James Bond must have parked just moments before). The small clutch of Porsche 911s seemed positively tawdry by comparison. Even in the pelting rain and valley mists, this collection of motors looked spectacular.

As I splashed through the puddles in my faded burgundy Mitsubishi Galant rental car, I could sense the Bel-Air style police getting ready to leap from the bushes and point guns at me. But the cops must have been on a lunch break because I pulled up unchallenged next to a green awning. A man stepped forward, walked around the car to my side, smiled and held his large golf umbrella over the door.

'Welcome to the Hotel Bel-Air, Sir. You must be Mr Brace,' he said. 'We have been expecting you, and we are so sorry about this weather.'

This was Bob, who has been with the hotel for more than 30 years and is one of the kindest, most interesting and genuine front-of-house hotel employees I have ever met. He escorted me across the Bel-Air's famous stone bridge, which arches over a small stream and the lower sections of the hotel's beautifully landscaped grounds.

There were live-oaks, yews, sycamores, massive coastal redwoods, a huge, solid *ficus roxburghii* sporting large wide leaves, a three-metre bird of paradise tree, and a tipu whose bright yellow spring flowers were being battered by the fat raindrops.

Ahead of me rose the hotel's centrepiece – the bell tower, peppered with red trumpet vine flowers. Large ferns were bursting from the undergrowth and the rain was drawing the scents of fruit trees and letting them linger on the damp and clammy air. Peach, pineapple, guava, lemon and orange were all floating through the hotel grounds. They could all get together later in a secret grotto down near the lake and make a smoothie.

The Hotel Bel-Air is not a hotel so much as a country retreat, with twelve acres on the edge of the city. This is where the concrete ends and the wooded Californian countryside begins. South from here sprawls one of the largest conurbations in the world, hundreds of square kilometres of steel, stone and freeway inhabited by more than fifteen million people and hermetically sealed with a smog blanket. North, over the rim of Stone Canyon, lies the fresh, clear air of the Santa Clara Mountains, whose peaks remain snow-capped until May, and beyond them is the southern fringe of the Mojave Desert.

The Bel-Air's position and its lush, florid grounds are a tonic for the soul but they serve a second purpose: they provide complete privacy for their celebrity guests. The hotel cannot be accessed from any direction without Bob and the security team knowing about it. Nor can paparazzi or movie-star stalkers spy on it from neighbouring properties. Also, the proximity of the canyon walls and the wind currents that they produce mean news helicopters find it almost impossible to hover overhead. And if guests want to avoid even the remote possibility of being snapped in the car park emerging from their midnight-blue Ferrari Testarossas, they can drive down a secret road at the rear of the property and be smuggled in safely.

The Hotel Bel-Air has become the hotel of choice for guests who want to relax and recharge without having to worry that a picture of them in a bathrobe is going to turn up on the front page of *The National Enquirer*. They have either danced in the media limelight for years and do not want to do it anymore, or they are the media-hating type of celebrity who has always loathed attention unless it is to promote a new film/book/wife/husband/lover (delete as necessary).

A large number of guests stay semi-permanently. They check in for several months while their new home is being built up the road, or while their old one is being refurbished and redecorated, with new wings being added for their growing family of chihuahuas.

They are not just protected from the glare of people beyond the hotel's boundaries, however. The lushness of the gardens and the design of the narrow brick walkways, small arbours and grottos mean they are screened from fellow guests too. They can spend days out of doors strolling through the grounds, loitering under the orange trees and having naps on green lawns, and hardly see anyone else.

Bob saw me to the door of my suite and wished me a pleasant stay. A log fire was crackling in a wide grate, and a welcome card was sitting on the desk. My luggage had arrived, with the raindrops wiped from its shell and locks.

I like to set myself challenges in luxury hotels, and at the Bel-Air it was to do what the hotel promises cannot be done – spot a celebrity. I know the place is crawling with them because my good friend Patrick Stewart, the Shakespearean actor also well known for his role in the *X-Men* films and the *Star Trek – The Next Generation* TV series, got married here in 2002. Another friend, also from England, told me he spent part of his stay rummaging around in the undergrowth observing plants and had found the singer David Crosby loitering in a bush. Oprah Winfrey is well known to take the Chalon Suite – the biggest and best – and adore every second of her stay. And the driver of the Beverly Wilshire's house car – a black Rolls-Royce Phantom – told me about meeting Sylvester Stallone in the Bel-Air's car park. Sly was vigorously polishing his own Rolls-Royce and lamenting the fact that he could never get the paintwork as shiny as the other Rolls-Royces he saw cruising around Hollywood.

Stallone wasn't in the car park when I arrived, but it might have been his Roller parked there. Later that afternoon I could have sworn I heard his gravelly voice outside my suite. Two figures walked past and I ran to the window, but their faces were obscured by large golf umbrellas. One was muscled, tanned and dressed in a tight black T-shirt; he was about the right height for Rocky and Rambo …

I grabbed my pocket-size digital camera, ran to the door, flung it open and splashed out in my bare feet, slipping and sliding around the corner just in time to see the umbrellas disappear into the doorway of another suite. In my haste I had forgotten my key and was left standing wet, bedraggled and celebrity-less on the brick path. It was at that precise moment that the Hotel Bel-Air's charming and debonair managing director, Carlos Lopes, marched around the corner inhabiting an immaculate suit and tie and sporting a serious expression.

I leapt from the path into a flower bed and pushed my way behind a large fern, making it shudder and send down a shower of raindrops. I crouched among the azaleas, my feet sinking into the soft black loam and the rain running in little tickling streams down my neck and back.

Lopes passed by, discussing with a colleague the finer points of how to clean the new bespoke chinaware that had recently arrived from Florence. Had he spotted me, my illustrious career as a luxury travel writer would surely have been over. I looked more like an escaped convict than a five-star hotel habitué. I skulked in the undergrowth in soaking-wet clothes, with my wild hair plastered to my head and my bare feet now completely immersed in mud. I had no room key, no identification, and to make matters infinitely worse I had a digital camera in my pocket with a blurred photograph of what might have been Sylvester Stallone under an umbrella. I had broken just about every Hotel Bel-Air guest code within half an hour of checking in.

'Señor, are you all right?' asked a small Mexican gardener who had spotted me. He seemed unsure whether I was genuinely in trouble or whether he should call a SWAT team to evict me.

'Oh, yes, hi, yes, I was just, erm, examining the plants. So many varieties of fern. Quite incredible. Also, I have locked myself out of my suite and I'm a little damp now. Could you maybe help me get back in? I'm Matthew Brace, I'm a travel writer. I'm in Suite, erm, Suite … I can't remember the number off-hand. It's that one there, on the corner. I have only just checked in,' I said.

The gardener smiled and told me to wait back at my front door and he would fetch someone from management.

'Okay, thanks, but not Señor Lopes,' I said in an urgent whisper. 'He's very busy and I am meeting him later and I, erm, maybe somebody else, not Señor Lopes, please.'

In the distance I could hear the familiar rumble of a tidal wave of shame which was about to break over my head. To her great credit, the woman from reception who arrived with a master key did not laugh, nor did she frown. She merely said, 'I hope you have not been waiting long, Mr Brace. Would you like the restaurant to make you some tortilla soup to warm you up?'

I said that would be terrific and disappeared into my suite, furiously spreading out some pages of the *Los Angeles Times* on the carpet so I would not tread mud into it.

The tidal wave had receded to merely a rather large ocean surge, but still it left my ego feeling as if it had been dumped and spun around several times by the surf. I would not have blamed the receptionist for wetting her knickers with laughter the minute she was around the corner and out of earshot, and broadcasting among her colleagues a description of the British travel writer who had been found crouching like a hobbit among the azaleas in the rain.

One day all the hotel staff who have found me in compromising positions – and there have been many – are going to get together and have a Matthew Brace Shame Convention, complete with PowerPoint presentations showing how my behaviour has degenerated from mildly eccentric to utterly inexplicable.

Such humiliation was not enough, however, to distract me from my celebrity-hunting mission. Not long after I stepped from a hot shower, which had brought some warmth back to my body and washed the California mud from between my toes, I heard some luggage roll along the walkway outside my door and stop by the suite adjacent to mine.

'Thank you,' someone said in a slow, deep and deliberate voice.

'Thank you, Mr Nicholson. I hope you have a pleasant stay with us,' replied the porter.

Jack Nicholson! Had to be. Next door. Bloody brilliant. I put down my bowl of tortilla soup and bounded to the door again, but this time I stayed inside, kneeled on a chair and peered through the fish-eye lens of the peephole. A laugh came from inside his suite, and it sounded as if somebody dropped something on the floor with a thud, but nobody came out.

I ran through a plan in my head: when he came out, or if I found him doing push-ups on the lawn in a silk dressing gown, I'd go out pretending to be very busy and on my way to an important meeting. I'd bump into him casually and say, 'Oh, hello Mr Nicholson, we appear to be neighbours. I'm Matthew Brace, I'm a travel writer. It's nice to meet you. Maybe I'll see you later at the bar,' upon which he would probably chop me into small pieces with an axe for being such a five-star loser.

So obsessed was I with meeting Jack Nicholson at the Hotel Bel-Air that I spent the better part of half an hour glued to the door, not noticing I was leaning awkwardly on my right leg and was getting quite severe pins and needles down my shin. I moved away for a few seconds and shook my leg as if I were trying to get an ice-cube out of my trousers, but it was too late – my foot was asleep, and presumably Jack Nicholson was as well.

That evening at dinner I sat alone in the outdoor section of the restaurant, in a semi-circular banquette. It was still raining, so plastic windcheaters had been lowered to keep the wet and the chill away from guests' shoulders. Three diners breezed in past me as I was ordering the smoked oyster and watercress cream soup, the artichoke ravioli and a glass of Sequoia Grove Cabernet Sauvignon. They followed the maître d' and as each passed my table they executed a blisteringly sharp and precise eyes-right that would put the Queen's Guard of Honour to shame. This was the Hollywood salute – you get a second and a half of someone's attention as they are en route to a power meal. If you're famous, they will say hi. If you look famous, they will say hi. If you look even remotely like you might one day become famous and they can exploit you in some way, they will say hi.

None of them deigned to say hi. In fact, they all looked vaguely ashamed with themselves for wasting an important glance which could have been saved for someone far more influential.

Instead they slid into their banquette, surrounded themselves with steel heating umbrellas and went straight into a
star-studded conversation. They talked about 'Arnold' and
'Russell' and 'Tom', and used superlatives I had never heard
before, like 'fabtabulous', 'bootilicious', 'mainframe' and 'so
OC, baby'.

'On set, ya know, Tom really has to work to be fabtabulous whereas Russell's got that whole, ya know, mainframe
look thing goin' on, baby,' one of them said, laughing at his
own hyperbole.

'It's so OC, so OC,' said another. 'I think I want the pork
belly but I don't want any fat with it – can they do it without
fat? Excuse me, can you do pork belly without fat? I want
pork belly without fat. Can we make that happen?'

Los Angeles, especially Hollywood, has been full of
fabtabulous people like this for decades, making things
happen. So I wasn't hearing anything new, and I was able
to tune out and concentrate on doing some work: taking
important journalistic notes from the 54-page wine list. I
was particularly intrigued by the Chateau Lafite-Rothschild
Premier Grand Cru Classé 1961, which was obviously a
complete steal at $3,200 a bottle. But once I had recovered
from the shock of the price tag, for which I would have had
to negotiate a small mortgage, I found my attention being
drawn back to my three fellow diners. I listened more intently and realised they were not just blah-blah-ing idly but
actually seemed to be pretty well-connected. I guessed they
were celebrity agents or casting directors, and Arnold, Russell and Tom were almost certainly Schwarzenegger, Crowe
and Cruise.

'Arnold's such a humble guy, ya know, considering what
he does and who he is, ya know?'

'Maybe because, like, ya know, he's from over there, ya

know, in, erm, wherever. Not California, anyway.'

'Ya, you're right, baby, you're right on the money, baby, could be. I love him, ya know, totally love him. I …'

The waiter returned with bad news from the kitchen and the fusspot's face fell.

'Oh, you *can't* do pork belly totally without fat. Does it really? It always comes with a little fat? Oh, okay. Hmm, oh dear, erm, that's really what I wanted. Erm, okay, well, I'll take a salad. And, can you turn these heating umbrellas up more, because I'm real cold.'

I could sense the waiter gritting his teeth and contemplating telling the woman that she was probably cold because a human body actually needs to be alive to feel warmth – as she was so clearly dead there was no chance of her ever warming up.

'Of course, Madam. I'll check into it right away,' he said with a graceful half-bow of the head.

The door to the bar opened and a young woman staggered down the stone steps wearing large sunglasses, which are essential in Los Angeles at 8 PM on a dark, rainy evening in case there is a sudden blinding interstellar explosion and your retinas are damaged for ever. She flashed a drunken, sexy grin at me and mouthed the word 'hi' a bit like Marilyn Monroe used to do to salivating journalists in trilby hats. It was my first Hollywood 'hi'. Clearly, she had the foresight to realise that I would be famous one day. Then she whispered very loudly into her Louis Vuitton mobile phone: 'Gwyneth said yes, can you believe that? I was like, oh my God!' She jumped up and down on the spot like a giddy schoolgirl and disappeared behind a hedge, which shook when she fell against it.

I summoned the waiter, ordered a top-up of Sequoia Grove Cabernet Sauvignon and sat back with a half-smile.

I had not actually seen any famous movie stars at Los Angeles's most discreet hotel, but I had almost certainly photographed Sylvester Stallone's umbrella and heard Jack Nicholson drop something in his suite, and at supper I had been in exclusive reach of several people who were obviously best mates with Arnold Schwarzenegger, Russell Crowe, Tom Cruise and Gwyneth Paltrow. I felt sure that if I put all of these semi-celebrity claims to fame together it would equal one actual positive sighting.

That's so OC, baby!

A few miles into the dense plastic jungle of Hollywood is another discreet hotel favoured by celebrities. The Sunset Tower in West Hollywood manages to be both subtle and fabulous at the same time. This is mainly due to the fact that it attracts Hollywood's classier and more refined 'old school', but also because it is surrounded by louder, brasher, gaudier establishments that are so desperate for publicity that they might as well stage press conferences for the paparazzi to announce in which rooms celebrities are staying, and what the best ways are to get candid snaps of them taking cocaine by the pool.

This is Hollywood, after all, full of men and women who last week were petrol pump attendants from County Donegal and waitresses from Arkansas saving their spare cash in glass jars, and who are now overnight silver-screen idols making more than $20 million a year. Invariably, they all go nuts, buying Harley-Davidsons and concept cars, entire wardrobes by Versace, and more drugs than they could take in a year. Public displays of wealth and excess and reckless attitudes are essential for the Hollywood player, especially the ingenues, and the best places to flaunt them are funky hotels, so it might not be all that surprising that this is where the flashy, à la mode celebrity establishments are located.

What is surprising is that the Sunset Tower is in the middle of them, standing as a beacon of style, sophistication and subtlety above a sickly sea of ephemeral schmaltz. It has not done anything particularly defensive to protect the celebrities who visit. There is no stone bridge to keep out the unwashed masses. There are no high hedges to block views, or secret back roads along which famous faces can be smuggled in blacked-out limos. The closest they get to deliberate secrecy is a private entrance to the Argyle Salon & Spa, which means regulars like Minnie Driver and Dan Ackroyd can breeze in for hair stylings and wellbeing treatments without being hassled by the paparazzi.

Rather, the stately and mature Sunset Tower relies on the attention-seeking semi-luxurious teenagers around it to draw the media flashbulbs away. To the west lies the Ian Schrager-designed Mondrian, whose Skybar is Hollywood's 'it' venue, and to the east is the funky Standard, which thinks it is so achingly groovy it needs to paint its grass blue and display its sign upside-down. And opposite is the Hyatt, known locally as the Riot, a major party house which is taken over each weekend by rock bands and hordes of music fans, who flock to this part of the Strip to see gigs at the House of Blues. A quick travel tip: at the Hyatt, ask for a room facing north to the Hollywood Hills rather than one which looks south to downtown. The south-facing rooms overlook Sunset Boulevard, which rocks and pulses 24/7 – sleep is rarely an option.

With all the action going on elsewhere, the Sunset Tower can take a deep breath and welcome its loyal clientele with ease. In the Tower Bar, which used to be gangster Bugsy Siegel's hang-out when the building was luxury apartments, the hotel's ebullient and far-sighted owner, Jeff Klein, ordered me the most powerful martini I have ever tasted and began to tell me about the regulars.

The 1950s silver-screen sex-goddess Jane Russell still drops by some nights for a martini. Nancy Sinatra comes often, ordering brandy and dry gingers and occasionally singing a number for the cool crowd of diners. Bill Murray loves the Tower Bar and dines here at least once a month. And Johnny Depp and his family drop by to inhabit one of the suede-backed semi-circular banquettes.

The Bar, and indeed the entire hotel, has been so stylishly refurbished that it feels like an elegant 1930s establishment, and this commands a certain respect and civility. It is the sort of place where if a Hollywood luminary sat down at the next table, you would be overwhelmed by the feeling that taking a quick picture or even bothering them for an autograph is just not the done thing. Nobody tells you that you cannot do this – it's just, ever so quietly and subtly, understood.

How Klein has created this genuine oasis of chic in one of the most crass and synthetic neighbourhoods on the planet is not entirely clear. I fear magic might have been involved. His vision is inspired, his eye for design and detail sharp and incisive, and his concept – which he has mirrored at his City Club Hotel in Manhattan – is my personal ideal.

'I believe that the old-school hotel has sort of been lost, especially in America,' he said. 'My whole concept is: whatever happened to the tiny little jewel that only you and your aunt know about? That secret little chic place with the impeccable service and the stylish décor? That's really what I want to create.

'There was a hotel in Paris, which is no longer there, that my parents and I used to visit. It was on the Left Bank and it was fabulous and very chic. It was owned by this older gay man who collected antiques and had impeccable taste. He just was amazing. He attended to every little detail, and just being in that hotel made you feel special and in awe of your surroundings. I feel like that art has been lost and I want to get it back.'

And he has at the Sunset Tower, where every room is a mini-museum to art deco.

'My market is sophisticated,' said Klein. 'There are many wealthy people who do not understand sophistication and do not want to understand it, and that's fine if that's your thing, but they are not my market. They are loaded and have Ferraris but no class. I don't want people coming in here with zero class.

'When I was opening the Sunset Tower, people in Los Angeles said, "Oh, you should have a DJ in the lobby, house music everywhere," and I said, "No, that's not what we're about." They said, "You don't know this town, they don't want elegance in LA," but the hotel has proved to be a hit, so I think people *do* want this elegance and sophistication.'

I sincerely hope I am not jinxing the whole operation, but I predict Jeff Klein's style and sophistication will catch on. Staying at one of his hotels is like eating the finest, freshest crisp California citrus salad with a glass of clean dry champagne, after a lifetime's diet of hamburgers and fries. It is new, different and utterly refreshing.

Despite falling in love with the Sunset Tower and vowing to return and dive into more martinis, I still had not spotted any celebrities, and was becoming more and more confident that this hotel, like the Bel-Air, really had mastered the art of privacy. I checked out the Argyle Salon & Spa, but Minnie Driver and Dan Ackroyd were nowhere to be seen. There was a woman paying her bill who looked a lot like somebody in *The OC* – or was it *Knott's Landing*? I'm so useless at celebrity-spotting it isn't funny. My brain is just not wired to remember faces and put names to them. It might help if I actually watched television for more than an hour a week, and if I spread my interest to shows other than nature documentaries. If there had been some Tasmanian forty-spotted pardalotes flying around the Argyle Salon & Spa I would have been able to identify them in a heartbeat. I soldiered on, thinking I might have more luck down in Beverly Hills. A 15-minute cruise from the Sunset Tower, along Sunset Boulevard past Joan Collins's five houses – one rented to Al Pacino – and down Rodeo Drive, is the Beverly Wilshire.

You will almost certainly recognise the French-Italian Renaissance façade of the hotel from the film *Pretty Woman*. Under the dramatic arches and through the big gold doors strode Julia Roberts dressed as a Hollywood hooker, but, contrary to popular belief, none of the scenes was filmed inside the hotel. The lobby where she was stopped by the demure general manager was not the lobby of the Beverly Wilshire. Instead the film was shot mainly on a set.

Scores of guests think the scenes in Richard Gere's suite were filmed in the hotel's rooftop suite up on the top of the Wilshire Wing, but they weren't. But that doesn't stop everyone calling this the *Pretty Woman* hotel.

It is ironic that the hotel has become known for the beauty of a woman, because over its 80-year history it has been populated by far more of Hollywood's leading men, including Elvis Presley, Warren Beatty, Steve McQueen and Kermit the Frog. It became a hotel where the privacy code was simultaneously enforced and flouted. Fans and the media knew the stars were staying there – it was Hollywood's worst-kept secret – yet the imposing design of the hotel, more like a Manhattan fortress than a relaxed, low-built West Coast resort, was such that they were kept at bay.

A lot of stars preferred to camp out in the rooftop suite. The suite is remarkable. It is a separate brick-walled studio apartment built on the flat roof of the hotel's older Wilshire Wing. It sports its own walled Italianate garden with potted plants, and the views from it are spectacular. Any guest must feel king of the world from up there, or king of Hollywood, at least. From where else can you look straight out across the Hollywood Hills to the famous 50-foot-high Hollywood sign and then down your nose at the shoppers on Rodeo Drive?

It is intensely private, which is exactly what Elvis Presley wanted when he checked in back in 1964 with his musician buddies. The King used the suite as a rehearsal space, mainly because his studio believed it would allow him to concentrate without being constantly badgered by fans at hotels in downtown Los Angeles. It worked, and the only attention he received when he was ensconced in his suite was from the occasional balloon floating past his window with an adoring fan's love letter tied to it with string.

About a decade later, Warren Beatty moved in to the rooftop suite just before he started filming *Bonnie and Clyde*. It was to be his home for the next decade. Can you imagine the cavalcade of women who must have clip-clopped up the stairs in their heels to spend the night? If only the walls of that suite could talk, we would have the most salacious Hollywood exposé yet written.

What we do know, thanks to the hotel's excellent official history, *The Beverly Wilshire Hotel: Its Life and Times*, by Horace Sutton, is that Beatty shared this eyrie with Julie Christie, Joan Collins, Leslie Caron and the late Natalie Wood.

With Beatty, when it wasn't women and film it was politics, and he was deeply involved with Robert Kennedy,

George McGovern and Gary Hart. He used his suite for fund-raising dinners and a booth in El Padrino (the hotel's former celebrity restaurant) to observe people and also to meet with Hubert Humphrey, Gary Hart and other Democratic hopefuls.

To devoted Beatty fans, the hotel became a shrine. They would leave him letters, cards and presents on an almost daily basis. One woman hand-delivered a long letter every week for a solid year while Beatty lived at the hotel. Elvis may have been known as the King, but nobody launches balloons for him at the Beverly Wilshire anymore. Letters for Warren Beatty, however, still arrive.

Another long-term guest, according to Sutton's history, was Steve McQueen.

In his suite, Steve McQueen kept a keg of beer, a 1941 Indian motorcycle and an old silver-plated cash register which he rang up when he needed to tip a bellman. He had a canopied bed and a sauna and railway sleepers. He grew a full beard and moustache and was pleased that these hirsute decorations concealed his identity.

The hotel's reputation was boosted further in April 1988, when the novelist Jackie Collins picked the Beverly Wilshire as the best hotel for having an affair, mainly because it had a branch of Tiffany's in the lobby.

A newspaper quoted her as saying that if you happened to run into someone in the lobby that you would have rather not seen you just say, 'Oh, I was just going into Tiffany's' to avoid suddenly being on the front page of the *National Enquirer* the next morning.

This star-studded history has ensured that the hotel has evolved into one of the big Hollywood celebrity hang-outs. I am not saying the Beverly Wilshire deliberately promotes its famous guests, but neither does it hide them. The result is a refreshing ambience where you can walk into the quite public, open lobby restaurant for lunch and find yourself sitting next to Danny DeVito, Lauren Bacall or P. Diddy.

There are no off-putting security guards in suits talking into hidden microphones in their shirt cuffs. The maître d' in the restaurant does not give you attitude. The lobby staff are welcoming, whether you are a millionaire basketball player or a farmer from Kansas who has wandered in to take a photograph of the chandeliers. The public areas have the feel of a friendly after-event party.

The hotel's dazzling PR director, Jennifer Cooke, took me for lunch in the restaurant. We discussed the menu, and I dutifully took notes in my little notebook, but then I put forward a far more important request.

'Can you tell me when we see some celebrities?' I asked.

'I won't have to,' she said. 'You'll see them.'

I'd heard Bill Clinton was there, and that Sidney Poitier was a regular. According to two star-struck guests on my floor, an actress called Molly Sims was also present. Where was my wife when I needed her? Molly Sims, Molly Sims … My brain was hurriedly engaging its rarely-used celebrity recognition sector, but it didn't know Molly Sims.

'Who's Molly Sims?' I had asked the guests.

'She's in *Las Vegas*. Don't you get that show in England?'

'Yes we do, and I think I might even have watched it once. Who does she play?'

The star-struck guests told me she was the really beautiful one with the long hair, which did not narrow things down much as I seemed to remember everyone in the show was beautiful and had long hair.

'She plays James Caan's daughter. You know, the guy who runs the Montecito Casino? Anyway, she's here. We saw her this morning.'

The Beverly Wilshire is also famous for hosting a lot of rap stars. Usher is one of its biggest clients, and Beyoncé has bounced out of a sports car there on a number of occasions. To my dismay, the rappers are apparently among the quietest and best behaved guests. Hotel staff told me they don't have wild parties but usually go to bed really early. So, all that macho 'Yo, watch me, I party til dawn wid my bitches 'n' my homies' bravado is just a load of hype. They're all in bed with a cup of hot milk by 9 PM.

The hotel's flamboyant general manager, Radha Arora, was doing the rounds of the tables in a pin-striped suit and bright yellow tie. He was the best-dressed person I had seen in the room. He was the best-dressed person I had seen in Beverly Hills. He stopped at our table to shake hands, welcome me to the hotel and confirm that many celebrities were in the house today, and that I should take a walk and see if I could bump into them.

Celebrity jackpot. Jennifer and I munched our way through a delicious McCarthy Salad, the house speciality, as she explained how the restaurant works.

'Most of the people here are big Hollywood players. They are producers, agents, industry types. A lot of movie deals are done in this room,' she said.

They use it like another office, a place to bring potential business partners, to woo clients, to seal deals, show off and generally be fabulous in a very public setting.

Jennifer took a call on her mobile phone and said we should probably go. Maybe our table had been booked by P. Diddy and some models. I left one of my business cards on the seat, just in case. As we reached the restaurant's front steps, the far-too-helpful waiter rushed up behind me and gave me my card back.

'You dropped this, Sir.'

Damn those efficient waiters. I was trying to network with Diddy and make a fortune. That's so *not* OC, baby.

Jennifer had to go but I loitered by the lobby lift in case someone famous came out. I felt like a nervous fan waiting to pounce on my idol and get them to autograph the back of a beer mat. After about a quarter of an hour the doors opened: standing in front of me, looking very tall and smart and rather pleased with himself, was Bill Clinton.

I flicked out my right hand faster than a Wild West gunslinger, and felt Clinton's security detail (two black men so huge they could easily have passed for four black men) stiffen and reach for their pistols.

He stepped from the lift to meet my outstretched hand, and I smiled and rattled out: 'Mr Clinton, it's very nice to meet you.'

'Hi,' he said. His 'hi' was slightly hoarse and stretched like a piece of chewing gum. 'Are you English or Australian?'

Perceptive.

'A bit of both. English really but lived in Sydney for the last eight years,' I blurted.

'I luuurve Sydney,' he said, as if he were talking about a long-lost friend who had died far too young.

'That harbour you got there. So beautiful. You take care and enjoy the hotel.'

And he was gone, shielded by his bodyguards, and misty-eyed for Sydney Harbour. In my excitement I had stepped into the lift and was now travelling up to wherever Clinton had come from. I jumped up and down with excitement, held my fists above my head and silently yelled. My first celebrity in Los Angeles. It had taken me a week, but never mind – I had Clinton's aftershave on the palm of my right hand, so nothing could stop me now.

The lift stopped, and I alighted to find myself in what was obviously the final stage of a very enjoyable charity lunch. People were talking loudly and laughing and slapping each other on the back. They were fumbling for car keys, swapping business cards, promising to catch up at the weekend, and making those telephone signs where they extend the thumb and little finger and hold their hand to their ear like a telephone receiver. In Los Angeles that one gesture symbolises a whole sentence: 'Look, I'll try to call you but, ya know, I'm a pretty busy, important guy and I've got that whole mainframe thing going on, so don't expect it soon, okay?'

Around the corner and through the throng came two men, one black and one white. They were 70 at the very least and looked rather frail. The crowd parted and let them through, patting them on their shoulders as they passed.

Sidney Poitier and an elderly friend were walking straight towards me as I stood in front of the lift.

'Going down, gentlemen?' I asked, sounding more like a lift porter than a luxury travel writer.

'Thank you,' said Poitier, his rich velvety voice as true as ever. The other man did not speak and spent most of his time staring at the ground. The two looked as if they were holding each other up, like a pair of old pals emerging from an all-night poker game.

They didn't smell of booze, so I figured maybe they were just getting on in years and these lunches were beginning to wear them out.

'Was it a fun lunch?' I asked.

'Yes, thank you,' said Poitier, not looking at me. A very soft, quiet belch issued from the other man. I half-hoped he was going to throw up on my shoe just so I could say Sidney Poitier's friend once threw up on my shoe in a lift at the Beverly Wilshire. For a thrilling moment I thought it was

Walter Matthau, but he had passed away a few years before, so unless Hollywood has worked out a way of reviving dead film stars – and I wouldn't put it past them – it couldn't have been him. I didn't have the nerve to push the conversation, such as it was, for the two friends looked like they were ready for their afternoon naps. The lift reached the lobby floor once more and they shuffled out.

I eagerly peered out to see which famous face would hop in to my lucky celebrity lift next. I could ride up and down in this all day meeting famous people. James Caan, maybe, fresh off the Montecito's executive jet and looking for Molly Sims? P. Diddy and his models, heading to a suite for an afternoon playing Scrabble?

The next face I recognised was Jennifer's.

'Having fun?' she asked.

'You bet. Bill Clinton and Sidney Poitier so far, and some other guy who I thought for a moment was Walter Matthau, but I think there are loads of famous people using this lift so I am staying in it,' I said.

In the Matthew Brace Famous Faces Hall of Fame Currency Exchange, a Clinton or a Poitier is each worth at least two Caans, 50 Sims, and about 100 P. Diddys.

Later that day, delighted with my celebrity haul, I retired to my suite to lie down with a bowl of celebratory blueberries. I flicked on the television and made myself watch the E! entertainment channel to ensure I did not miss any other important celebrity spots, and to find out what Molly Sims looked like.

As I was saying my goodbyes to Jennifer the next day and getting into a taxi I spied a girl on the steps with big sunglasses talking on her cell phone. Blueberries, E! entertainment channel … I could feel my celebrity recognition systems grinding in my head.

The girl was wearing a three-quarter-length coat and large sunglasses and was pacing up and down the steps, talking animatedly into her phone and trying her best to look as conspicuous as possible. Molly Sims. I actually recognised her.

I slid into the back of the cab, and back into reality once more.

Chapter 10

Sex and Romance

QUICK QUIZ: WHAT is the world's most romantic place?

Hands up for Paris? Venice? Barcelona's Barri Gotic? Central Park in spring, shopping on Fifth Avenue in the early evening? Courchevel on skis at New Year with beef carpaccio and grappa for lunch? Samba dancing at the feet of Corcovado in Rio in the sultry summer heat? Ice-climbing in the Scottish Highlands, all decked out in bright red gaiters and crampons and snug little gloves?

Or whale-watching from the Mornington Peninsula or Margaret River? Perhaps a hammock on your own beach at Negril in Jamaica, with nothing but rum and smooth marijuana to keep you horizontal? How about sitting on the slopes of Iceland's Hekla volcano on Midsummer's Eve, drinking Rekya vodka in the glow of the midnight sun?

I highly recommend all of these, but you are going to need a suitably fabulous and sexy hotel to maintain the romance or the heady cocktail will be diluted and your trip ruined.

That is where things get tricky. You might think the luxury travel writer would be spoilt for choice in this regard, and that the only problem would be choosing which hotels not to mention. But because what we each find romantic is so intensely personal, no hotel will ever succeed in meeting the requirements of all its guests all of the time, no matter how many sunken baths, rainforest showers, sunset ocean views and Hermès accessories they offer.

For some, the ultimate in romance is scoffing down a full continental breakfast in bed in their suite. Personally, I can thing of nothing less sexy. Eating on an angle makes me feel slightly queasy, and I hate having to pick flakes of croissant out of my sheets. Even though I know someone is going to come in and change the bed linen in a few hours, I would feel guilty for leaving a coffee stain. Bed is for sex and sleeping, and nothing else.

Some guests have a penchant for being serenaded at dinner by a squeaky violinist playing a romantic tune, usually very badly. They even pay good money for this appalling invasion of privacy. I'd pay them to leave me alone and go and squeak at someone else's table, preferably in another hotel and on another continent.

One eye-poppingly expensive establishment I stayed at (roughly £1,000 a night if you please, plus light plane transfers) decided it would be romantic to allow couples to dine out on floating platforms in the bay. Not a bad idea in principle, but they put the platforms so close together that there is no hope of a private conversation, let alone a secret wedding proposal. You might as well sit at the same table as your floating neighbours.

They also decided it would be a smart idea to serve all the courses at once, bringing both you and your food to the platform together in a tinny fishing boat and leaving the trays of food there, covered in aluminium foil. There is nothing like having your supper left at your feet wrapped in cheap kitchen foil to make you feel really romantic. I wish I could identify this place but it would undoubtedly result in a legal writ. See me round the bike sheds afterwards and I'll whisper it to you.

The main problem is that romantic holidays are big business. Every luxury hotel has convinced itself that it is up to the challenge of satisfying kissing couples, honeymooners and fiftieth wedding anniversary guests, and of relieving them of their hard-earned cash. They certainly have perfected the latter objective, but the question of satisfaction often leaves a lot to be desired. As well as being a luxury hotel addict I am a die-hard romantic and, in my well-travelled opinion, only a tiny percentage of luxury hotels are truly and unquestionably romantic.

You might disagree with my personal choices and wonder why I have left certain places out. Croissants in bed, squeaky violins, and dinner wrapped in aluminium foil might be at the top of your list. If they are, you won't find me sharing the hotel with you – but then you probably would not want that anyway. I tend to be a bit picky and annoying.

What the following hotels all share is one thing – a magical, almost indefinable, romantic spirit. It is partly due to their natural surroundings, but mainly it is because of the inspired vision of the designers, owners, managers and staff. They have seen the potential, understood the desires of romantic couples, and delivered. They, too, I feel sure, are die-hard romantics who have simply thought: is this sexy enough for me to want to bring my partner here and fall in love all over again? The recipe is immensely hard to perfect, but I believe these romantic hotels have all got it.

My first pick is in Australia. The Observatory Hotel was the first luxury hotel I stayed at south of the Tropic of Capricorn. I had read about it in an in-flight magazine en route to a particularly non-luxurious news assignment in Texas: I interviewed a prisoner on Death Row, shared a cheap ground-floor motel room with a family of moths, and listened all night to the young men of Houston swear at each other and occasionally shoot a handgun somewhere in a nearby street.

Not daring to turn my light on for fear it might draw their attention, I grabbed my torch and shrank under the covers to read the article once more and dream of diving into the Observatory Hotel's pool after a hard day doing not a lot on Sydney Harbour. When I finally came to stay there in 1999, to write a pre-Olympics travel story for the *Guardian*, I found that the hotel was even more spectacular than I had thought and the moment I stepped into its discreet and chic lobby, I had no doubt that was the beginning of a beautiful friendship.

The Observatory Hotel is not like other luxury hotels. Of the hundreds I have stayed in and reviewed over the years, it is one of only four or five that I genuinely miss. I reminisce about the place when I am far away or squeezed into an aeroplane and craving a king-size bed. It is still my temporary home when I am back in glorious Sydney.

There are several reasons why it has remained in my Hotel Heaven Top Ten since then.

First of all, there is no question you are in Sydney: the rooms look over the rooftops of the historic Rocks district, the site of the original convict settlement of Port Jackson. The settlement was built on a narrow peninsula whose sandstone outcrops jut out into the harbour – and now support the southern buttresses of the Harbour Bridge.

The vista also includes East Darling Harbour which used to be the lifeblood of Sydney's maritime trade. This was the port area before the Botany Bay terminals were built further south near the airport to handle almost all the freight.

Bright yellow and green Sydney ferries beaver about daily across the harbour, bringing commuters to work and then reloading with sightseers for day trips. The yellow and black chequerboard markings of water taxis dash about between them, skirting around the small sailing boats on leisurely harbour cruises.

I was enjoying a nightcap on my balcony one late summer evening when the view was interrupted by the departure of a gigantic freight ship, which had spent the day disgorging its cargo of Korean cars. The thousands of tiny metal boxes were all neatly lined up on the port's asphalt apron, shimmering like jewels in the moonlight, when their mothership set off on its return journey. I dreamed that night of the ship's voyage and wished it calm waters as it headed back to the Korean winter. I woke at 7 AM to find an even bigger cruise ship had taken its place. Sometime in the dead of the warm night, it had squeezed underneath the coathanger of the Harbour Bridge and eased up to its moorings. Its eager passengers were hurrying off the gangplanks like a colony of ants which had recently scented a very large honeypot. I could feel the thrill of their anticipation: a new port, a new city, a new continent.

Sadly, the ships have recently stopped docking here but their graceful hulls still glide past silently to alternative moorings nearby.

The view also takes in the main part of Darling Harbour with its museums and restaurants, and from the front entrance of the hotel it is a short walk under the Moreton Bay fig trees and past the solid and stately sandstone buildings of the Rocks to the Harbour Bridge, and to the site where the First Fleet landed in 1788 and set up Port Jackson.

While the views from the Observatory Hotel left me in no doubt where in the world I was, there was a much more powerful feeling engendered: a palpable sense that I was travelling in style. I have since read descriptions of the hotel – I might even have written them myself – which suggest it has rekindled a touch of genuine old-fashioned travel romance. While this is true, it is far from being some stuffy tribute to Victoriana. The owners, Orient-Express Hotels Trains & Cruises, have taken the best ideas from the first Golden Age of luxury hotels and fused them with the demands of modern travellers.

The hotel's logo is a three-masted clipper sailing over the top of the globe, with the Southern Cross shining down from a night sky. It's the sort of classic travel image you might find in old English gentlemen's clubs or in the hallowed halls of the Royal Geographical Society in London, yet it has become a modern iconic symbol among Australia's hotels. With the exception of the sparkling Hilton and the Four Seasons, I can group the rest of Sydney's luxury hotels together, although they will hate me for doing so. They are relatively ugly metal towers hugging the harbour front and commanding views of the bridge, Circular Quay and the white sails of the outer harbour.

The Observatory stands alone, both physically and stylistically. It is removed from the glitzy peacock crowd. It is different, maybe slightly aloof, but then it has reason to feel superior. Its finesse and charm have engendered jealousy among its less sophisticated rivals.

Another five-star hotel went to some lengths to tell me the Observatory lied about its celebrity guest list but let me tell you, if I was a celebrity in Sydney for a film premier, I wouldn't even look at another hotel.

I have no reason to doubt the Observatory's claims to have played host to Gwyneth Paltrow, Ewan McGregor, Hugh Jackman, Priscilla Presley, Kylie Minogue and Monty

Python globetrotter Michael Palin. Anyway, they have all signed the guest book. And I know the famous violinist and the world's most ardent Aston Villa Football Club supporter, Nigel Kennedy, stayed there because I bumped into him in the lobby as he was running out for a rehearsal at the Opera House.

The last time I saw him there he was having a wardrobe malfunction involving a missed button on his trousers. If not for the diligence of the concierge they might have fallen to his ankles that night on stage halfway through Vivaldi's *Four Seasons*.

My paparazzi acquaintances in Sydney back me up on the hotel's celebrity count too, saying they have spent many a night huddled outside on Kent Street waiting to snap celebrities coming or going.

Fun as it is to bump into famous guests, what satisfies my luxury hotel addiction is that the Observatory is chic, elegant and romantic all at the same time, and it always makes me feel special. It goes beyond merely giving me enough to write a glowing review – it transcends into the personal. It is the only truly world-class hotel in Australia, and the luxury benchmark for all others to aim at.

The intimate and cosy Globe Bar is lined with oak-panelled walls and shelves of books – just the kind of place where you might expect to be approached, with all the speed of a glacier, by an antique waiter who has been working there for 156 years and can barely hold his pen straight to take your order. In fact, you are met by young, confident, preppy Australians who don't need pens and paper and who can reel off the drinks menu and most of the wine list from memory.

The hotel's restaurant, Galileo, has been a Sydney favourite for years. It is where, back in 1999, I had one of the best

meals of my life. I am the sort of travel writer who risks letting my food go cold in order to find out exactly what part
of the New South Wales coastline my oysters have come
from, and which river system in the Northern Territory
is tapped for the barramundi. I feel the need to discover
why the Margaret River Cape Mentelle Cabernet Sauvignon
goes better with duck than with filet mignon, and why Sydney – like no other city on the planet – has so much exquisite fresh produce year-round, and then share this valuable
knowledge with my loyal readers. Galileo knew it all and
was even happy to share a couple of recipes with me.

During the eight years I lived in Australia, and having
spent a deliciously substantial proportion of that time dining in hotel restaurants, nothing came close to Galileo's
stellar performances. Chefs may have come and gone, and
the menu may have morphed and evolved with Sydney's
rapidly changing trends, but a recent return visit left me in
no doubt that the restaurant is still at the top of its game.

The Japanese executive chef, Harunobu Inukai, is dreaming up Franco-Japanese dishes that guarantee diners new
tastes. Not only is the food gastronomically precise and delicious but it's also fun. I am seriously considering waiting
for Chef Haru in a sidestreet of The Rocks and mugging
him to get hold of his recipe for cos lettuce soup and capsi-
cum ice-cream.

And, while I'm at it, I might grab hold of the sommelier
as well. Never in a decade of luxury travel writing have I
had wines as exquisite as those he offered at a degustation
evening recently. I am told he engages in endless research to
find obscure and different wines from around the world. I
doubt if anyone else could have persuaded me to try a Salo-
mon Undhof 'Wachtberg' Gruner Veltliner from Austria. It
sounded more like a 1960s Porsche racing car. Does Austria

even make wine? Well, yes it does – and the Gruner Velt-liner is a little cracker, and the perfect accompaniment to Chef Haru's salmon terrine.

I am unbearably fussy when it comes to so-called 'fine dining', and I hardly leave a restaurant without at least half a dozen niggling little faults scrawled angrily in my note-book. Not at Galileo. There is simply nothing wrong with it, apart from the fact that, eventually, you have to say good-bye, pay the bill and be shown the door.

The Observatory Hotel scores big for romantics too. It is the most dreamy property in Australia, with its sister ho-tel Lilianfels (in the Blue Mountains) running a close sec-ond. The rooms are intimate, decorative and cosy. There's a hint of Louis XVI and some splashes of Aussie floral deca-dence with big bold curtains displaying flowering purple plant patterns. The rooms are intimate and decorative, with low ceilings which add to the cosy ambience. Downstairs is a subterranean spa and pool that owes much of its de-sign to ancient Rome. After you have dived in, surfaced and expressed your pleasure by issuing a long and relaxed 'aaaah', you can float on your back and look above you to find a scaled-down version of the night sky laid out on the ceiling.

It continues the astronomical theme of the hotel, but is also one of the most powerful trompe-l'œil devices that any hotel has come up with. For a few seconds you actually believe you are stargazing. Steam rooms and saunas are just off to the side and on the floor above is the spa, a series of rooms offering everything from your standard deep tissue massage to treatments involving Tibetan bells and glow-ing coloured lights to realign your charkas. The Romans would have loved the Observatory Hotel. Had they extend-ed their empire a little more broadly, they might have found

Australia, built a huge complex of baths that looked something like this, then shipped in as many concubines and
amphorae of wine as their ships could handle.

If your inner Roman ever takes over and you find yourself driven by the notion of re-mortgaging your house to
fund a private orgy, try to persuade the Observatory to rent
out their pool. Invite your sexiest friends and pay the staff
big tips to go home early, say nothing and lock the doors
behind them. I imagine Orient-Express Hotels would have
to refuse your large cheque in order to maintain their reputation for style and finesse, but it would be fun trying.

While we are loitering Down Under and speaking of
things Roman, here's a news flash: there is a new resort just
opened on Hamilton Island up on the Great Barrier Reef,
which is called qualia. The lower-case 'q' is not a typo, it's
how the hotel likes it. Lower-case, low-key. Get it?. Latin
scholars will immediately be able to translate this into
something like 'the properties of sensory experiences'.

A confession first: I have not visited this hotel so I cannot give you a critique. It opened just a few weeks after I
had moved to live in the Middle East but the place looks
drop-dead gorgeous, and apparently they have gone all-out
on the dining. It also looks a lot more private and secluded
than many Great Barrier Reef resorts which can be a bit,
well, Costa del Aussie shall we say. I'm packing my bags.

Majestic dining is also a big factor at another of my favourite romantic hotels, the Sila Evason Hideaway resort,
which occupies the far north-eastern tip of Koh Samui,
Thailand's original party island.

Koh Samui is past its sell-by date but ignore that because
the Sila Evason Hideaway is most definitely fresh and enticing and well-placed at the far end of the island so you
can completely avoid the fleshpots further south. When you

land at the island's cute little airport and pick your bags off the ingenious wooden luggage carousel, find your driver – dressed in a beige Sila Evason Hideaway outfit – and follow the Monopoly principle: go straight to the Sila Evason Hideaway, do not pass Go and do not go to Lamai or Chaweng.

Reception is a wide deck, floored with old railway sleepers shipped over from the Thai mainland. The designers had great vision – the view is captivating. The deck looks out over a channel, towards the northern island of Koh Phangan. When I first visited Koh Samui and Koh Phangan in 1989 with my school friend Adam, we were unwashed, layabout backpackers looking for hedonism on a shoestring budget. We found it here. We employed a 13-year-old fishing boy to take us over to Koh Phangan with some American and Canadian girls we had befriended. The trip took just under an hour in the boy's longtailed boat, which broke down in the middle of the ocean channel a number of times. But we had bottles of beer and two or three joints, the sun was shining, we were tanned, lean, healthy and free from all commitments, and we were all going to have sex later that evening on a beach, so we could not care less.

Back in 1989 I eschewed anything five-star and considered a night on a strange tropical island lying under the stars on a rush mat with a warm, fragrant and free-thinking American backpacker to be the very height of luxury.

It felt strange returning to Koh Samui more than fifteen years later – not quite so healthy and with numerous commitments – and staring down at that same stretch of water. Now I wanted luxury everything, and I have been known to descend into a black mood if I do not get it.

'You check in?' a voice said, dragging me back from my reverie.

I apologised to the Sila Evason Hideaway's guest relations officer, handed over my credit card and said I was the travel writer, here to write a review of the hotel. I also asked, 'Do you get this a lot, people having difficulty checking in with that view to distract them?'

The girls behind the desk laughed and covered their mouths with their hands.

'Yes,' said one. 'Sorry we laugh, but yesterday two guests come here and check in, from Australia, and they start cry. It was man and woman. They met here 30 years ago – over there on that island.' She pointed to a small rocky outcrop in the channel known as Laem Samrong.

'This resort was not here then. Now they married. The woman get out of the car and look at the island and the water and she just cry, right there,' said the girl, pointing to the edge of the deck from where the view is best.

'And the man?' I asked.

'He cry too. Both cry. So much cry, could not check in. Had to do check in later in the villa.' The girls giggled so much they almost started crying.

'Yeah, they are a bit like that in Australia,' I said. 'They're a sentimental bunch.'

I knew how the couple had felt. That view is enough to make grown adults break down and cry for joy, whether it brings back memories of where you found the love of your life, or just of some chill-out time with a backpacker from Salt Lake City (I think her name was Stella).

It is the only reception area of any hotel that has induced such an emotional response from me. Usually lobbies and reception desks are formal places where I greet managers, announce myself, swap business cards, say how delightful it is to be there, pass on regards from editors, and generally do a lot of travel writer diplomacy.

The managers do it too. It is a mutual back-slapping session which can last from a couple of minutes to a full hour. I am trying to convince the manager that this is strictly business and not a free holiday, and that at the end of it I am going to have to write a fair and honest review. The managers are thinking: 'We're giving you the best suite and not charging you a cent, you had better bloody like the place.' On 95 per cent of occasions we get on famously and everything works out fine. It can be very enjoyable, especially when we find we have mutual friends on different continents and can show off to anyone else who is listening.

'Have you seen the new Shangri-La in Abu Dhabi yet?'

'Yes, isn't it marvellous? Did you eat at Bord Eau?'

'Yes, we did. Superb.'

'Did they send a Rolls to meet you at the airport?'

'Splendid.'

'Marvellous.'

And so it goes on, this travel expert tennis rally, with each of us heaving gloating forehands over the net. It must be painful for anyone nearby, but I quite enjoy it because it reminds me that even though I get paid a pittance to write these articles I do get to lead, at least for part of each year, a seriously jetset lifestyle.

I knew right away that the Sila Evason Hideaway was going to be different and special, because the usual reception arse-kiss session was devoid of even a peck on the cheek.

The Swedish general manager, Eric Hallin, magically appeared from a secret stairway in the floor behind the desk, and greeted me with a warm, soft handshake. He was dressed all in white and had a wide, easy smile. He was so utterly relaxed that I wondered if I had disturbed him from a nap or a spa treatment. Being a hotel manager is one of the most stressful jobs known to humankind, yet Eric had the placid demeanour of a yoga teacher who had just spent two weeks attaining nirvana at a Buddhist retreat.

I had not seen anyone this blissed out and calm since the afternoon I spent interviewing the reggae star Eddy Grant at his Blue Wave studio in Barbados. Eddy and I lazed around talking about music, and he spent half an hour telling me how the Rolling Stones had recorded their Voodoo Lounge album there and how the record got its name: Keith Richards rescued a kitten from a drainpipe in a rainstorm and christened it Voodoo. Then he found a shoebox for the kitten to dry off in and wrote 'Voodoo's Lounge' on the side.

Not a lot of people know that.

Eddy could have told this story as quickly as I have here, but on that long, blurry Barbadian afternoon it took forever.

Eric Hallin and I did not discuss other hotels or travel editors or when we were last in Monte Carlo, or the Rolling Stones for that matter. We did not discuss anything at all other than which villa my partner and I were to stay in, and if we would like to join him for lunch.

Eric was, I came to learn after a day or two at the resort, one of life's naturally relaxed people. The benefit of this for guests is that they are put at ease from the moment they arrive. I cannot tell you how many luxury tropical island retreats ruin the magic of their location by having overly officious staff or busy little bustling managers who flit in and out of doorways pretending to be important, and speedwalk down corridors as if they are heading towards a fire that needs putting out.

There are no signs, but I am pretty sure the Sila Evason Hideaway has a walking speed limit of a half a mile per hour, and that is precisely the pace you want when you are escaping from the city and work and family and stress.

The soporific atmosphere is intoxicating. After a day or two, the 150-metre walk to the hilltop restaurant seemed such a struggle to my partner and me that we lay like discarded towels on the day bed by our pool, and flipped a frangipani flower to see which one of us had to get up and crawl to the phone to call our butler and ask her to bring a spicy Thai salad and some more Singha beers.

One day we managed to slouch down to the spa where, in private treatment rooms overlooking the ocean, we lay next to each other while no fewer than four Thai masseuses (two each) gave us massages, rubbing us with smooth river stones coated in aromatic oil. We floated back to our villa on the afternoon breeze, unable to speak or carry anything heavier than a hibiscus blossom. We tried to read books and failed. Instead, we smudged the first pages with sunscreen thumbprints and let them fall to the wooden decking around the pool.

I tried to write my review and spent hours over each sentence, unable to concentrate. My eyes followed a wagtail as it hopped along the ridge of our villa's thatched roof, and then flew over to the one next door and did the same skipping dance. Then I caught sight of a tropical bird soaring higher and further out over the waves. My partner dragged herself to her feet and fell into the pool, taking so long to surface that I thought she had fallen asleep on the bottom. I joined her, and together we floated hand-in-hand, gazing up at the wagtail and the tropical bird and the opalescent sky.

We were reconnecting, rediscovering each other. We were falling in love once more. No words had to be spoken. All we had to do was drift and drink in the blissful beauty around us. This is what Sila Evason Hideaway does so well.

The views of the sparkling expanse of the Gulf of Siam;

the beautiful teak-wood villas with their sensuous white beds and silky smooth plunge pools; the delightful, breezy hilltop restaurant; the quiet protected beach; the little Thai butlers who scuttle in and out unseen, bringing pots of green tea and leaving small sachets of fragrant oils under the pillows; and the general contagious torpor. They all work seamlessly together to dissolve the pressures of every-day life and leave guests with nothing else to do than love and be loved.

The only downside to Sila is that space is at a premium on this rocky outcrop at the tip of the island. Some villas are close together and are overlooked by others, and the foliage between them is scant – so ask for one that is higher up the hill so you can do the overlooking.

Here's the most romantic bit of all: after a day of frenetic activity lying horizontal by the pool, you can hop into your outdoor shower (plenty of room for two), dress up in your best tropical evening wear, stroll down the hill and have supper with your beloved on a huge wooden deck under the stars. The deck is a masterpiece of engineering, jutting out several metres from the rocky shoreline and over the crashing waves below. There are eight or nine different levels and areas, so you can spread out and whisper sweet nothings away from your fellow guests. The balmy night air wraps around you, the candlelight sparkles in your partner's eyes, and somewhere in a secret kitchen out of sight and earshot a German chef called Thomas is busy creating culinary delights – like Maine lobster with wasabi ice-cream, iced tom-yum gazpacho, and Barbarie duck with chutney and fennel.

The dark seashore is gradually illuminated by the sway-ing lamps of shrimp boats as they prepare for a night's trawling. High in the heavens, shooting stars fall from the sky. If you have been waiting for the perfect location to propose, this is it.

In a decade of luxury travel writing, I have only found a handful of truly romantic beachside resorts. There are heaps of terrific beach hotels for hedonism, for culture, for diving and for generally showing off in a pair of Speedos, but surprisingly few that hit the romance buttons.

Another joining the Sila Evason Hideaway in my Hotel Heaven is Fiji's Yasawa Island Resort. Yasawa means 'heaven' in Fijian, so I had a pretty good feeling I would be on to a winner when I organised to stay.

There, too, the romantic principle is the same: provide sumptuous food and immaculate service in a breathtaking location and let lovers do what they do best when the weather is warm and their time is their own.

The resort is on one of the Yasawa Islands off the west coast of Fiji's main island, Viti Levu. You get there by boat-plane, which is a thrill in itself, and touch down dramatically just offshore. Jumping into the knee-deep water is one of the best feelings anyone can have at the start of their holiday, but if you are wearing your best Manolo Blahniks call for help; there is bound to be a strong Fijian man nearby to carry you to the beach.

When I dropped in to stay I was welcomed quietly and calmly, and my bags disappeared so quickly that I felt sure the tide had carried them off. To my immense relief, there weren't any of those infuriating welcome songs that so many South Pacific resorts put on for guests when they arrive or depart or whenever the staff need a bit of singing practice. You can see them gathering and strumming their ukuleles as your plane prepares to land. I know the vast majority of guests love it and recount to their friends how the staff 'sang' them in and out of their holiday. Maybe I am being a big old snobby grouch here, but it all seems so phoney.

The only welcome song I can bear is the one performed by a guy at Rarotonga Airport in the Cook Islands, and I only pay any attention to that because the poor bloke has to stay up all night to greet bewildered, time-twisted fliers who invariably land at 3 AM. He is always chirpy and pleasant and he's got a pretty good voice. The rest of them should be banned from ever singing or playing an instrument.

I detest 'hello' and 'goodbye' songs at hotels and resorts with as much passion as I loathe forced group activities and wretched, wretched dinner entertainments and cabarets. I had to run out of a restaurant in a resort in Samoa once because a fabulously beautiful Polynesian dancer was pulling me from my seat towards the stage, encouraging me to make a complete arse of myself by doing a hula with her. I had just consumed a vast plate of sashimi, followed by at least a full quarter of a yellowfin tuna, several yams and a bottle of respectable Chablis, but I still managed to wriggle free from her clutches and sprint for the door.

Yasawa has none of that nonsense. It is a beautiful, sexy, romantic beach resort for beautiful, sexy, romantic adults. There are no kids running around demanding ice-creams, sticking their inquisitive fingers into crabs' claws and getting their feet skewered by sea urchin spines. The clientele is rich, intelligent, successful and romantic. They want the finest food, wine and service, preferably on a par with what they get back home in London, New York or Sydney. They want things to work. They want their demands met on their time, not Fijian time. And they want peace and quiet. Yasawa delivers on all counts.

On the Yasawa's dive boat I fell to talking with a stockbroker from San Francisco who had been a hippy in the 1970s

and had devised a personal strategy for being both capital-
ist and socialist at the same time. I was deeply jealous and
begged him to tell me his secret. He was also an expert on
hammerhead sharks, of which I was less envious.

In the sublime pool I met a business consultant from New
Zealand who was taking some time out with her husband
from a hectic year. We flopped about in the tepid water,
drinking gin and tonics and nibbling at rectangles of Kapiti
blue cheese, discussing the merits of web-based travel agencies and how it could be that our magical ice-cubes were not
melting in the sunshine.

In the wonderful Baravi Spa, opened only late in 2006, I
drifted off into a secret world as two masseuses performed a
synchronised rhythmic massage known as Baravi Rhythm,
which they do in time with the waves crashing on the beach.
It is the only time I have fallen fast asleep in the massage
table. It took a lot of head-patting and shoulder-shaking to
wake me.

At pre-dinner cocktails I met a man from Sydney who
had made his fortune from selling roses to love-sick Sydney-
siders. He was determined, gutsy and interesting. His wife,
fresh from the altar, was dazzlingly beautiful, and arrived
at dinner each evening in a new designer frock. Collette
Dinnigan followed Lisa Ho followed Scanlan & Theodore.
I felt sure she had disobeyed the strict fifteen-kilogramme
weight limit for luggage on the boat-plane and wondered
how she had got away with it.

At dinner we all dispersed to private tables, where the
romance could continue. The staff were clearly all summa
cum laude graduates of the Hotel Heaven School of Love and
Romance. I watched them as they approached each table to
serve or clear or refresh glasses. About ten metres out from
each they made a lightning-quick assessment. If it looked

like a man was about to drop to one knee and propose, they pulled up deftly and diverted to another table, like a jet on final approach which has suddenly spotted another plane on its runway. They waited for breaks in conversation or for the interruption of laughter before approaching, lest they disturb the moment. It was fascinating to watch. I had only seen such skill twice before: at the Savoy in London and the Istana in Bali. I made joyous notes in my little notebook.

Many luxury resorts in Fiji say they can only train their staff to a certain level, because then the laid-back island culture kicks in and lethargy takes over. Yasawa disproves this entirely. The staff were impeccable and yet they retained their Fijian cheekiness. Some guests encouraged them, and the waiters and porters duly dropped their guard and chatted and laughed. Other guests did not, and the Fijians remained alert and formal. Any beach resort that wants to be considered a truly romantic escape should tell its managers to catch the next boatplane to Yasawa to see how it is done.

Another major romantic plus for Yasawa is that the price includes all meals, which means couples who are not loaded and who have saved hard for their stay do not have to worry about a mounting hotel bill as they dine each evening: the lobster is on tap 24 hours a day. I naively thought the booze was too and asked for a look at the wine list. My eyes stood out like organ stops when I spotted a bottle of 1990 Louis Roederer Cristal. Could this be possible? A place on the beach, washed by balmy night breezes, and a bottle of Cristal champagne as part of my rate? Not quite. Booze is extra, which is understandable given that champagne lushes like me might be tempted to skip off home with a few bottles clinking in their beach bag.

If you book Yasawa far enough in advance you can secure the Honeymoon Suite, which is one of the places from where I have had to be dragged kicking and screaming to reception for check-out. They call it Lomalagi, which also means 'heaven' in Fijian. So you can quite legitimately tell your friends that while you were on your holidays, your temporary address at Lomalagi Villa at Yasawa translated to 'Heaven, Heaven, Fiji Islands'.

Lomalagi is separated from the rest of the bures, tucked away at the northern end of the beach. It has a big deck, a large and luscious freshwater pool and a hammock built for two, all shaded by coconut palms. You can choose to walk up the beach for supper or call the front desk, who will send a man in a four-wheel-drive to escort you there and back along the bumpy road that snakes up and down the low hills at the back of the beach. If you want complete privacy, place the painted coconut at the edge of the villa steps. It acts as a romantic forcefield, repelling all visitors.

Of course, luxury and romance do not just meet hand-in-hand on a tropical beach. Some of the world's most romantic hotels are in cities. One is within a few steps of Piazza San Marco in Venice. Despite the occasional pungency of Eau de Venice when the tides do not adequately clear out the canals, you must go there at least once in your life. It is achingly romantic. Stone bridges arch gracefully over side-canals, gondolas drift quietly through the 'streets', the waters lapping at their jet-black bows.

My introduction to Venice could not have had worse timing. I had been commissioned to write an article about the romance of the city, yet found myself flying in to Marco Polo Airport just a month after the painful but necessary break-up of an eight-year relationship. Suddenly I was plunged back into the wide and bewildering field of singles and dating and cooking for one. I was floating, disheartened and anchorless, at the dark, far reaches of the romance galaxy. To add to my gloom it was late January, the bleakest and most mournful of times.

Venice was enveloped in sea mists that seeped along the canals and sucked the last bits of warmth from its ancient stones. People walked about in long black coats and capes with hoods. It felt like a town in the grip of a secret cult, as if the Illuminati had risen again and were making a stronghold here in Venice. The Venetians spoke in whispers, and even the echoes of their fine Italian soles were dulled by the omnipresent fog. They emerged from the opaque gloom quite suddenly, snuggling their chiselled cheekbones inside their fox and mink furs to keep warm. And that was just the men.

It was shortly before Carnivale, when masks, harlequin pantaloons and velvet capes of the Commedia dell'Arte are donned and Venice becomes a city of hijinks and flirtation. This was the grey sober cloak before the parties begin, wine flows, and the colour and the tourists return to chase the grey phantasms back out to the distant reaches of the lagoon.

Yet, even in this breathless, paralysed corner of the year, when the rich ochres and terracottas of the roofs and doorways are drained of pigment and the late winter agues weep under doorways, Venice is still romantic.

I woke early one morning, before even the priests were stirring. Somewhere out east, beyond the Lido and over the Adriatic Sea, a feeble dawn was trying to break. The sun would be kissing the wings of the 747s at 35,000 feet as they headed west across Europe's sleeping plains and mountains bound for Heathrow, but no sun shone in Venice.

I walked damply across Campo Santo Stefano, which is one of the biggest squares in Venice, but that morning it seemed small and claustrophobic in the clinging mists. The cafés were still closed. I followed my little wet map to the Ponte dell'Accademia and made my way up the cold wooden steps and over to Dorsoduro. The first morning *traghetto* was feeling its way across the Grand Canal. Four people, tall and straight, stood in the bottom of the boat wearing black coats and hats, silhouetted against the dirty-white haze of the early morning. It looked like an advert for something refined and expensive, like a single malt or an American Express Platinum Card.

I waited for the *traghetto* to motor back to the Dorsoduro side of the canal, boarded and returned to the Santa Maria del Giglio boat stop. This time it was just me in the advert, a lone figure, alone in Venice and no longer in love. I walked for an hour more, taking unknown alleyways and paths along canals in an attempt to get myself lost.

In some squares the only sound was that of Venice's small army of street-sweepers performing their dawn ballet, brushing and pirouetting around each other dexterously, and scooping up into green buckets all the small biscotti wrappers and nub-ends of cigarettes left by yesterday's Venetians. They left the alleyways and piazzas swept and fragrant with the scent of orange blossom, the same unmistakeably Mediterranean smell that lingers on the air in Seville in the weeks before the Easter festivities each spring.

In a corner of Campo Santa Maria Zobenigo stood two black coats, joined as one. Their hoods met and moved slowly, in sync. They twitched and two plumes of breath rose into the clammy air. The sound of laughter floated across the square. The coats parted, just about a metre, before rejoining. More breath and more laughter. Time seemed to stand still, for the lovers and for me. I felt I was intruding on their passion so I moved on, alone, across Ponte

dell' Ostreghe. As if to goad me and remind me of my soli-
tude, the cooing echoes of their love followed me, ricocheting off the ochre brick walls of the palazzi.

I wondered what it would be like here in summer, with
men in white flowing shirts and women in flower-print
skirts and large sunglasses, and American tourists wearing Ivy League blazers and steering their mahogany motor
launches along the canals, pretending to be Roger Moore as
James Bond. People say the humid air in July and August
can smell rather like that of a bag of dead cats, but I bet it
would still be romantic. I made a mental promise to return
in July, with a lover.

Along Calle Larga XXII Marzo, past Gucci, Bulgari and
Ferragamo, I found the telltale arches near the Museo Correr and, in ten strides, was stepping out across Piazza San
Marco, just as the mists were beginning to thin and Venice
was re-emerging from its cocoon.

Florian's Café was just opening for another day of nerve-
wracking prices. A white-jacketed waiter emerged and began
setting up the wicker chairs. From somewhere deep inside
the café came the strains of Vivaldi and the faintly burnt
smell of coffee being ground. Across the square walked a
man in evening dress and a woman in a cocktail number,
a white cashmere shawl and impossibly high heels, heading home from a long night out. They felt neither the chill
nor the mists of that early hour, only each other's glow. She
carried a white rose. He pulled her towards a café, saying
he needed a quick espresso, but she tugged him onwards,
to bed. He shrugged his shoulders to the waiter setting up
the café and they broke into a run. At the far corner of the
square near the Museo Correr, where my recent footprints
still marked the wet flagstones, he lifted her like a ballerina,
making her scream with delight.

Otherwise, the piazza was deserted. Even the pigeons were still asleep. I must have chanced upon it on the only morning of the year when it was free from tourists.

The sky was lightening, shade by opaque shade, and beyond the Campanile and the statue of St Mark himself, and around the edge of the Palazzo Ducale, I saw the hotel in which I had spent the night and from whose warmth I had slipped two hours earlier, the Londra Palace. I was just in time for breakfast.

It took me a few years, but I did return to Venice in the summer. This time I had a lover, which was good, but she was in Australia and not with me in Venice, which was bad. At least I was in love; to visit Venice twice in a lifetime and be single, unloved and unanchored both times would surely be cause for concern. Only one canal smelled of dead cats, and that was because floating along in the green slime at the canal's edge was, in fact, a dead cat. Elsewhere the alleyways and piazzas were full of the scent of coffee and freshly baked panini, and lashings of Italian aftershave.

I took the public water bus (*vaporetto*) on day trips to the islands of Murano and Burano, and the Lido. I wore my finest Italian shoes, all the way from Milan via the Westfield Shopping Centre in Bondi Junction, and my bold-check trousers, which looked extremely smart and expensive but were in fact a £7 steal from an op-shop in New Zealand. Each day I made a habit of hopping off the *vaporetto* opposite Harry's Bar near Piazza San Marco and ploughing a furrow through the mumbling masses of tourists to get back to the Londra Palace.

It had a new general manager and had been through a radical style overhaul, which had left it looking even more fabulous than ever. The designers had managed to maintain the glories of the Venetian palazzo style, while bringing a lighter, modern touch to the lobby and restaurant. On shelves and tables were positioned spectacular sky-blue glass vases, made in the workshops of nearby Murano. More blue glass had been fashioned into corrugations and graced the front of the bar and the reception desk. The door handles of the rooms were also made from Murano glass – turquoise and sunshine-amber.

On the walls were artworks by Tiziana Priori, an Italian artist who had taken much inspiration from Tibetan prayer flags but had given them a Mediterranean feel. The hotel's most famous room, Room 106, had also been refurbished. This was the one that the Russian composer Pyotr Ilyich Tchaikovsky stayed in when he was living in Venice in 1877, gazing over the Grand Canal while writing the Fourth Symphony. His desk is still in use today.

The general manager, Mauro Zanotti, swept into the lobby from behind two theatrical curtains, looking as if he had just spent a few hours with his tailor, his hair stylist and then his grooming coach. He was the epitome of style, and in an instant I felt my fine Italian shoes and flashy New Zealand pants to be little more than cheap tokens offered at the altar of fashion by an obvious amateur. He spoke finer English than I did, breaking off only once to switch into fluent Spanish and French for two VIP guests who arrived shortly after me. He also speaks fluent German, and has a fair stab at Russian. He is handsome to boot, a natural wit and a pilot who flies his own plane. If he had not been charming, calm, genuine and kind, and someone with whom I struck up an instant rapport and began what has turned into a solid professional relationship, I would have lain in wait for him down an alley and pushed him into a canal for being so perfect.

Where was Mauro Zanotti when Roger Moore was filming

Moonraker in Venice in 1979? He would have been the perfect Venetian Mr Fix-It for 007 to rely upon. He would have had his own supercharged mahogany motor-launch, and made it available to Bond at the drop of a hat.

Mauro had saved Room 508 for me. It has a magnificent terrace and some of the best views in Venice. You can look out over the Bacino di San Marco, at the eastern end of the Grand Canal, across to the statuesque Campanile and dome of the Palladian basilica of San Giorgio Maggiore, which fatly occupies its own island. Next to Maggiore and separated by the narrow Canale della Grazia is the eastern tip of the Giudecca and the five-star Cipriani Hotel, one of the world's real greats. On my terrace I sipped mineral water and watched the Cipriani's motor-launch cruise back and forth every few minutes, carrying oil tycoons and their flamboyant wives.

A huge cruise ship appeared, dwarfing Maggiore and the rest of Venice. It sailed slowly past, on its way out to the Adriatic, with its passengers waving furiously from the decks. I did not wave back, but I thanked God and San Marco that I was not on board and rather was ensconced in what was fast becoming a Hotel Heaven Top Ten favourite.

The terrace in Room 508 is another perfect place for a marriage proposal, but you need to get your timing right. You could stay up all night, walking the streets and being romantic, and then get back to the room in time to open up the shutters, walk out on the terrace and pop the question at dawn as the first rays of sun wash the Campanile and the dome of San Giorgio Maggiore with warm yellow light. Or, you could wait until noon, when the bells of San Zaccaria, Basilica San Marco and all the other churches of Venice go off at once and the air is filled with their echoing music. I am convinced that every day somewhere in Venice a black-cloaked priest walks across a piazza with a large set of keys, opens a heavy and ancient wooden door, locks it behind him, and climbs some well-worn stone steps to a secret tower, where there is an elaborate computer display and a single button that he presses to trigger all the church bells simultaneously.

Or you could save the proposal and the soft murmurings of love for the hotel's waterfront Ristorante do Leoni. An impossibly beautiful Roman couple tried this while I was there. The man didn't get down on one knee, but whatever he said to his girl worked because she leapt up and sat on his lap and kissed him as if it was her last minute on Earth. The neighbouring tables burst into applause and the waiters gathered round to shake hands and offer complimentary liqueurs.

I was so fascinated by this scene that I had to pause from my delicious fegato alla Veneziana (calf's liver and onion) and glass of Chianti Reserva 2001 Il Grigio San Felice, and then I remembered that, despite being in love I was physically alone here in Venice. The only thing accompanying me at my table was a pile of press releases about the Londra Palace and a rather battered flight schedule, which flapped limply in the evening breeze coming off the Bacino San Marco. I kept my glass of Chianti going until 11 PM, when a glass of Vin Santo dessert arrived, courtesy of the manager. I nursed it for almost 40 minutes, bade *buona notte* to the waiters and went for a midnight walk around the deserted alleyways and canals. The ochre walls of the palazzi were still warm from the day's scorching temperatures, and in the corner of a piazza a couple folded around each other and became one. I was back in the Campo Santa Maria Zobenigo, where I had stood watching the lovers years ago in the February mists. Was this the same couple? Was this their special place, where they had always gone to be romantic in private, and where they would always go in the future, even when they were old and grey and held together with titanium bolts and braces? And would their ghosts continue to haunt this corner of Venice among the phantasmagorical fogs and the warm summer nights long after their bodies were returned to the earth? I liked to think so.

These hotels are all undeniably romantic and definite gateways to Hotel Heaven, but I have saved the best four until last. They are all in Bali. As I cannot decide which of them I like best, I try to stay at all four as often as possible. If you want to find Hotel Heaven, I highly recommend you adopt the same tactic.

Down at the beach in the cool, funky suburb of Seminyak stands the imposing Legian Hotel. Its walkways and water-courtyards are reminiscent of a Moorish palace in Morocco or Andalucia, while its stone staircases are more a homage to a Mayan temple in Yucatan.

I love this hotel, possibly more than any other. I love it for its staff, who have become like part of an extended family through my numerous stays. I love it for its double-infinity pool right next to the beach; you can swim to the edge of the big one and flop over a low wall into the second smaller one. I love its tandoori oven, from which comes the best Indian food I have eaten anywhere, including in India. I love it for its long, soft lounge chairs, where you can while away the day in the sun, reading and sleeping and recharging, and being brought cool, lavender-scented towels, iced water and face-freshening spritzer sprays. I love it for its afternoon teas of sticky rice cakes and pots of ginger tea, which appear at your lounger around 4 PM each afternoon and get you in the mood for cocktails and dinner.

I once saw a couple who were clearly as enamoured

with the hotel as I was. I spied them up on their balcony, the man standing behind the woman as the two of them danced slowly together in their bathrobes. 'How romantic,' I thought. They were obviously getting hot doing this dance, for the woman threw open her bathrobe and bared a pair of full, formidable breasts, kissed by the late-afternoon sun. The man was shorter and smaller than his partner and was all but hidden behind her solid Amazonian frame. His left hand was visible on her left shoulder and his right had firm hold of her long dark hair. He pulled her head back every now and then and she smiled. They were not dancing. They were having sex.

The formidable breasts swung backwards and forwards. Her hair fell down either side of them, brushing the nipples as she swayed in rhythm with her partner. I know all this detail not because I am a luxury hotel pervert, but because a) I am a trained observer of life and always take great interest in matters of the human spirit, and b) it is not every day you see a public demonstration of sexual abandon.

Contrary to what you might be thinking, I was not gawping at them through a pair of binoculars, open-mouthed, salivating and steaming up the lenses. In fact the situation was far more delicate and awkward. I was sitting with Hans Meier, the Legian's genial and charming general manager, having afternoon tea at a table near the lawn and conducting a formal interview for an article for the *Sunday Telegraph* in Sydney. He was facing the ocean and I was looking back at the hotel – as it happened, directly towards the amorous couple.

To their credit, they were silent, but the scene was somewhat distracting. I valiantly continued with my list of questions, keeping my focus on Hans and the teapot, and not on the soft-porn film that was showing over his right shoulder. I began to sweat a little and Hans suggested we move into his air-conditioned office, but I was scared he would stand up, turn around and see the lovers at it, and then worry that I might think this behaviour unbecoming of a luxury hotel. The tiniest things can throw the panic switch in a hotel manager, especially when he has a travel writer in-house.

'No, I'll be fine, I like it out here,' I said, before going into the finer details of occupancy rates and the plans he had to expand the restaurant. I asked him who designed the bathrobes and he told me they were made from a very tough, long-lasting cotton. I watched the man on the balcony putting considerable pressure on his partner's robe as he clung to it and moved in time with her – the robes would have to be tough to make it through that kind of assault unscathed.

A waitress arrived with two cold towels, which we used to mop our brows. I pressed mine to my face for a second or two, which helped things immensely, and as I took it away the show was over. The couple had disappeared back into their room and the balcony was deserted.

I hurried back to my room to impart the full detail of the public shagging to my partner. I suggested that, as this was such a romantic hotel, we might like to try something similarly naughty on our balcony – but maybe after dark, in case Hans spotted us. My eager, red-blooded suggestion elicited from her a long look of incredulity and a series of very rude words ending in '… must be bloody joking'. She was right, of course. Our balcony was even more open and public than that of the amorous couple. We might as well have done it on the lawn.

If public sex is not your ideal way of expressing love for your partner, then you might like to move to the Legian's deeply romantic private villas. Across the road from the main hotel, and through a well-guarded security gate, is a little bit of paradise called the Club at the Legian. Ten exquisite villas exist here, each within their own walled compound. They have three-metre walls for complete privacy, and are roughly 30 square metres in size.

Each villa also has its own plunge pool, which provides respite from the heat during the day and becomes a sexy plaything at night, when it is illuminated magically by lights built into the walls. There are few things more sensual than a naked midnight swim with your lover in your own pool, in your own secure and private villa, on a warm tropical night with the scent of frangipani in the air.

About half of each compound's area is occupied by its villa, which is fully air-conditioned and designed with simplicity and symmetry. A spacious living area sports a huge television and a DVD library, a sound system with Bose speakers, and – wait for it – a free mini-bar. But it is not just any mini-bar. There are three long, tall glass bottles marked W, V and G: whisky, vodka and gin. One of the tasks of your personal butler is to make sure these are fully topped up, 24 hours a day. The butler can also organise sumptuous meals in the villa or in the cute dining pavilion outdoors by the pool. All this means that lovers can operate on their own timeframe and not be reliant on set cocktail hours, mealtimes or other unromantic rules and regulations.

The villa bathroom is large – I have seen studio apartments in Sydney with less floor space – and features a 'rainforest' showerhead big enough to drench two people: ideal for lovers who cannot bear to be apart from each other, even for a moment.

Through a sliding door is an outdoor sunken bathtub. On my first visit I asked my butler to sneak in during the evening and fill it with water and scented oils and rose petals, and to arrange a cathedral's worth of candles around the edge, as a surprise for my partner. It looked dynamite. You know that look of wonder that flashes across your lover's face when you really get the romance right? It flashed.

And so to bed, in a four-poster made of dark-stained hardwood and with soft white muslin drapes to keep the mosquitoes out and to envelop you and your partner in blissful union.

If this has whetted your appetite then you will be delighted to learn that the Legian has an equally sexy sister, the Chedi Club. It is similarly designed, but is located up in the cooler highlands of Bali near Ubud. It occupies the 4½-acre private estate of Tanah Gajah near the Goa Gajah (Elephant Cave). Unique design features make this hotel overwhelmingly romantic and they all rely on one breathtaking element: a large, working rice field which lies adjacent to the property, offering peaceful views across a sea of vivid green, broken only by small prayer flags fluttering in the breeze.

Clearly a die-hard romantic designed the place, because some villa compounds have imaginative sliding bamboo doors which can be opened to allow an uninterrupted view of the rice field. Occasionally a discreet and demure Balinese rice farmer will walk past and say hi, but otherwise you have this paradise vista to yourself. You can drift in your pool and gaze on this scene for hours, letting the tranquillity wash over you. A similar view is offered to anyone who joins the yoga class at dawn most mornings, and those who indulge in the spa treatments, for both the yoga studio and spa rooms are built on the edge of the paddy and look straight out over its wide expanse.

I indulged my passion for volcanic mud wraps in the Chedi Club's spa one morning, and within half an hour was coated head-to-toe in grey sticky lava paste. This is my favourite spa treatment, mainly because it makes me feel wonderful but also because it makes me look like one of those terrifying tribal mud-men from Papua New Guinea. This satisfies my childish humour when I look in the mirror and do a mud-man dance, wearing nothing else but those flattering little paper panties that spas give you in a feeble attempt to cover your private bits. What you should never do when having a volcanic mud wrap is be seen by anyone other than your spa masseuse. Unfortunately, when I was ready to wash it off and have a steam bath, I mistook the door to the spa's bathroom for one to the outside porch, opened it, stepped out and elicited an Oscar-winning scream from a passing Japanese guest.

The Chedi Club wins the Hotel Heaven award for most romantic restaurant, too. The chairs and tables sit on a six-metre stone platform, which juts out dramatically into the rice field. At night it appears to float on a dark, whispering lake, lit only by small torches on stone pillars dotted around the rice field. Rice-paper candles light the tables.

A third guaranteed Bali romantic is the Balé, a minimal-ist white limestone-walled temple to luxe on the coast near Nusa Dua. The Balé is hardly a hotel at all but a clutch of 29 private villas, which climb up a gentle slope from the ocean.

Guests arrive in the semi-circular driveway and take an open, white terrazzo pathway past smooth columns and rectangular pools. At the end is a white space with white, modern, square chairs and sofas, and an eight-metre empty terrazzo counter. The only thing that confirms this is the reception area and not an art gallery space is the quiet hum of a phone and the smile of a diminutive receptionist peek-ing over the counter.

No other hotel I know can so rapidly induce a state of peace and tranquillity as the Balé. You instinctively know you have made the right choice and that every moment here is going to work wonders at repairing the stress-damage that life has caused your body and mind.

From the reception area, a wide staircase climbs up to a central piazza with more water features and the hotel's restaurant. It's here that first-time guests start to wonder if they are in Bali at all or if they have been transported to a *pueblo blanco* in Andalucia or an Arabian sultan's palace. The white walls, elaborate waterways and interlinking pools are straight out of a Moorish formal garden. The illusion is strengthened by the accent of the avant-garde general manager, Jose Luis Calle, who hails from Spain's secret, desert province of Extremadura. Jose is passionate about his beloved Balé and his staff.

'We want guests and staff to be part of one family – but at the same time our staff know they are here to be as professional as they can be,' he said. 'So far this system works well – it's a happy family.'

The architects have also brought some quirky touches to the hotel. Rather than having big signs saying 'Ladies' and 'Gents', which would detract from the minimalist smoothness of the central piazza, they positioned a line of wooden ducks leading inquisitive guests to the toilets, which are tucked away around a corner and behind stone walls.

'When guests ask, we can say, "Just follow the ducks, you will find your way there,"' said Jose.

Each of the Balé's villas is incredibly sexy and deeply romantic. The bed is huge and positioned on a raised terrazzo platform, and the wooden cabinets and panelling are dark chocolate in colour. There are some cute touches, like fresh flowers, and a collection of handmade soaps presented in different-coloured papyrus wrappers. Each villa has a small lawn and garden with frangipani trees and a king-size day bed, and some have views of the ocean. Each also has a divine plunge pool. The Balé must tap a low-calcium aquifer somewhere, for the pools have the softest water. It is like diving into wet silk.

Dedicated butlers wait in the wings, eager to supply bottles of champagne and frighteningly healthy meals from the spa menu. They are also ready to pass on the latest weather report and advise when the car is ready to take you down to the Beach Club for more lounging around and the promise of dinner for two under an arc of Balinese stars.

What is so refreshing about the Balé is that it is unswervingly adult. It is designed for couples who want to reconnect, be quiet and private, and luxuriate in each other's company. Some guests check in to their villas and never set foot outside until their butler comes to escort them to their airport transfer. Some will leave once a day only, to float down to the bar for a bellini at sunset.

And to cap it all off, Jose has introduced an inspired series of master-classes with healers, chefs, Chinese medicine practitioners, yoga teachers, colour therapists and other holistic experts, who stay at the hotel for tours of duty. There can be few spas anywhere in the world that offer the range of treatments found at the Balé: you can get well and truly cleaned out with colonic irrigation, get a dose of crystal therapy, take some shiatsu prodding and pummelling, and then have your colours balanced and your mind meditated. That's just day one. Guests who have been recently irrigated might find the line of ducks handy, in case they cannot make it back to their villa in time.

The combination of restrained décor, quiet luxury, a small clientele and a plethora of deep relaxation techniques makes the Balé one of the world's undeniably romantic hotels.

The fourth Bali beauty is little Tugu, a small but perfectly formed property right out at the beach in Canggu. The hotel is run by an endearing manager, Lucienne Anhar, whose father, Anhar Setjadibrata, owns the place and has filled it with the most incredible collection of Asian (mainly Indonesian) antiques. A magnificent seven-metre statue of a mythical bird called a garuda towers over the lobby.

Anhar Setjadibrata even transported an entire eighteenth-century Kang Xi temple from Java, where the demolition gangs were about to go to work on it. The teak pillars and beams were dismantled, shipped to Canggu and reassembled. It now offers an ideal spot for some very private dining.

Tugu also houses two delectable and dead sexy suites called Puri Le Mayeur and Walter Spies. They are both named after painters – Belgian and German, respectively – who loved the island. The suites are personal and quiet, just the sorts of places where you might find über-trendy designers like Kenzo and Ferragamo.

Sadly, the currents off the beach are so treacherous that you are likely to be carried over to Java in about half an hour, but that means you and your loved one have the perfect excuse to stay inside, curl up on a daybed and just be.

Chapter 11

In Excess

IN THE EVOLUTION of the luxury hotel, a mantra for success is not so much survival of the fittest as survival of the fattest. Whereas most luxury hotels are happy to offer excellent service, award-winning cuisine, drop-dead gorgeous suites and views over private white-sand beaches, a distinct clutch of properties feel this is nowhere near enough, and step everything up several gears. They simply cannot help themselves when it comes to excess. They do not just want to be big and bold; they want to have multiples of everything: kitchens, sports cars, private jets, wine cellars. So much so that you wonder how they can possibly afford it all, even when the rates are in excess of £1,000 a night.

Sometimes these overloads of luxe bring to mind the licentiousness of ancient empires. They believe life should be lived 24/7 at maximum volume and ultimate exclusivity with no restraint, and they make sure their VIP guests get seriously regal treatment.

It is the unfortunate lot of the luxury travel writer to infiltrate this largely unseen, diamond-encrusted world as often and as deeply as possible, and to experience what life really feels like up there in the stratospheric heights of overindulgence. This means travelling way beyond the standard luxury hotel sphere, for these hotels are in a category of their own.

Such immersion in gluttony is essential if you're to write accurately of the wonder of it all, which is why I found myself sliding gleefully into the back seat of a shiny black Mercedes in Hong Kong's Central region en route to the InterContinental Hong Kong Hotel and clutching my bright orange Hermès bag.

Just between you and me, I must confess I have never shopped at Hermès (because, annoyingly, I never seem to have a spare £3,000 in my wallet to buy anything), but I found the empty bag discarded in a Qantas business-class seat after a flight to Los Angeles and thought it might come in handy. It looks fabulous and always prompts approving glances whenever I check in somewhere posh. I usually put something light in it – an old T-shirt or a pair of beach shorts – to make it look as if I really have spent lots of money at Hermès. Then I seal the top just under the handle with orange tape, just in case the frightfully cheap and worn item falls out and my scam is uncovered. So far it has worked like a dream.

The Chinese driver of the shiny black Mercedes wore a smart grey suit and a peaked cap, and he had stood to attention and held the door open for me. Had he not had his right hand on the door handle I felt sure he would have saluted me.

'Good morning, Mr Brace. The traffic is good today, so we should be at the InterContinental Hong Kong in about fifteen minutes,' he said. He was obviously impressed by my Hermès bag.

'Shopping good today? Hermès very quality. Very expensive,' he said.

'Yes, very,' I said, trying to be nonchalant but secretly

wondering if he had taken a sneak peek inside the bag as I slinked into the car.

The Mercedes had tinted glass and electric everything, and between the two front seats was a small contraption with square spaces nursing chilled water bottles. The chauffeur eased the Mercedes into the traffic on Queen's Road, and promptly veered across several lanes with the confidence and authority of a driver in the US president's motorcade. The red taxis hooted their horns and made rude gestures but nothing ruffled the chauffeur.

He glared back at them with an expression that said: 'Look, pal, I'm big, black and shiny, I'm from the very important InterContinental Hotel and I have a VIP guest in the back, so get out of the way.'

This was style, this was luxury, this was what Alexander Walker told me about on the rooftop restaurant of the Hôtel Méditerranée in Cannes. I had made it to the pinnacle of hotel luxury. I sat back and smiled a self-congratulatory smile to myself.

'So this is what the hotel's VIPs get driven around in, is it?' I asked the chauffeur.

'Yes, Mr Brace,' he replied. 'But also no. Not every VIP.'

'Just the really special ones, eh?' I said.

'Well, actually we have better cars for other VIPs.'

My heart sank and dragged my ego down with it, to a dark and miserable place somewhere under the black leather seat where the balls of fluff and crumpled Hong Kong dollar notes go to die. There were other cars? Other cars better than my car?

Somewhere in this city some VVIPs who were more VI than me were being ferried around in the hotel's big, shiny black Bentley and a big, shiny black Rolls-Royce, and then overhead were a lucky few UIPs (Unbelievably Important

People) who were whirring in by helicopter. Those who get the Mercedes are Number 3 VIP. It is the bronze-medal position. One position lower in this automobile pecking order and you're hauling your bags on to the Star Ferry and catching the subway with everybody else.

Suddenly my Hermès bag did not seem so flashy. Suddenly I realised I still had a long way to go to taste the real succulent heart of absolute luxury. We shot into the tunnel that runs under Victoria Harbour and connects Hong Kong Island to Kowloon, flickered through the orange and white lights, and then shot out the other side and stopped at a set of traffic lights. I buzzed the electric window down and saw a small crowd of Japanese tourists waiting on the pavement and squinting at me, fumbling for their cameras. Big, black, shiny cars and chauffeurs usually mean celebrities. They expected to find a rock star filling their viewfinders, or a footballer, or at the very least someone from the television, but their confused and disappointed expressions told a different story. I was a bronze-medal nobody. They urgently turned their cameras to one side and started flashing away, because next to my big, shiny, black Mercedes was now standing the hotel's bigger, shinier, blacker Bentley. The drivers looked at each other and nodded a polite but subtle greeting. I looked in at the guests sitting in the back of the Bentley, who were reading copies of the *Financial Times* and the *South China Morning Post*. They did not look back. The lights turned green and, as if to remind me of my lowly VIP status, the Bentley with its VVIP cargo pulled away first, leaving my chauffeur to limp along in its slipstream like a courtier grovelling at his master's heels.

The VIP car hierarchy is now a part of all luxury hotels with a penchant for excess. And nobody does it better than the Burj Al Arab and the Emirates Palace in the United

Arab Emirates. The InterContinental Hong Kong and the Beverly Wilshire in Los Angeles might have one Rolls-Royce each, but the Burj Al Arab has a fleet of sixteen. They are all white and all dazzling and all available around the clock for guests. So whether you are heading for a business meeting with the ruler of Dubai, His Highness General Sheikh Mohammed Bin Rashid Al Maktoum, or popping down to the supermarket for a Mars bar, your Roller awaits. Presumably the drivers were kept busy in May 2006, when, according to the world's media, supermodel Naomi Campbell spent $1.8 million to book out the entire hotel for a three-day party to celebrate her thirty-sixth birthday. No doubt Naomi bedded down in the Royal Suite – the hotel's most expensive – which is on two floors, and has its own lift and revolving bed.

The Emirates Palace hotel, 125 miles down the coast from Dubai in Abu Dhabi, also has a garage worth millions. It might appear to be a relative pauper, having only two Rolls-Royces, but it makes up for it with a pod of two Maybachs and sixteen brand new 7-Series BMWs. My Pakistani chauffeur was not going to let any Bentley burn him off at the lights. Instead, after picking me up shortly after dawn at Dubai's airport, he decided to show me what the new snow-white BMW could do on a road with virtually no traffic. On the wide open freeway that links Abu Dhabi and Dubai he cruised out into the fast lane and opened her up to 90mph. We shot through a mini-sandstorm as it spun across the asphalt, leaving the dust swirling in our wake. At 100mph the big blue road signs became hard to read as they flew past, and the white and gold long-distance taxis we overtook looked like they were stationary.

At 110mph I had to stop taking photographs of grazing camels through the window because the desert landscape was blurring. At 120mph the car seemed to lift slightly from the road, reducing the friction to a mere soft hum. The chauffeur braked hard for a speed camera. 'I know exactly where they all are along this road,' he said with pride. Then he accelerated once more: 125, 130mph. He was going for the luxury hotel VIP land speed record. We peaked at 136mph and I felt the engine could have powered on to further with ease, but there was a distinct possibility we would become airborne at that speed and end up in a sand dune, which would have taken a lot of explaining to the Emirates Palace management.

'Some guests like to go very fast,' said the Pakistani chauffeur. 'Some of them have their own sports cars and racing cars at home so they like to see how fast we can go. Some guests ask for fastest car and fastest driver. Emirati police will catch you when you are speeding, but they also like going fast in cars so sometimes they say, "Okay, go, no ticket … nice car."'

Luckily for us the Emirati speed police were otherwise engaged that morning as the BMW rocket-ship tore up the highway. I was deposited at the vast drive-in reception area at the Emirates Palace in what seemed like minutes. Even the chauffeur looked at his watch and gave himself a congratulatory smile.

'Not my best time, but not bad.'

I asked his name.

'Michael Schumacher,' he said.

I watched Michael Schumacher purr his BMW back out into the sunshine in preparation for another quick lap of the United Arab Emirates before lunch, and headed inside feeling not unlike a *Star Trek* captain coming down to walking pace after a few hours of travelling at Warp Speed 9.

When it comes to luxury hotel excess, cars are flashy and

fun – but the real outrageousness is on display in the property itself, and you cannot get much more outrageous than the Emirates Palace, which opened in 2005 after an estimated construction cost of $3 billion. I doubt it will ever win any prizes for design, but for sheer audacity and shameless opulence it cannot be beaten.

Mere mortals like millionaires and luxury travel writers get dropped off and welcomed at the main reception area on Level 4, but for presidents, kings and emperors there is a separate entrance. I don't just mean a different door but an entirely different road. Back out on the highway, as you approach the hotel, and just past a huge smiling portrait of Abu Dhabi's much-loved and revered former President, His Highness Sheikh Zayed Bin Sultan Al Nahyan, stands Abu Dhabi's own Arc de Triomphe, a sandy stone arch with security bollards, guards and traffic lights, and a white dome and golden spire on top.

When the truly mighty rulers of the world come to stay, they enter the hotel here. Police stop traffic at a large roundabout, which, handily, has a VIP road right through the middle of it for special occasions – can't have the rulers driving around a mortal's traffic island, now can we.

The bollards under the Arc are ceremoniously lowered, the security guards stand to attention and the majestic ones are ushered in. This saves them driving another quarter of a mile down the road and then winding through the grassy lawns and flower beds of the hotel grounds, and it brings them directly to the fifth floor, the dead centre of the hotel, where a small clutch of super-secret, impenetrable and über-luxurious suites are located: sixteen Palace Suites and seven Ruler Suites.

The hotel built these suites (the most expensive of which cost more than £6,000 a night) so it could host meetings of the Arab League, which comprises 22 countries. All the heads of state can now stay in the same level of accommodation. Cataclysms of a Biblical nature await any hotel that shoves the King of Saudi Arabia or the Sultan of Oman into slightly less salubrious rooms than their counterpart rulers from Bahrain or Kuwait. All it would take is for Libya to invite Jordan over for a bowl of dates and a hubbly-bubbly, and suddenly the Jordanians would discover that the Libyans had an extra bed or more comfy sofas in their suite, or extra quantities of toiletries, and diplomatic relations would spiral dangerously out of control.

I did my homework on the Arab League's business and social diaries and planned my trip well away from their summit meetings. Had I been there during the shindig I would probably have had security guards stationed at either end of my bed, even though my room was a good hike from the Palace Suites, at the end of one of the hotel's two gigantic wings. And if you think this is an exaggeration, bear in mind that the hotel building covers 300,000 square metres, which is roughly 42 full-size football pitches. (The overall site, including the pools and gardens and beach, is one million square metres, and a walk around the boundary will cover roughly one and a half miles.)

I usually have a good sense of direction but I still got lost. I had tried counting the number of palm trees and Swarovski crystal chandeliers (the hotel has 1,002 of the latter), in the hope I could count the same number back again and retrace my steps. Not the brightest of ideas, admittedly. Luckily, the hotel has contemplated the 'lost guest' scenario too, for it simply wouldn't do to have wealthy inhabitants collapsing of thirst on the premises after walking for hours to find the swimming pool – you can do that just a mile away in the desert. So, 30 interactive touch screens are located strategically throughout the hotel, with maps and directions, along with an overwhelming number of signs, and there is an army of 1,000 Emirates Palace staff members to send out search parties to rescue you. They even have little golf buggies which can locate guests in minutes and scoot them off to their destination in comfort. One corridor is almost long enough for any golf-mad Arab sheikh to practise his long, low drive without having to go outside into the heat. Just watch out for the chandeliers, there's a good chap.

Being at the hotel between Arab League meetings meant the suites were free for me to take a quick sticky beak. So what do the world's richest and most powerful rulers get for their squillions of dirhams and rials? Oodles of floor space, made with wood and inlaid marble, and covered with carpets so soft you would swear they had been weaved from the coats of a couple of thousand mink. What I thought was the main part of the suite turned out to be merely the reception area, complete with gold and silver pillars, mosaic-tiled alcoves with vases of fresh flowers, and Swarovski crystal chandeliers hanging from the high ceilings. At least ten employees of the Emirates Palace work as a team to keep the Swarovskis free from dust and muck. I feel sure there is scope for a niche hotel employee convention somewhere in the not too distant future. The Swarovski chandelier-dusters from Emirates Palace could spend two or three days swapping notes on the intricacies of cleaning very expensive things with the gold-leaf toucher-uppers from the Ritz in London, and the vacuumers from the Ritz-Carlton in Singapore.

Each suite has several bedrooms: one for the all-powerful majestic one, and the others for wives, foreign ministers, secretaries, financial advisors, life coaches, personal trainers, pillow-fluffers … take your pick.

The main bedrooms are so big that they make the king-size bed look more like a pull-out futon, and their ceilings feature deep, golden, inlaid domes illuminated by recessed lighting. For day-time lounging there is a beautifully up-holstered chaise longue by the window, and numerous other sofas and armchairs scattered around the rooms. They make doing nothing seem highly appealing. There are silver-plated sinks in the bathroom, a private dining room (more Swarovski, more Arabic alcoves), and a private terrace overlooking the Persian Gulf, so the leaders can wander outside and wave hello to their oil reserves.

The front doors of these suites lead you into the hotel's huge central atrium, above which arcs the biggest of the property's 114 domes, which, at 42 metres wide and 68 metres high, is one of the largest in the world. It is finished with a mosaic of silver- and gold-coloured glass tiles, and on the apex sits a gold finial. Those among the wondrous rulers who are not vertigo sufferers can peek over the fifth-floor atrium balcony and watch the peasants walking around below on the expansive multi-coloured marble floor, whose octagonal centrepiece mimics the vast dome above it. From this core the two wings of the hotel stretch away east and west. Each is the size of a fairly substantial city hotel and yet houses only 151 rooms.

The hotel has only 400 rooms in total, which means that even when it is full the staff still outnumber the guests. But it boasts 130 kitchens and kitchenettes, and seven restaurants, one of which has a sommelier to guide you not only through the wine list but also through the 40 varieties of olive oil clanking together on a little trolley. Near the lobby there is the Havana Club, where you can sip a 'James Bond' cocktail, and where a glass of Rémy Martin Louis XIII cognac will set you back more than £100.

There are 49 conference rooms, a huge space that seats 1,100 and can host live entertainment, a 2,500-seat ballroom where Christian Dior likes to stage fashion shows, and two helipads. The all-singing, all-dancing auditorium is wired to allow simultaneous translation of events into nine languages, and has a state-of-the-art digital voting system and broadcast facilities, so television crews just have to plug in their cables and they can send sound and vision all over the hotel, the UAE or the world.

Emirates Palace has 1,300 metres of private beach-front, and two gigantic pool complexes with large expanses of open water, wooden bridges and hot-tubs. One pool is for adults to lounge about in and swim, and the other has waterslides, flowing 'rivers' and plunge areas so kids can pretend they are on their own fantasy island and can devise elaborate games, escape from pirates and conquer sea-monsters.

A team of bath butlers is on-call 24 hours a day to devise ingenious flavoured baths for all guests, and if you are feeling really fabulous and have several thousand pounds at your disposal, you can opt for the champagne version. Yes, your bath really will be filled with champagne, which I can only imagine is rather cold and sticky.

Emirates Palace is also lusciously extravagant when it comes to technology. At check-in I was given a golden plastic disc for a room key. It resembled a piece of the chocolate money I used to hang on the family Christmas tree when I was a kid.

'Wave it in front of the door panel and say "Open Sesame",' the receptionist told me. I dutifully did as I was told, but it was only on the third entry to my room that evening after supper (as my bemused neighbours were watching me) that I realised I did not actually have to say 'Open Sesame' at all. In fact, the ingenious system is based entirely on transponder technology. It was using a radio frequency to unlock the door, not my magic words.

The receptionist had also taken the trouble to explain very carefully and patiently how to use the touchpad in the room that controls everything from the lights to the television. On my first evening I approached the touchpad with trepidation, talking to it quietly as if it were a disobedient dog that might bite me at any moment. It was the size of a table mat and the thickness of a laptop computer, and was made of grey plastic. There was a thin grey stick that you removed from its cradle and used like a pen to activate the device. The screen sprang to life, showing me several options in boxes.

I pressed the spot on the screen which said 'TV'. Nothing happened. I pressed the one that said 'Bathroom Light'. Nothing happened. Then I tried 'Air Conditioning'. Nothing happened. Suddenly my huge plasma screen was full of Britney Spears, the lights in the bathroom were flashing on and off, and the ducts above my head were blowing ice-cold air down my neck.

I panicked and searched for the 'Off' switch, but super-high-tech gadgets in modern luxury hotels do not have 'Off' switches any more. They expect their users to have at least an ounce of tech savvy and to be able to figure out how to shut down using the pads on the screen. Britney was making my eardrums tremble and I felt sure I had fused the bathroom lights and would have to shower in the dark from now on, so I decided to revert to my trusted Luddite method of just pulling the batteries out and starting again. Even this approach failed – there was no compartment for batteries. The thing was alive.

I touched the 'TV' part of the screen again and Britney disappeared, leaving for a split second a faint echo rattling around the room. All was quiet. The cold blasts of air retreated into their labyrinth of tubes with a disappointed sigh.

Still determined to conquer the technology, I had another go – but in a few seconds my room looked like a scene from *The Exorcist*. Lights were going on and off in every corner. The television was flitting deafeningly between Aerosmith videos, yoga lessons on a yacht in the Caribbean, and a shopping channel that was flogging trays of hideous gold bangles. Then it flicked through the Arabic stations, where men with prodigious beards were sitting on cushions and discussing the merits of the Koran; then back to shots of the inside of Steve Tyler's cavernous mouth.

I ran to the television, looking for a mains lead and a plug, neither of which was there. I tried turning off the lights using the switches on the wall, but they came back on again. The air-conditioning was blowing warm air now.

As suddenly as this technological poltergeist had begun its mayhem, it stopped. The room was silent once more. The lights were off and the air-conditioning had reduced to a low murmur. I laid the Table Mat of Fear down on the carpet very carefully, crept into bed and lay there breathing silently. It made a blip noise, flicked on for a few seconds, filling the room with ghostly blue-white light, and then shut down.

At breakfast with the hotel's PR director the next morning, I said I had had a spot of bother with the remote-control system. She asked what I had done and as I answered it became instantly apparent to me that the fault had been entirely with the incompetent user. This device had been used perfectly efficiently by thousands of guests and was considered a major advance in luxury hotel technology. I sat there feeling defeated and small, and consoled myself by pouring delicious camel's milk on my Coco Pops and munching on preserved figs, peaches and a zaatar croissant.

I retired to the beach to get away from the wires, the ether, the transponders and all the other futuristic gadgetry that the hotel offers, only to be asked by a waiter in white shorts and a T-shirt: 'You have your laptop, Sir? The whole beach is wireless, so you can access the internet here if you wish.'

'Just a gin and tonic, thanks,' I answered.

The wealth that has built the Emirates Palace has come from oil. Abu Dhabi holds roughly 9.2 per cent of the world's oil reserves and 4 per cent of its natural gas. It also owns the Emirates Palace. Big and lavish as it might be, the Emirates Palace has a more expensive rival, if we are measuring excess by land value: the Hotel Bel-Air in Los Angeles.

As I said a little earlier, the Bel-Air is the equivalent of the luxury hotel stratosphere. Everything to this point has been the ascent – now you are levelling out at 35,000 feet, and the view is sublime.

Excess is everywhere, starting with the cost of the land itself, which is $10 to $12 million per acre. The Bel-Air has twelve of them, including one given over to a delightfully relaxing herb garden, where the basil, rosemary and oregano provide undoubtedly the most precious hotel restaurant garnishes in the world.

Guests are pampered in 91 lavishly decorated and furnished rooms and suites, which feel more like wings of a private country estate. There are wood-burning fireplaces, paved patios for alfresco dining (some with Andalucian tiled fountains), hardwood floors, bespoke French fabrics and Italian chinaware, custom-painted ceiling murals, vegetable-dyed Persian rugs, and marble wet bars.

In a recent refurbishment regular guests were asked what

they would like to see kept or changed. Some guests mentioned their favourite colour palettes, and the designers took notice. I can think of no other hotel in the world where guests get to decide how the suites look.

As an added amenity for its long-term guests, Hotel Bel-Air offers monogrammed bathrobes and linen. These are kept in a cedar storage closet until they're required, and returned there afterwards. Guests who come and go several times a year can also leave their own clothing in their closet.

The bar stocks at least 30 varieties of coffee, because you just never know who is going to turn up. And if guests are feeling frisky, virtually any request is executed with dazzling efficiency. Catering for a party in your suite for six friends? No problem. Booking a private jet to the Napa Valley for an afternoon of wine-tasting? Ready on the runway for you in an hour, Sir.

When the restaurant had a dress code, it used to have a wardrobe full of Ralph Lauren jackets for men who showed up without one. But the dress code has gone now, which makes the place much friendlier. Lauren himself used to stay here too, by the way.

A good proportion of the day is spent dreaming up new and ever more lavish schemes to offer devoted guests. In 2006 the manager, Carlos Lopes, introduced small ice-packs in little bags for sunbathers at the sublime oval-shaped pool, and 'frozen eye-patches for the ladies'. To this theme he added frozen grapes and berries, all designed to cool people down.

Some guests mentioned casually that, due to the increases in airline security, they were getting sick of travelling with their laptops and having to take them out at every screening post. Lopes listened calmly and made mental notes. Soon afterwards he ordered 20 new laptops for guests to use free in their suites.

The guests aren't the only ones being pampered to within an inch of their lives at the Hotel Bel-Air. Probably the most cosseted swans ever to have lived – Eros, Athena, Artemis, Apollo and Hercules – dwell at Swan Lake. They are guaranteed five-star treatment equal to that offered to Hollywood's elite, and get to dine daily on hearts of romaine lettuce. It's as if they have their own Presidential Suite by the lake.

And speaking of Presidential Suites, the latest Golden Age of hotels means war has broken out between the big hotels over who has the most. The clear frontrunner at present is the Waldorf=Astoria in New York. At the last count it had 26 – one Chief Presidential Suite, and then another 25 for normal presidents. The main reason for this outburst of excessive luxe is the proximity of the United Nations building, just a few blocks away. When the General Assembly meets, the Waldorf=Astoria has had as many as 24 heads of state staying on the one night.

As with the Emirates Palace, packing many of the world's leaders and their envoys – all from different backgrounds, belief systems and sometimes conflicting customs – into a confined space has the potential to spark global mayhem.

So the Waldorf=Astoria hired a full-time director of diplomatic affairs, Marina Jiang, who is the closest thing on Earth to a real-life Superwoman. She speaks four languages fluently, and knows intimately the etiquette of just about every country you could name. She is the person you'd push to the front of the crowd if Martians landed, to explain Earth to them in a few simple sentences and to try to persuade them not to liquidate us all.

If the heads of state of France are having trouble sleeping because their suite is next door to England's and

England is drinking beers and watching Arsenal vs Chelsea live on cable at 5 AM, Marina can act as a go-between to make sure the Poms pipe down and the Entente Cordiale is maintained.

When the heads of state descended on the hotel's Waldorf Towers (the most exclusive section) in 2005, for the annual United Nations General Assembly and to celebrate the sixtieth anniversary of the UN, Ms Jiang had her work cut out for her. Ever alert to the needs of her guests, she assigned to each delegation a service manager fluent in their particular language to assist them during their stay. Jiang had half-a-dozen suites repainted in colours that would be particularly pleasing to the incoming VIPs. She and her team ensured that the flowers in the suite for Hu Jintao, President of the People's Republic of China, were red, which is a sign of happiness in that country.

Saudi Arabia's Crown Prince Sultan Bin Abdul Aziz was making his inaugural visit to the USA, so Jiang decided it would be fitting to transform the living room in his suite into a royal court resembling a palace back home. She even hung olive branches on the walls.

This expertise in etiquette has been honed over the hotel's prestigious history. When Aliza Begin (the wife of the Prime Minister of Israel, Menachem Begin) dropped by, the staff were prepared with boxes of her favourite bubblegum. The founder of Saudi Arabia, King Abdul Aziz Bin Abdul Rahman Al Saud, wanted nothing so western. During his stay, he was provided with bucket-loads of fresh goat's milk.

No doubt this elite clientele is the reason behind the hotel's new Guerlain Spa, which was due to open on the 19th floor shortly after this book went to press in spring 2008. If it is anything like the Guerlain Spa on the top floor of the

Martinez in Cannes, the princes, sheikhs and diplomats are in for a truly rotten time being pampered with the finest spa treatments on the market.

Sometimes it is quality, not quantity, that counts when it comes to Presidential Suites. The InterContinental Hong Kong has only one Presidential Suite, but for my money it knocks the socks off the rest of the world. At 2,400 square metres and with five bedrooms, it is the largest suite in Hong Kong. It is positioned at the western edge of the hotel, which itself is perched on the shore of Victoria Harbour, offering the best views of Hong Kong's bejewelled skyline.

The suite cost £1.25m to build and took 253 days and 76,120 man-hours. It has a double-storey living room, with plate-glass windows to make the most of that million-dollar vista. There is an expansive rooftop swimming pool, also overlooking the harbour. It costs about £5,500 per night and includes 24-hour personal butler service, round-trip airport limousine service in either the Rolls-Royce, the Bentley or the Mercedes. Anyone who picks the Mercedes when they are paying that much must be out of their mind.

For guests who would prefer to gaze at an ancient rather than a modern wonder of architecture, Venice is the location and the Cipriani Hotel the place to stay. The Cipriani is one of the world's most famous hotels, and for good reason. It's so amazing in every way that it is difficult to pin down all the factors that make it so, but one is the northern flank of the hotel, where two fifteenth-century buildings – the Palazzo Vendramin and the Palazzetto Nani Barbaro – offer the most opulent and private rooms and suites. This is where you get private butler service and a view that will take your breath away – right over the Bacino San Marco to the famous square of the same name. Nani Barbaro has five junior suites and the Vendramin 11 apartments, but those who have seen both say nothing compares to the Dogaressa Suite.

'Dogaressa' was the title given to the wife of the Doge of Venice, the ruler of the city. She was the First Lady, if you like. The suite was named after the Dogaressa Loredana Mocenigo Marcello, wife of Alvise Mocenigo, the 85th Doge. When I dropped by, more than 450 years too late to have a glass of Chianti with the Dogaressa, the suite was taken – presumably by a modern duchess. I did not get to see the suite's sitting room, the largest in the Palazzo Vendramin, which is decorated with original eighteenth-century Coromandel screens, antique Chinese lamps, and Fortuny and Rubelli fabrics. Nor did I get to experience the pink-marble bathroom, and I shouldn't think I will any time soon as this suite is one of the most sought-after in the world.

Instead, I had one of the best hotel lunches I can remember, dining on beef carpaccio and chilled grappa with the hotel's long-standing managing director, Dr Natale Rusconi, and his son Pietro. Dr Rusconi has been in charge since 1976 and has learnt a thing or two about service, etiquette and being the perfect gentleman to every guest. Twice during our lunch by the Olympic-size swimming pool (the only one in Venice) he excused himself briefly, wiped his mouth with his starched napkin, leapt to his feet and greeted guests as if they were long-lost friends.

'When guests come here, they are visiting their holiday home,' he told me. 'It's the Cipriani family.'

I asked if I could join.

'You will,' he said, beaming from inside his immaculate suit. 'You will.'

Several top-ranking luxury hotels have followed the Bel-Air's lead in providing guests with every possible courtesy and satisfying their most extravagant desires. Just when you think it cannot get any more fabulous, it almost certainly does.

At the Martinez, the grand art deco palace on the beach-front Croisette at Cannes, a secretive princess books out the top-floor Presidential Suite for three months each summer. She checks in around early June and lives there until late August, coming and going amid a human forcefield of security – both her own and that of the hotel. The hotel knows precisely when she is leaving and when she is coming back several minutes in advance, so security can commandeer a lift for her and prevent her having to wait by the door.

Such a summer holiday would probably cost something like $1 million, but no doubt some hard deals are struck behind the scenes to knock the odd $100,000 off the bill in return for the financial comfort of a three-month let. For that fee, the princess gets what the hotel modestly calls a slice of 'Seventh Heaven': 1,000 square metres of space, including four bedrooms, two living rooms, two saunas, two jacuzzis, and a teak-decked terrace with two 100-year-old olive trees and an unsurpassed panoramic vista of the Mediterranean. The olive trees were uprooted from a field in Provence and flown in by helicopter.

There are statues, African masks, lamps by Felix Aublet and Mariano Fortuny, and original lithographs by Picasso. Oh, and if you get bored up there, call for your butler, Alain, he can arrange for one of three sports cars to be made ready. You can take your pick between a convertible BMW, Mercedes or Porsche, depending on which day it is and how your mood takes you. Apparently Sunday is very popular for taking a Porsche for a spin around the perfumeries of Grasse, or giving the gearbox a workout up the twisting roads of the Estérel mountains.

The suite is situated dead-centre of the top floor and right under the big neon glowing letters that spell out the hotel's name.

'The Martinez sign basically covers the Presidential Suite. It is part of the idea, part of the identity of staying in the suite,' said the hotel's international sales manager, Sebastien Legrand.

One year the princess booked the Martinez for July but then skipped off to Portofino for a change. Apparently it was no match for the Martinez, so she made a call in her cutest foreign accent and begged to come back. Since then the Presidential Suite has been hers every summer.

Whereas you might not recognise the princess emerging resplendent from a private lift and breezing past you, you would certainly spot Woody Allen, Francis Ford Coppola, Colin Firth, Natalie Imbruglia, Jennifer Aniston, Quentin Tarantino and Clint Eastwood, who are all regulars at the Martinez during the Cannes Film Festival each May. One year, before the princess flew in, Jodie Foster warmed up the Presidential Suite for her during the festival. At this annual orgy of cinematic mutual appreciation, the hotel is fully loaded with stars, checking in, checking out, drinking too much, being loud, leaving tips that a waiter could use to buy a decent-size Renault, and singing after hours in the bar with long-term resident pianist, Jimmy McKissic.

Witnessing Jimmy play classics, dressed in his trademark red and yellow stage costume, is a spiritual experience in all senses of the word. Jimmy, who has lived at the hotel for 21 years, firmly believes he is there 'because of God's wisdom and guidance'. The view from the hotel's suites is so heavenly that I did not doubt him.

I was lucky enough to be granted an audience with Jimmy before he retired in 2007 and I asked him what his most memorable night had been. Jamming with Brad Pitt and Jennifer Aniston, maybe? Accompanying a clarinet-blowing Woody Allen perhaps? But the experience he remembers more than any other involved someone way bigger and more powerful than anyone Hollywood could serve up.

'The most memorable night I have had at the hotel is the night I saw God. I lived on the seventh floor in a two-bedroom suite, and I would feed the seagulls every day,' Jimmy told me. 'Then one day I felt God's presence, and it felt so good and I said, "I would love to see you now, but I do not know what you look like and if you appeared in that doorway now I would die out of fright." So after work I went to bed, and at about 3 AM I woke up to go to the bathroom. I turned on the light and there was a big seagull in my bedroom – but I never fed the birds in my house, I always fed them on the terrace.

'I thought before that if I saw God I would be worshipping him, praising him, kissing him, but I was frightened, and then God said, "I knew if you saw me, you would be frightened." I will never forget that; that is the most wonderful experience I have had at the Martinez, the night I saw God.'

I know what you're thinking – it's possible it might just have been a regular seagull rather than the Almighty elaborately disguised in feathers and a red beak, but I believed Jimmy. He's come a long way from his Bible-belt childhood home in Little Rock, Arkansas. He has met and played for presidents and other world leaders, and has graced the stage of Carnegie Hall in New York. He's seen a fair bit of the world in his 67 years, and he's got a heart of gold, so I reckon he could spot a divine, omnipresent seagull from a mortal, fish-and-chip-eating one. Amen, Jimmy, Amen.

The bar heaves day and night with characters from the

worlds of fashion and design who look as if they have just walked off the set of *Zoolander*. One man who was sipping champagne was dressed head-to-toe in patriotic tricolour blue, and sported a dramatic sweep of blond hair that had been blow-dried to perfection. He wore an enormous pair of sunglasses, easily big enough to be used to do some heavy-duty welding. This, I was later informed, was Michou, the most famous cabaret owner in Paris, the *Prince et Reine de Montmatre* himself. He owns and runs Chez Michou, between Sacré Coeur and the Moulin Rouge.

He broke off from his gang of friends as I passed by with Sebastien, greeted him with a warm handshake and turned to me. He looked me up and down, and I felt sure he was devising an outrageous part for a luxury hotel reviewer in his latest cabaret revue. I fully expected an invitation to Paris to come sliding dramatically under my door that afternoon.

A hotel as extravagant as this must have a restaurant to match, and the Martinez leaves guests in no doubt that their gastronomic eatery, La Palme d'Or (named after the ultimate award at the film festival), is the place to eat in Cannes, and possibly even in the whole of the south of France.

La Palme d'Or has two Michelin stars and without fail provides some of the most magical moments you will ever spend in Cannes. It occupies a long, low balcony, looking down on the pool and out to the ocean. From here you can gaze upon the motorcade of black Ferraris as they grind up and down the Croisette trying to get out of first gear, and then bury your nose in the menu.

Unfortunately, even the most refined French restaurants still like to provide English translations of their dishes, which often end up being embarrassingly literal. My favourites at the Palme d'Or included 'the Sea Bass in his Box', 'the

Tense Hand', and 'the Young Pigeon', which turns out to be nothing to do with pigeon at all but a tartare of tuna with cannelloni and Swiss chard. But the Palme d'Or award for the winning dish title must go to the bowl of shellfish marinière with a puree of celeriac and a froth of coconut, which goes by the unashamedly exuberant name of 'Hello O'Clown!'.

I am acutely aware that it is very bad form to burst out laughing when you read the menu in a *restaurant gastronomique* in France. Chefs have killed for less. So it was a great relief that I did not get the opportunity to eat there during my stay in Cannes, for I would almost certainly have offended the staff by chuckling over my grissini. Nor was I offered a free lunch by the hotel – maybe they knew I would snigger like a schoolboy on reading 'Hello O'Clown!'. To be fair to the Martinez, it was high season when I rocked up on their doorstep, rather at the last minute, and the dear old Palme d'Or was fully booked for days in advance with people no doubt fighting to get in to find out what 'Hello O'Clown!' looked and tasted like. Can somebody please let me know?

Instead, I went back to the Méditerranée, which is now a Sofitel, and had lunch in the rooftop restaurant in memory of my surrogate uncle, the *Evening Standard*'s veteran film critic Alexander Walker, who died suddenly in 2003. My father used to tell me how Alex would sweep his hand across the view and say, 'This makes doing the shorthand course all worthwhile.' The cuisine had gone even more up-market, followed closely by the prices, and the truly elegant types were replaced with new, mainly Russian, money, who wore T-shirts with little fake diamonds stuck on them that made up the names Dior and D&G. But the view over the Port de Cannes was the same, the yachts, the jetties, the

Mediterranean twinkling like a crystal chandelier in the Cote d'Azur summer light. And, just for a moment, Alex was there too, receiving a note from a waiter which would summon him away to meet someone far more important than me.

Even when guests become irrational and crazed, hotels will bend over backwards to make life as luxurious as possible for them, as long as they keep paying the tab. The Sunset Tower in Hollywood once bowed to a strange request from its long-term guest John Wayne, who was gradually becoming one of his Western characters in real life and missed life on the range so much he insisted on bringing a cow to his penthouse apartment, letting it live and graze out on the balcony. By the way, if you managed to stay awake through the clinical and catatonic remake of *The Italian Job* in 2003, you might have spotted Mark Wahlberg and his fellow thieves discussing their dastardly plot on this very same balcony.

In the mirrored hallway of the Silver Corridor of New York's Waldorf=Astoria, the hotel's 1930s designers made sure the steel-fronted, ornately decorated lifts were built extra-wide to cope with the voluminous ball gowns of the time. The management of the Waldorf=Astoria knew it must spare no expense. This was where the snow would be dusted from fur coats as Vanderbilts shook hands with Rockefellers and invited each other to Cape Cod when the weather warmed up some, so everything had to be of the most extravagant standard possible. The hotel's restaurant was one of the first in the world to serve prime Angus beef, and it hosted the first society gala in the USA outside a private residence. It even built a private train track under the hotel for President Franklin Roosevelt – it connected to Grand Central and allowed him to come and go with ease and safety.

And who in Australia could forget their former leader, John Howard, checking in to the Royal Suite at the St Regis Grand Hotel in Rome during a diplomatic tour in July 2002? He spent $42,000 (roughly £20,000) of Australian taxpayers' money on a four-night stay. It is generally considered protocol for host governments to pay accommodation expenses for heads of government visiting on official business, but once the Italians took a look at the bill they choked on their biscotti. There was a cool diplomatic stand-off between Rome and Canberra, and for a while it looked like Australian taxpayers would end up footing the entire bill. They should have each demanded a St Regis pillow chocolate at the very least.

An Australian Senate committee hearing in May 2003 was told that Mr Howard checked in on 5 July 2002 and left on 9 July. He was in town for talks with his Italian counterpart, Silvio Berlusconi.

The room cost around £4,500 a night, but that did not include extras such as the butler who is on hand for guests in the Royal Suite, nor any mini-bar charges, telephone calls and movies, and it didn't include any of the costs of the PM's security entourage.

What I really want to know is why he didn't want to check in to his namesake hotel, the delightful Casa Howard near the Spanish Steps? In May 2002 it had just opened its Part II, with five more beautifully appointed rooms. Clearly Mr Howard thought Casa Howard was for plebeians while the St Regis Grand was worthy of his Caesaresque status. Strangely Mr Howard, who lost not only power but also his seat in the last general election (and to a female journalist, no less), was not available for comment on the issue.

Some luxury hotels are now even trying to second-guess their guests by offering outlandish luxury before it is requested. The San Ysidro Ranch in Montecito, California, offers room service not just for you but for your pets as well. Your pampered pussy or pooch signs in and can then be treated to a filet mignon or a massage. At the Phoenician in Scottsdale, Arizona, why not order your very own martini butler? For $350 an hour he will don a tuxedo, wheel a large drinks trolley into your suite, and shake and stir whatever flavoured martinis your heart desires. He will also teach you how to become a martini-aficionado, a skill that every dedicated luxury hotel addict should master.

Or, for $80,000 you can check in to the Ritz-Carlton in New York – down near Battery Park – and get a room with a spectacular view over the mouth of the Hudson and, at a pre-arranged time, pop a champagne cork and watch your very own firework display over the Statue of Liberty. If you feel a little guilty shelling out this amount on yourself and your loved one instead of donating it to the homeless or buying several small wells in an African village, fear not. Think of all the homeless people camped out on benches in Battery Park and elsewhere in downtown Manhattan who will lift their heads and say, 'Ooh, fireworks, that's nice.'

Slightly cheaper fireworks were on offer in Cannes on my last summer visit. I could have paid a couple of hundred pounds to watch them and have a special supper at the restaurant of the Hôtel Carlton, but instead I opted for a spot of warm wall on the Croisette. The fireworks rambled on for close to an hour, but not in a spectacular, breathtaking way like in Sydney or Venice on New Year's Eve. The routine wandered aimlessly, as if the *feu d'artifice* lighters were getting so bored that they stopped every now and then for a Gauloises and then remembered that several thousand very rich people (including a princess and Michou, the Parisian King of Cabaret) were waiting to see the rest of the show. The display took so long that an ocean breeze picked up and blew the smoke and gunpowder back towards land. The warm wall I was sitting on disappeared into the fog, as did the Ferraris and the entire Croisette, and then the fabulous hotels where dinner guests were trying to decide if shelling out a couple of hundred pounds to be smoked like a haddock in your best white shirt was really worth it.

You're in Cannes. C'est la vie!

Chapter 12

Future-luxe

DURING THE PAST 150 years, luxury hotels have pushed the boundaries of extravagance repeatedly; now, we lucky guests find ourselves at a stage where the seemingly impossible is achieved with the opening of each new property. As the virtual age takes hold, scientific innovation abounds, and as the luxury hotel addict becomes more attuned to the possibilities of excess, you can bet that the hotels of the future are going to be nothing short of amazing.

Not that many years ago it was considered fairly incredible that a hotel could be built in the middle of a desert. What about the water, they cried. And the heat? Now, in Australia, you can fly direct from Sydney to Uluru (formerly known as Ayers' Rock) and transfer to your private, permanent, air-conditioned and highly luxurious teepee at Longitude 131, slap bang in the Red Centre of the continent. In Dubai in July when the mercury is boiling up to 50 degrees you can crank up the air-conditioning and recline in a fluffy bathrobe in your sky-high suite at the Burj Al Arab, order a hot chocolate and run a warm bath to keep off the chill.

We are just beginning this second Golden Age of luxury hotels. If you think Longitude 131, the Burj Al Arab in

Dubai and the Emirates Palace in Abu Dhabi are high-tech and futuristic, just wait until you see what is around the corner.

The Emirates Palace claims to be the world's only seven-star hotel, although it recognises that officially the star-rating system only goes up to five. But its claim might be disputed by the Flower of the East when it is completed in 2009, just across the Strait of Hormuz on Kish Island in Iran. If the German architects get it right, the hotel will rise from the flat lands of the Kish Island's Iranian Free Trade like a gigantic spiralling flower vase waiting for a giant to splash past and drop a sunflower in it.

Then there is the rise of the fashion hotel. Versace started it, followed by Bulgari, and now everyone is at it. The Italian fashion label Byblos has opened the Art Hotel Villa Amista near Verona. Outside it has retained the stately warmth and style of the restored fifteenth-century villa it inhabits, but through the main doors you jump through time to an ultra-modern temple of pop art and futurism. The latest fashion house to diversify into accommodation is Missoni, which signed a deal in mid-2006 to build 30 new hotels designed to complement the brand.

The real thrills and spills, however, are going to come from the hotels whose bankers and designers are focus-ing on the two big new frontiers for their ambitious future plans: the oceans and space.

Two submarine hotels are planned: the Poseidon Under-sea Resort fifteen metres beneath the gently lapping waves off Fiji, and Hydropolis off Dubai in the Arabian Gulf, which is aiming to comprise two Hydropalace hotels with 220 suites. One is to be built in shallow water just beneath the surface, while the other will be down on the sea bed. Ten years ago I would have written an article on Poseidon and

Hydropolis with a sarcastic, satirical twist, poking fun at the preposterous nature of such harebrained schemes, criticising the designers for reading far too much Jules Verne, and wondering who would ever want to go and stay there, even if they could build them.

Now, I have been inside the rocket-ship Burj Al Arab, I have watched the Milky Way through a telescope while sipping whisky at Sossusvlei Mountain Lodge in the middle of the Namib Desert, and I have travelled in diagonally moving lifts in Las Vegas. The future is already here, so rather than mocking Poseidon and Hydropolis I am frantically contacting the owners to try to be one of the first travel writers to review them the minute they open.

The Poseidon is scheduled to open in early 2009 and is advertising itself as the 'world's first permanent one-atmosphere sea-floor structure and the world's first true undersea resort'. Guests will access the resort by a tunnel and an escalator, which means non-divers can also come and stay. The interior is constantly at one atmosphere, meaning there is no difference between the atmospheric pressure inside the resort and pressure at the surface, and it will be completely air-conditioned and humidity-controlled.

Suites are like pods, arranged in two lines of ten on either side of a central walkway. At either end of the walkway is a large structure shaped like a curling stone, which will house communal facilities and the hotel's operational logistics, and the world's first sea-floor restaurant. Just in case this is not exciting enough for you, the restaurant will revolve, giving you a 360-degree view of your temporary ocean habitat.

'You will be able to take a table near the acrylic windows and then complete a full revolution in about one hour,' said Bruce Jones, the multi-millionaire submarine-builder behind Poseidon. 'Cuisine will be strictly five-star, with an eclectic selection of some of the world's best dishes prepared by master chefs and served by skilled, personable and attentive waiters and waitresses.'

Each undersea suite will have a king-size bed, a jacuzzi and sofas where you can while away the hours watching the daily commute of tuna, turtles, sharks and reef fish of Fiji.

Rooms will be made from tough, transparent acrylic walls that will afford views out onto coral reefs. Guests will have fingertip control of their environment. They will be able to alter the lighting on the reefs and even release food to attract fish. This five-star accommodation will set submarine guests back a cool £7,500 per week.

Bruce Jones was inspired by underwater pioneers such as the French 'aquanaut' and inventor of the aqualung, Jacques Cousteau, and the French architect Jacques Rougerie, who built three conceptual underwater buildings in the late 1970s for marine research. Sadly, none of them was ever immersed and tested.

According to Jones, the design and engineering of the underwater portions of the resort are now complete. 'The company is currently focusing its attention on location selection, permitting, property options, licences, and so on,' he said. 'The economic viability of the construction of the resort is predicated on the in-house manufacture of the monolithic cell-cast polymethyl methacrylate viewports, so work is underway on the planning of a manufacturing facility.'

My only fear is that, as Fiji is one of the world's premier dive spots, you might not be able to walk about your suite in the nude, or get too friendly with your partner – you might find a school of divers staring in through the glass and taking photos. But Bruce Jones has thought of this awkward scenario as well.

'The suites are set up with a reflective film so that it is nearly impossible to see into them during the day. At night, guests will be able to opaque sections of the view-ports to increase their privacy,' he said.

The Poseidon will also have a library lounge which doubles as a conference room. There will likely be a diver lock-out chamber so qualified scuba divers can enter and exit the resort in their wetsuits. Their luggage will make its way down separately via a porter, nice and dry.

Jones told me the resort would have its own run-around vehicle, a deep submersible that could take guests on exploratory trips to nearby reefs and walls.

Onshore the resort will have a reception area, café, swimming pool, luxury spa and hydrotherapy centre, gift shop and tennis courts. There will also be a dive shop and a car rental facility, along with a complimentary limousine service to take guests to and from the airport.

But here is the ultimate in underwater luxe. A much deeper two-bedroom private undersea bungalow, cantilevered off a reef wall 300 metres down, is planned – Poseidon's Lair. The Lair will only be accessible by the submersible. The bedrooms and jacuzzi will be sealed with transparent acrylic spheres which will allow unsurpassed viewing of the ocean depths. For this step into the unknown, guests can expect to pay £10,000 a night, but they will also get their own private submarine captain and butler.

But if Jones builds the Poseidon, will they come? He has spent seventeen years designing, refitting and selling submarines, and is convinced a market is there.

'Everybody who comes off a tourist submarine loves the experience,' he said. 'Last year in America over 100 million people went to aquariums, so there's a tremendous amount of interest in the sub-sea world – it's growing all the time. We can entertain people, but also educate people and promote environmental stewardship. Only in really experiencing what it's like underwater can you really motivate somebody to protect the natural resources of the sea.'

Halfway around the world in the Arabian Gulf, the hotel visionaries of the United Arab Emirates are busy developing their own Atlantis. They claim their resort, also due to open in 2009, will be the 'world's first luxury underwater hotel'. Hydropolis will include a 'land station' where guests, fresh off the plane, will check in. Then they will be shown to a connecting tunnel, where a little train will transport them along a self-supporting steel rail to the resort's main area.

From there they will go to one of the 220 suites within the submarine leisure complex. From the plans, the $750-million Hydropolis is a large kidney-shaped complex, about 260 hectares in area. All that can be seen on the surface is the reception area, a low, sloping and curving roof, and some palm plantations on a beach.

Beneath the waves lie the various levels on which are located the suites. It is as if a big city hotel has been towed out to sea and scuppered, drifting down to the sea bed.

This futuristic vision of designer and developer Joachim Hauser is about to take shape beneath the waves just off the Jumeirah Beach coastline in Dubai. The hotel will incorporate a host of innovations that will take it far beyond the original concept of an underwater complex worthy of Jules Verne.

Hauser has said that despite several attempts and visions, by Jules Verne, Jean Gusto and others, no-one has ever managed to colonise the sea and make living underwater possible.

There will be restaurants, bars, meeting rooms, themed suites and a ballroom located at the nerve centre of the complex. Open-air events will be staged under a vast roof which can open to the sky like a blooming rose.

The developers, Crescent-Hydropolis, are now planning a chain of underwater hotels, and nine countries have shown interest.

According to the Hydropolis website, the 'Hauser dream has always focused on fusing the nexus between man's quest to conquer the seas and living peaceably in its environs alongside aquatic life'.

It continues:

'Hydropolis enables us to explore our inner sanctum that originates with the sound of fluids in our mother's wombs. Now, we will be able to do so in an oceanic environment that lifts the spirit, refreshes the mind and heals the body with nature's most abundant resource – water.'

Personally, much as I love her, I would rather not hear the sounds of my mother's womb again. I got over that 40 years ago when I was born. And I am adamant I do not want to explore my inner sanctum – I don't even know where it is and if I did, goodness knows what I might find lurking in there. But I do most definitely want to live under the sea, even if it is only for a few nights in a suite in Hydropolis.

Macao is also developing its seabed, building an undersea casino called City of Dreams – or, presumably, Ocean of Nightmares if you lose. The Government of Macao Special Administrative Region (SAR) has agreed to lease 113,300 square metres for the proposed scheme, and the roulette wheels are due to start spinning in 2009. The casino should have capacity for 450 gaming tables and 3,000 one-armed bandits, and it will be surrounded by water and marine life. The $1 billion resort will also house, above the waves, deluxe apartment buildings, 2,000 hotel rooms, a shopping mall and a 4,000-seat performance hall.

I hate to pull the plug on the enthusiasm and colourful hype of these three big projects, but I feel it is only fair to point out that the world's first undersea hotel has been operating for some time off the coast of Key Largo in Florida. The Jules' Undersea Lodge is nowhere near the scale of the Poseidon or Hydropolis, but it is definitely a hotel, is certainly underwater, and is extremely cute. To enter, guests must dive down seven metres through the mangroves of the Emerald Lagoon. As they approach, they can look in through the 42-inch porthole windows and spot the comfy beds and fish cushions that await them. Access to the hotel is in true James Bond style, through an opening in the bottom of the structure. Once you have de-wetsuited and flicked off your flippers, it's time to take a hot shower and slip into evening dress and a dry martini before supper.

If you take advantage of the hotel's Luxury Aquanaut Package, you can also benefit from the gourmet delights prepared by Jules' very own 'mer-chef', who will dive down with all the ingredients and a spatula or two, and rustle up something fishy and delicious for you on the sea bed. You can even engage the mer-chef to prepare cakes for birthdays or wedding anniversaries, but most fun of all is dialling out for pizza. A local shop on Key Largo is quite used to getting calls from the depths ordering a king-size pepperoni to go. Presumably the hotel staff diver who delivers the pizza can pick up the extra anchovies on the way down, but how they keep it from going soggy is a mystery.

And – if I am being terribly pedantic – there are a couple of other underwater accommodations I should mention. Huvafen Fushi in the Maldives offers treatments in an underwater spa room; the Utter Inn in Sweden has a small underwater cottage seven metres below the surface of Lake Mälaren. And the Hilton Maldives Resort and the Red Sea Star in Eilat in Israel both have underwater restaurants.

What the Poseidon, Hydropolis and the Macao chaps are doing is taking this philosophy, this Jules Verne dream, chucking in many millions and thinking very big indeed. Their projects will undoubtedly revolutionise once more the rapidly evolving concept of the luxury hotel.

But the future does not stop there. There are visionaries who are being even more ambitious, who are dreaming of checking in to the ultimate hotel destination of all – space. A Dutch architect has already drawn up comprehensive plans and blueprints for the first hotel on the moon. Hans-Jurgen Rombaut released his first set of diagrams and proposals for the aptly named Lunatic Hotel in 2001.

'When designing a building on the moon,' he told me, 'you have to come up with practical solutions for the extreme conditions, such as the high radiation levels, the extreme temperatures that range from approximately −120°C to +120°C, the lack of atmosphere and the low gravity (one-sixth of the Earth's gravity).

'While some of these conditions pose problems, they also offer some exciting opportunities. For instance, with low gravity and because of the lack of atmosphere – and hence a lack of wind pressure – it is possible to design constructions that could not be built on Earth.

'I intended to stress the possibilities of low gravity in the design, and offer visitors a stunning view of both the lunar landscape and the Earth in the ink-black lunar sky,' he said.

The temperature range is tough enough, but it's the deadly radiation which makes moon holidays even trickier. Stories of guests getting zapped and melted by cosmic rays would do little to promote the destination, so Rombaut's design includes 50-centimetre-thick walls made from two layers of moon rock and a 35-centimetre-thick layer of water held between glass planes in the windows.

Because of the astronomical costs of rocketing materials from Earth, Rombaut designed the hotel so that almost all materials could be mined and produced on the moon. Only tools and machinery would have to be flown up.

'For instance, part of the hotel is below the moon surface and is dug out of moon rock,' he said. 'The material removed from this construction area can be cut into rock slates and then used to cover the towers. Glass and moon-dust tiles are used as well, and they can be manufactured on site with materials that are abundant on the moon.'

Rombaut has suggested the Lunatic Hotel should be built at Rima Prinz, a deep rille not a million light years away from where Apollo 12 touched down on 19 November 1969. Just in case you take this book with you into space in 40 years' time but forget your moon map, head for the Sea of Rains and take a left towards the Ocean of Storms. If you hit the Bay of Rainbows you've gone too far. There's sure to be a sign, anyway. And judging by Rombaut's thrilling colour impressions, which look like my old Ray Bradbury novels, the hotel will be eminently visible. Two 160-metre needle-like towers soar over the rim of a deep canyon as Planet Earth hangs in the sky between them. At the highest point of each tower will be a bright red light, presumably to warn passing spacecraft.

Timing your visit is crucial. One lunar day actually lasts fourteen Earth days – half the length of time the moon takes to make a complete orbit of the Earth. As there is nothing like a romantic sunrise or sunset while you are on holiday, most tourists will be staying for at least a fortnight.

But what exactly is there to do up there during your 336-hour day? I can hardly imagine the hotel organising picnics, golf outings or hikes to the Sea of Tranquillity.

'Actually, moonwalks would probably be very popular, but they would require a spacesuit and could only be taken in organised tours, as they can be quite dangerous,' Rombaut said almost matter-of-factly.

'Moon excursions in a vehicle are probably a bit more comfortable and may take you to some interesting scenery, or perhaps even places of historical interest, such as the Apollo landing sites, where the footprints of Neil Armstrong and Buzz Aldrin are still visible in the lunar dust as if they were made yesterday.

'Unlike most holidays, you will spend a lot of your time in the hotel but I like to refer to it as a "sensation engine" rather than a hotel. There will be a range of activities and features. You can choose between the spiritually oriented tower and the physically oriented tower.

'In the spiritual tower, you can watch over the lunar landscape or gaze to the Earth that hangs in the ever-black sky, or you can observe it through powerful telescopes, offering you a view you have never had before. Meditation and spa facilities are available in this tower as well.

'In the physical tower, you can experience low gravity by taking part in gravity games such as abseiling, swimming (you can almost jump out of the water like a dolphin) or even flying, which requires a bat-like suit and a bit of a daring mind.'

Yep, that's me. I have the daring mind; just please, please, give me one of those bat-like suits. You can keep the Presidential Suite at the Waldorf=Astoria, tower rooms at Chateau Marmont, and even a Palazzo Vendramin suite at the

Cipriani. I would give up almost all my usual luxury hotel addictions to shoot off into space, dress up like Batman and launch myself from a balcony at the Lunatic Hotel like an interstellar lemming.

Mind you, I can see the lack of gravity posing major problems for rock bands who wanted to defenestrate televisions and fish tanks – they would just float back up again.

The Lunatic will also have a number of bars and restaurants, each with stunning views of the moon and the heavens, and exercise will be crucial. Because of low gravity, muscle tends to deteriorate quite quickly, so visitors will be encouraged to avoid lifts and instead use the steep, tilted galleries to move from one level to another.

'When tired, you can return to your hotel room, or your capsule,' said Rombaut. 'These capsules are compact living units – a bit like teardrop-shaped spaceships – each equipped with a bedroom and private bathroom. They hang freely from thin steel cables in the tower, and can be lowered and rotated by a remote-control, so that visitors can alter their view themselves. Guests will feel they are still travelling on through space. At night-time, these capsules serve as giant light bulbs and illuminate the inside of the towers.'

If this has tempted you to scamper off to Flight Centre and see if they have got any Lunatic packages, then you might want to hold off for a few years. The Lunatic is probably not going to be open for business until at least 2050, by which time, in Rombaut's words, 'there will probably already be some primitive "first generation" settlements on the moon'.

Mad-cap and thrilling as all these adventures sound, back down on Earth and on dry land, a far more subtle revolution in hotels is taking place, and it is the vision of one man.

You will know by now I am a fan of Jeff Klein's art deco wonder, the Sunset Tower Hotel in West Hollywood, but one of the reasons I like this hotel so much is that it could be the start of a new direction in luxury accommodation.

Klein is a fascinating blend of characters. He was a wealthy New York socialite before he was a hotelier, but he also worked his way up from the bottom. He admits to being a luxury hotel addict from an early age, and after college got a job as a porter at a Manhattan property and in time became manager of housekeeping, a position he still considers probably the most important in any luxury hotel. Now he has both experience and lots of cash, and is causing a bit of a stir.

He is not afraid to air vociferously his hatred of ephemeral hotels that are designed for flashy openings and to be lauded in the press, which then disappear within five years.

'I wanted to start a buzz, but not by creating a fake scene,' he told me as we gazed out over an uncharacteristically wet Los Angeles skyline from the super-cool Tower Bar at his hotel. 'Consumers will be fooled by a fake scene for a few months, maybe even a year, but eventually you need to deliver good service, good food and good beds, without attitude, ridiculousness and gimmicks.

'I loathe the concept of boutique hotels,' he said. 'My goal is to create places for people who want something more sophisticated than having a DJ in the lobby or a nightclub on the first floor. I'm really not interested in hotels as theatre. I want to get back to a sense of style and functionality.

'Minimalism was all very well a few years ago, but it has lost its edge now. One very important aspect of my philosophy is that a traveller needs a place to work and play comfortably, a room in which they can get a good night's sleep, and a hotel where they feel stylish and chic. You wouldn't think that blend was much to ask for, but it is incredibly hard to find.'

In his New York hotel, the City Club on West Forty-fourth Street in Midtown, he created an anti-lobby, a place to check in only and not to loiter.

'I did not want a scene in the lobby, or people to think they could come here to hang out. I wanted it to be a place where guests are wowed by the architecture and design, then can check in smoothly and quickly, and move on up to their rooms to unpack and settle in,' said Klein.

'It's shocking, I know, to create a tasteful, discreet and elegant hotel. How old-fashioned!' he joked. His success with the Sunset Tower and the City Club means he is now mulling over plans for future projects in the USA, Paris and beyond.

'I could fail miserably, or I could be a brilliant success,' he said.

As a certified and discerning luxury hotel addict, my money is on the latter.

Acknowledgements

MY SURROGATE UNCLE, the late Alexander Walker, deserves considerable posthumous thanks for getting me hooked on luxury hotels.

My wife, Erin Brady, has been a source of comfort and support, as well as being the kind of über-stylish travel companion that no self-respecting luxury hotel addict should be without.

I owe a huge debt of gratitude to the multitude of hotel managers, PRs and staff who went out of their way to help me research *Hotel Heaven*.

Big thanks to Katie, Wulf and Luca in London for much-needed confidence; to Sarah, Scott and Ruby for the spare room and temporary office in Sydney; Edward Gray in London for expert opinion; Jack and Fran in New York City and Namibia for humour and encouragement; Sofia de Meyer, Lizzie Corke and Shayne Neal for showing me a sustainable luxury hotel future; and Sam Carter at Old Street Publishing in London for having faith in me.

A quick nod to my musical travelling companions and sources of inspiration: Jools, Curtis, Beth, Barry and Donald.

Most importantly, thanks to my parents for encouraging me to write and giving me the will to take roads less travelled.

About the author

Matthew Brace is an award-winning travel writer and journalist. He was born in Stratford-upon-Avon, lived in Australia for eight years and now resides in the United Arab Emirates. Matthew has been a reporter, foreign correspondent and travel writer for the broadsheet press for fifteen years. He has travelled in and reported from over forty countries.

He writes regularly for newspapers and magazines in the UK, Australia and the Middle East. He is the author of *The Bradt Guide to Tasmania* (2002) and *Heaven on Earth* (2008).

References

p.22: Binney, Marcus (1999). *The Ritz Hotel, London*. London: Thames & Hudson.

p.41: Information on the *Normandie* is taken from the September–October 1996 issue of *Carnegie Magazine*, published by Carnegie Museums of Pittsburgh.

p.64: Davis, Stephen (1997). *Hammer of the Gods: Led Zeppelin Unauthorized*. New York: Berkley Boulevard Books.

p.81: Rhoderick-Jones, Robin (1997). *A Very Special Place: Tales from the Goring Hotel*. London: Goring Hotel.

p.122: Binney, Marcus (1999). *The Ritz Hotel, London*. London: Thames & Hudson.

p.222: Sutton, Horace (1989). *The Beverly Wilshire Hotel: its Life and Times*. Cheney Communications.

pp.302–303: For more information on the Hydropolis project, see www.hydropolis.com.